Twitchhiker

summersdale

TWITCHHIKER

Summersdale Publishers Ltd
46 West Street
Chichester
West Sussex
PO19 1RP
UK

www.summersdale.com

Printed and bound in Great Britain

ISBN: 978-1-84953-074-3

Substantial discounts on bulk quantities of Summersdale books are available to corporations, professional associations and other organisations. For details contact Summersdale Publishers by telephone: +44 (0) 1243 771107, fax: +44 (0) 1243 786300 or email: nicky@summersdale.com.

Twitchhiker

How One Man Travelled the World By Twitter

Paul Smith

About the Author

Paul Smith (@twitchhiker) is a former Sony award-winning radio producer based in Newcastle. He currently has 11,000 followers on Twitter and blogs about travel at http://www. twitchhiker.com. Paul won the travel Shorty Award 2010 for the Twitchhiker project.

Foreword

It was a belter of an early summer's day in Austin, Texas, and I was sticking to the faux leather seats in the back of a yellow cab somewhere uptown. Late for yet another interview, I'd been so worried about packing the right kit that I hadn't checked the address. Rummaging around the web on my phone would cost a packet in overseas data charges, so I turned to Twitter. One minute and one message later, my posse had rescued me with the correct address and I put the cab driver out of his misery.

I'm professionally obliged to fiddle with the web, so when I started playing with Twitter in 2007 I had no particular expectations about what it could do or how much I might end up relying on it. I try out dozens of services and don't feel any obligation to battle with them if they are pointless or hard to use – so what was it about Twitter that worked?

Part group text message, part Facebook status update, part discussion group, part mini-blog – it might sound confusing at first but it is flexible, rather than complicated. And in the past two years, it has become indispensable in my job as a technology journalist.

It is a brains trust of the technology scene, linking me with all the people who are interested and engaged enough to want to be involved in news as it happens, and allowing me to ask advice of and share opinions with that network. It is an important organisational tool for meeting up with contacts, particularly at conferences where it also serves as an often irreverent back channel for debate. The network on Twitter ebbs and flows, leading you to new contacts and letting you maintain contact with others. It also serves as a medium for my own work, sending my latest articles to people interested enough to want to follow me. And perhaps most significantly, the real-time nature of Twitter makes it an important platform for breaking news and discussion on the burning topic of the day, from the true horror of the Haiti earthquakes unfolding hour by hour to the clumsily compiled UK Digital Economy Bill.

The most recent test for me was taking a nine-month hiatus from work to have a baby. In those lonely middle of the night feeding sessions I honestly felt that Twitter was a lifeline to the outside world. And taking all that into consideration, I wouldn't hesitate to say that Twitter is now my primary communication platform.

Twitter's network is largely idealistic and optimistic, perhaps because no one would want to follow anyone as tediously rude or unconstructively negative as your average Internet troll. Twitter is also still small enough that users feel a kinship with fellow users, in the same self-congratulatory finger waggling way as VW Beetle owners.

But no project has tested the optimism and sociability of Twitter as much as the Twitchhiker project. Which leads me to our young friend Paul.

It was very much one of those 'I wish I'd thought of that' moments when Paul explained the idea, and not just because I fancy going to New Zealand again. But I watched as the trip unfolded and Paul's eccentric idea grew, as people connected only through this modern word of mouth began to go out of their ways to offer a lift, or a bed for the night, or a ferry ride to a rock in the Southern Ocean, or... a party with Liv Tyler? I'm still not sure how he pulled that one off.

By the time I met Paul in Austin, Texas, for the South By Southwest Interactive Festival, he was nearly halfway to New Zealand. Slumped over his ribs and beans in that greasy BBQ house, he really did look like he'd travelled every one of those 8,000 kilometres, bless him. I wondered if he might have started to regret the whole idea, but he stuck to his guns. I don't think I ever doubted that he'd get there.

As Paul put it in his own inimitable way: he proved the world isn't full of rapists and bastards. And he raised money for charity, which is always worth doing. But he did so much more because he caught our imagination. At the heart of the idea was a test of good old-fashioned kindness and generosity, and if a powerful but oft-dismissed new technology platform can bring a little light and love back to the world then it has been A Very Good Thing. A Very Good Thing Indeed.

Jemima Kiss, March 2010

Chapter 1

It was quiet and still, the very dead of night when the dead themselves might consider turning in, and I had no business being awake. I'd deprived my body of a full night's sleep for a fortnight, occasionally through choice but mostly through circumstance. This time, however, I was of the unshakeable belief that the blame rested squarely with the mattress.

Despite the name, a folding bed shares few genes with its everyday equivalent, even when it's one provided by a Hilton hotel. Such mattresses are more a bucketful of rusty, tired springs thrown into a sack of damp dust. One spring in particular was attempting to puncture my torso, but I denied the wicked implement its blood-letting and instead sat up to peek through the curtains. Like any city centre in the pre-dawn hours, Austin was motionless, save for the occasional flicker of headlights straying between the building blocks. The Texan capital gazed back at the twelfth floor of the Hilton and recoiled in horror at the haggard bald head at the window.

'Nearly time to get up, mate.'

The voice belonged to the previously unmentioned Norwegian gentleman in the room. He was also in bed; not mine, but a real bed several feet away, with its real pillows and real mattress, plump with goose feathers and unicorn hair and kittens. There was still time to kill him and claim it. I thumbed at my mobile phone; the display momentarily blinded me. Half past five, it blared. No point resorting to murder and spoiling the sheets when we were due to receive a phone call any minute. And we did.

'Hi Paul,' said a man called Syd, a television producer. 'Good night's sleep?'

'Yes,' I lied.

'Awesome. We're just about set up for you down here.'

'We're nearly ready,' I lied again, standing in full view of Austin with my left testicle hanging out of my boxer shorts. 'We'll see you shortly.'

A hot shower massaged out the knot between my shoulders but did little to soothe the one in my stomach. I rooted through my bag for a set of clothes that didn't look like they'd been stuffed in a wrestler's thong for a week, and pulled out a red T-shirt I'd promised to wear for the occasion. The socks had been worn for only two consecutive days and so were reasonably fresh, and a woman called Cindy had donated a three-pack of boxer shorts in a Wichita car park two days earlier. Choosing what pair of trousers to wear was even less problematic, since one of the three pairs I'd packed was some 1,600 kilometres distant in a Chicago hotel, possibly still in the wardrobe where I'd hung them five days before.

'Come on then,' said Matt, the previously unnamed Norwegian gentleman with his previously unmentioned

Cheshire accent. 'Let's see you make a daft sod of yourself for the camera.'

The first time Matt and I met was in the very same hotel, twenty-four hours earlier. I'd agreed to bed down in his room barely twelve hours before that. We'd been perfect strangers less than two days ago, yet there we were accompanying one another along silent corridors to the elevator, where we descended to the ground floor and tiptoed through reception to the lobby bar. The previous evening's drunken roars from twenty-somethings in ironic T-shirts were replaced by the sound of a three-man production crew tearing duct tape to secure snakes of cable across the floor. A light stronger than the Texan sun singled out a chair in the centre of the room. Syd the producer gestured to me to sit down and stare into the light, while I sneaked a mic and an earpiece under my T-shirt to my neckline.

'Morning, Paul. You're looking really fresh today,' an excitable voice crackled into my ear. The owner of the voice had the all-American name Ted Winner, and he was a television producer talking to me from Times Square in New York City. 'Thanks again for doing this so early on a Sunday!'

'You're very welcome,' I lied once more as the cameraman bothered my face with powder. 'Just out of interest, how many people will be watching this?'

Through my earpiece, the disembodied voice of Ted suggested the sort of number scientists fling about with dizzy recklessness when describing how many stars populate the galaxy, or the number of atoms in a wheel of cheese. That couldn't be right. He must have meant thousands. Or tens.

The situation really wasn't making any sense. I couldn't discern a) what I was doing out of bed so early on a Sunday, b) why anybody else would be up at the same time, unless they were on fire, and c) why these people cared to interview me when viewers could no doubt be watching a non-stop *CSI* marathon on another channel.

'Bloody hell, really?' was my considered response. 'Were you having a slow news day?'

'Hey, you're big news, Paul. We're really lucky to have you.' Flattery will get you everywhere, I thought, except at ten to six on a Sunday morning.

'Nervous?' asked Ted.

'More so now you've asked the question,' I replied.

'Don't worry, you'll be fine.'

I was about to be beamed into the homes of several million viewers on ABC's *Good Morning America*, live from Austin, Texas. A fortnight ago, I was burning Yorkshire puddings in my kitchen, nearly 8,000 kilometres away in the north-east of England. In the space of fourteen days my world had become a blur of travel, of trusting strangers with my life, and there were plenty more moments of suspended reality to follow. I would go on to woo A-list celebrities, have film stars ejected from VIP lounges and gaze across the greatest natural beauty on earth – all while wearing the same pair of underpants.

How the hell did I get here?

Chapter 2

When we resign from a job that has made us progressively ill, miserable or mad as hell to the point of wanting to punch a nun, we pray the management will realise the error of their ways and beg us to stay. We hope the boss will break down in floods of tears, fall on their knees and wrap their arms tightly around our legs with childlike abandonment of shame, plead with us to reconsider, and offer more money than can be stuffed into a reasonably sized duffel bag.

We dream to be irreplaceable, indispensable, we want to be that vital cog in the corporate machine, to know our departure will bring about the end of days for the company and see those responsible burn in a festering trough of their own faeces, while we laugh heartily and skip into the golden sunshine of our future, having stuck it to The Man good and proper.

What we don't wish to observe under any circumstance is our line manager stand up and point at the door while screaming spittle into our face in a manner similar to Donald Sutherland during the finale of *Invasion of the Body Snatchers*. Or appear so unmoved by proceedings we question why they hired us in the first place. Or perform any other act which serves to reinforce how utterly worthless and pathetically inconsequential our contribution to the company has been.

Given the choice between these two scenarios, it'll come as no surprise whatsoever when you learn which one greeted my decision to exit a twelve-year career in the radio industry.

I developed a crush on radio when I was fourteen, while my friends were developing a taste for illicit sips of Diamond White, as well as still-developing girls. I didn't manage to kiss the fairer sex until I was seventeen, by which time several of my classmates were fathers; I'd become far too occupied with loafing about in hospital radio to waste time going tops-up. Wearing my dad's blazer and sharing the occasional can of Kestrel Super Strength with Adrian Taylor in the abandoned yards and wynds of Darlington town centre was the height of my recklessness.

As my affair with radio blossomed, my interest in academia evaporated; after two months at Leeds University studying physics with astrophysics, it was patently obvious that a) I cared little for a career as a rocket scientist, and b) I was never going to get laid if I kept studying it. I abandoned my degree and set about carving out a career at my local radio station, beginning as an unpaid dogsbody and quickly progressing to unpaid lackey. I also dabbled in on-air presenting but my brain ran at twice the speed of my mouth and I would constantly trip over my words. It was immensely gratifying, though; in the same breath I had an idea, it would spill out into the microphone.

I became friends with a local musician call Jon Kirby, a blonde-haired, blue-eyed, happy-go-lucky character, full of jokes and laughter and reputed owner of Darlington's largest collection of *Razzle* back issues, and who'd enjoyed modest chart success with north-east band Dubstar. Jon soon became a regular guest on the evening show I presented, and together we critiqued new releases. Perhaps our most insightful review was of the debut single by an unknown group called the Spice Girls, who'd perfected the sonic imitation of a bag of cats having their backs shaved. We didn't hesitate in ruling out any future success for girl power. You just can't buy that sort of intuition.

Those were heady days, when indie ruled the charts, England discovered they could play football again (so long as you were content with not winning anything), and I was a very minor personality after appearing on page eleven of the *Darlington and Stockton Times*. In the decade that followed, I whored myself at another ten radio stations up and down the country, as a radio producer, programmer and manager. There were the stratospheric highs of scriptwriting for Johnny Vegas and Hugh Laurie, and employing Richard Bacon for a whole five weeks, and the subterranean lows of getting up early to argue with Terry Christian before, during and after his daily breakfast show on BBC local radio, but I could only ever see myself working in radio. I adored everything about it – its diversity and immediacy, its warmth and intimacy.

Meanwhile, my friend Jon had been led away from the lifestyle of the jobbing songwriter by the allure of insanely repetitive playlists, and had joined the promotions department of a local commercial station. We daydreamed of working together again, and opportunity knocked while I was a producer at the BBC in Leeds – my editor John Ryan inexplicably entrusted me with a weekly show and allowed Jon to co-host, despite having only my word that it wouldn't be a diabolical shambles.

And so, Jon and I set the controls for the heart of the sun, with a blank canvas for trying out all the nonsense we'd dreamed up over the years. Our favourite feature was undoubtedly *My Mum's Better Than Your Mum*, which involved quizzing one another's mother to determine who had bragging rights for the following week. It was often my mum who proved the most entertaining – partly because she would flirt outrageously with Jon, but mostly because she was and remains as mad as a barrel of monkeys:

Jon: 'Right, Sheila, question one. What animal is also a type of shoe?'

Sheila: 'What type of what?'

Jon: 'Animal.'

Sheila: '... is an animal?'

Paul: 'Is a shoe, mother. What type of animal is a shoe?'

Sheila: 'I don't think I know that.'

Jon: 'Think of Winnie the Pooh, Sheila.'

Paul: 'He always helps you, doesn't he?'

Sheila: 'I know he does.'

Paul: 'No, I said, *he always* helps. *He always* helps.'

Sheila: 'He's what?'

Paul: 'Eeyore mother, Eeyore!'

Sheila: 'Oh, Eeyore!'

Paul: 'Yes!'

Sheila: 'Is the answer donkey?'

Jon: 'Yes Sheila, the answer is the donkey shoe. Well done.'

Eventually I was offered a job managing the presenters of a regional station in the north-east of England, where I wasted no time in taking on Jon as my deputy. We'd become best friends and I trusted the man with my life – admittedly, he'd probably have some excuse about the traffic when arriving ten minutes late to save it, but he'd turn up nevertheless. We were in charge of a station that broadcast to two million people and had a very generous budget to blow, so we'd nurse beers in our favourite bars, daring to dream of a new golden age of radio that teemed with big personalities and bold ideas.

We barely got started. I horribly underestimated the demands of senior management and amount of political bullshit I'd be forced to wade through. All I wanted to do was win the audience over with exciting, engaging radio, not play games and massage egos, which meant I spent my days either in a manic whirlwind of ideas and hyperactivity, or as an impetuous, miserable child with a face like a burglar's dog.

After ten months, the role broke my spirit and my passion for radio had bled away. I never saw it coming; there wasn't a defining moment that required a defining song, just a sequence of days and then weeks that increasingly saw more bad than good. And so without much of a clue as to how I'd pay the mortgage, I resigned. My managing director, a tall lady with a demonstrable addiction to Walkers Sensations Thai Sweet Chilli flavour crisps, barely ticked the boxes one should when faced with the resignation of a senior manager. A boss should at least feign the five stages of grief for the sake of the employee, yet there was only a smattering of denial, barely a whiff of anger, precisely no bargaining, a sliver of depression, with the acceptance of the situation arriving midway through a mouthful of crisps and far too quickly for my liking. In summary, my managing director wasn't entirely arsed.

I still had to explain my decision to the group director, who arrived unexpectedly a couple of hours later. He was a man I'd admired from afar since starting out in radio; an intelligent, well-respected operator who knew plenty about the industry, but who had smothered me with a lard-doused pillow since the day I arrived. Instead of allowing me to learn from my mistakes, he saw to it that I never made any; my frustration had led to conflict and resentment.

Our meeting was short and to the point. The lack of expression or concern on his face meant I was neither going to be sorely missed nor leave in a blaze of glory. And when I spoke of my frustrations and being held back from trying my big ideas, that's when he scooped my guts out and spilt them all over the carpet:

'It's not your job to have big ideas, Paul. It's mine.'

Ouch. All the plans Jon and I had, all our schemes to ensure the station saw its day in the sun, they were never going to happen. I clenched my jaw tight, hoping the furious rage chewing at my chest wouldn't reduce me to tears.

During those final few days of bitterness and misery and blubbing like the fat girl at the end of a party, I registered on a social networking website called Twitter at five minutes past nine on the evening of 20 October 2007. My account remained largely unused for the first few weeks – I was too busy figuring out what the blithering hell I was doing with my life. I only knew that I had to be in control, so that whatever ideas I had – no matter how idiotic or likely to fail – wouldn't have to remain a daydream.

My yearning for epic adventure was aroused many years before I plucked up the courage to walk out on my radio career. In fact, I was in the bath. It was a nondescript Saturday afternoon in September 2004, and if I had become accomplished at anything by my thirtieth year on planet Earth, it was submersing myself in lukewarm water for several hours at a stretch. That, and skilfully manipulating taps with my feet. I only ever shower when I can't justify writing off half a day for a bath, or when I can smell my own body odour. Bathing, on the other hand, is an activity for gentlemen – an altogether regal luxury enhanced by a chilled glass of 1988 Krug and an eagerly anticipated hardback autobiography. Or a can of Stella Artois and the free paper.

On this particular Saturday afternoon, the lazy autumnal sunshine filtered through the patterned glaze of the bathroom window and a copy of *McCarthy's Bar* was perched on my belly, nervously teetering above the waterline. Pete McCarthy was reasonably well known for his series *Travelog* on Channel 4, and his first book sold over a million copies. *McCarthy's Bar* was a rudely brilliant and deeply personal account of his journey through the backwaters of rural Ireland. It was impossible to read without tumbling into love with the notion of slinging on a rucksack and exploring the Irish countryside, seeking out the truly traditional Irish pub that proved so elusive to McCarthy, rather than those that celebrate St Patrick's Day by investing in foam hats. At that point I'd only ever travelled as a teenager with my parents to the Costa Brava, and on a package holiday to Egypt, which I recalled not so fondly as being one part Indiana Jones-esque temples and hieroglyphics, and two parts food poisoning and subsequent squits.

I digested a substantial wedge of *McCarthy's Bar* that afternoon and had all but lost myself in dreams of supping stouts as thick as porridge and dancing jigs with locals. Then I read McCarthy's explanation of why the timeless American tradition of the cross-country road trip was entirely absent from British culture. It wasn't an astonishing revelation, but one I hadn't considered before – there simply isn't enough road stretching in any one direction for very long. The distance from the snout of Scotland to the tail of Cornwall can be completed by car in fifteen hours – hardly an epic adventure.

I hooked the hot tap with the heel of my left foot and set about solving the challenge posed by the UK's geographical inadequacy. By the time the steaming water ran cold, I had the answer. A road trip lasting several weeks was entirely possible, so long as you travelled very slowly. I'd have to drive a vehicle that by its very nature would crawl along the road. A milk float! And so in that slowly cooling trough of dead skin and oily sweat, I spent another half hour fantasising about a journey along country lanes, trundling through picturesque hamlets, quaffing real ale in real alehouses and indulging in parochial gossip as a lusty, busty barmaid provocatively handled the wooden shaft of her beer pump.

Adventure ahoy! At least, it was until I clambered out of the bath, realised there were no towels at hand, scarpered bollock naked through the house to the airing cupboard to retrieve one, dried myself, dressed, sat down with my laptop and looked up the price of second-hand milk floats. Balls. I didn't have a spare £2,000 for my chariot of choice, but then since I was still in full-time employment at the time, neither could I take a month or two off in order to drive it. I put my plans for the open road to one side and slunk back to the day job of mucking about in radio stations.

Pete McCarthy died of cancer a month later at the outrageously young age of 52. His work had shaken me by the shoulders and dared me to travel, and in the years that followed I began to peek at what else the world offered. I travelled to the US for the first time and began a very public affair with New York. It was an explosive city, full of life, an adventure on every corner. Over successive visits I explored the nooks and crannies of Brooklyn and the Bronx, and became a regular in the bars of Hell's Kitchen, in particular a dive called Rudy's at 44th Street and Ninth Avenue. You'll remember Rudy's if you've visited there – a man-sized statue of Porky Pig eyes you up outside a bar you'd never consider entering in daylight. Or while sober. Inside is a God-awful mess of black ceilings, untreated brickwork and bulging red neon, with a washroom that appears to have been kicked down a hill. Promise me you'll visit.

When I walked out on my radio career, my gallivanting across the Atlantic was seriously curtailed. During the first few months, I didn't travel anywhere except up and down my own staircase as I re-invented myself as a writer. I picked up a semi-regular gig blogging for *The Guardian*, hardly enough to pay the bills but a good badge to wear when talking to prospective employers. Over time I assembled a ragtag roster of freelance jobs that meant I could turn up to work in my dressing gown and slippers without brushing my teeth or wearing underwear. My office was a desk in my dining room, from which I wrote and blogged and nipped next door to worry the fridge more than is considered acceptable by dieticians.

As a result, I became entirely dependent on my precious broadband connection for my livelihood. It was an emotional and precarious relationship, especially when the connection would occasionally fall over and die as a critical deadline approached. It was tantamount to paralysis, and not the sort of paralysis that sees you off to swim with dolphins for a week in Florida. I'd perform the Wi-Fi equivalent of CPR, turning the router off and back on, unplugging all the cables and plugging them back in again. Uninstalling software, reinstalling software. I'd regularly spend hours pouring my soul into the telephone while BT and Sky contradicted one another, unable to agree on who was to blame, only that somebody was but it wasn't them. In desperation, I'd kneel down and pray to God and little baby Jesus for my broadband to be resurrected. Admittedly not the best use of a prayer, and God would acknowledge this by doing nothing whatsoever.

Without broadband, life was meaningless – I was unable to communicate with the world around me. I was a 3D man in a 2D man's world, like Jeff Bridges in *Tron*. The greatest loss wasn't necessarily my ability to work, but my ability to tweet. After quitting my job, I'd begun using Twitter more and more frequently, to the point of addiction. Quarter to two in the morning. In the car. The bath. On the toilet. In fact, a great deal of my time on the toilet was spent reading the comments of others on Twitter. The prolonging of my bathroom habits eventually led to an acute case of haemorrhoids, but on the plus side I was saving money by no longer subscribing to *Total Film*.

If you've never used Twitter, let me tell you a little about it: Twitter allows you to post short updates on the Internet – no more than 140 characters – about your current thoughts or activities, which can be read by anyone else in the world. This initially sounds like a pathetically inconsequential exercise, the reduction of small talk to quantum minutiae. Who cares what you had for lunch? Does the world really need your point of view on *The Apprentice*?

But then it clicks. Twitter isn't a one-way broadcast – it's a two-way conversation. You can comment on a website, a news story, a sandwich filling, and if enough people are paying attention, they'll reply with their comments, their news, or seven ways to create an even better sandwich filling. You can follow what other people are saying and other people can follow you, and if you reach a critical mass of friends and followers then the exchange of conversation, news and information becomes not only addictive but indispensable.

In my case, Twitter had rescued me from the isolation of working as a freelancer in an empty dining room by delivering a new social circle, a support network of other writers and a bountiful supply of inspiration for feature ideas for commissioning editors to subsequently reject and ask a staff writer to produce when they thought I wasn't looking.

Twitter was transforming the way I communicated with individuals not only in this country, but around the world. And as I found myself prying into their lives, a fleeting thought flashed behind my eyes – would a stranger, who knew me only by a real-time, bite-sized commentary of my life, ever welcome me into his or her home? Could I use this new network to travel the world and meet these people? How far would one Twitter acquaintance – a tweep – go for another? Could I trust them with my life?

Chapter 3

An evening of gentlemanly excess enjoyed in the company of Captain Stella and his first mate Jim Beam had resulted in the hangover from hell, and a thousand lunatics wailed and clawed inside my skull for sweet release. My heavy-headedness meant I'd staggered out of bed far too late for a Saturday, and my punishment was to spend lunchtime amongst the living damned, known locally as Gateshead Tesco. The one and only rule of weekend supermarket shopping is you hit them early and hit them hard – in and out before 9 a.m. with military precision – otherwise you risk exposure to members of the public who will conspire to ruin your day. Specifically:

a) those who can't be trusted with a shopping list without having to call home and verify every item on it
b) the elderly, couples in particular
c) housewives who abandon their trolleys lengthways in the freezer section upon realising they've forgotten the carrots
d) parents with more than one child

e) anyone who goes to the supermarket to 'get out of the house for a while'

f) drivers who don't understand that Bluetooth headsets are for in-car use only

and, depending on my mood:

g) everyone else

My irascible mood was intensified by circling Tesco's car park for twenty minutes, during which time I swore at drivers who had straddled two bays, and raced at breakneck speeds to claim a free space, only to find some wanker with a better car than mine reversing into it. The filthy concrete hulk of Trinity car park stared down on my frustrated game of cat and mouse. Famous the world over for its role alongside Michael Caine in *Get Carter*, it was considered a 'culturally significant' structure by renowned architects – none of whom had to live in Gateshead and gaze upon its eye-shriekingly hideous form on a daily basis. It was a miserable spectacle under a heartbroken sky, and its very presence in my line of sight made me all the more furious on that day.

After nearly a year of logging in to Twitter on a daily basis I would use it to vent my inner bile, as many other users did. It was all very cathartic, being able to silently rant in public, and this day was no different. I'd barely made it into the vegetable aisle, before my access to the red onions was barred by a gentleman on crutches, all four limbs splayed like a baby giraffe wearing roller boots. He was accompanied by his wife, who reversed her scooter over my foot. A low guttural sound may have escaped from my throat but I quite definitely screamed 'Careless bitch!' within the confines of my head. Twitter learned of my despondency too, as I punched my thumb into my mobile:

> **paul_a_smith** The seventh circle of Hell continues to intersect the Earth at Tesco on a Saturday lunchtime. Why wait until now to road-test your mobility scooter? Gah.
>
> *1:04 PM Jan 31st*

It was around this time that the UK media began taking an interest in Twitter. Two celebrities were roundly responsible for generating press coverage of the service, albeit under very different circumstances. The first, Stephen Fry, registered on Twitter on 15 July 2008 and took to tweeting like a duck to orange sauce. My friend Andy quite rightly describes Fry as the country's favourite uncle – a tea-drinking, darts-fancying, intellectual cornerstone of British culture, his prowess in the fields of comedy, television, technology, literature and the arts ensured an intensely loyal fan base on Twitter. When Fry tweeted, both the public and the media followed.

Over four months later, on 30 November 2008, British TV and radio presenter Jonathan Ross signed up to Twitter. Whereas Stephen Fry's fascination with gadgets and gizmos compelled him to experiment with this new service, Ross unexpectedly found himself with plenty of time on his hands following a notorious incident involving a prank radio call on a Spanish waiter. The stunt raised thousands of complaints and Ross was subsequently suspended by the

BBC. The presenter retreated immediately from the baying mob and little was heard from him again – at least, not until he joined Twitter a month later. The media discovered they had access once more, and soon the tabloids filled their pages with sensational headlines spun from his throwaway tweets, inadvertently creating national press coverage for Twitter. When Ross returned from his suspension and discussed Twitter on his TV chat show (together with his guest Stephen Fry, naturally), the UK went bananas for it.

The media was unhappy with Twitter for an awfully long time, because they were having to report on a phenomenon they didn't fully understand themselves. Whenever journalists made an attempt to describe Twitter, they resorted to the tired stereotype of users offering nothing more than benign descriptions of their eating habits – the two-way nature of sharing and conversing was entirely lost on them.

That changed when Captain Chesley Sullenberger successfully landed Flight 1549 on New York's Hudson River. The story broke not over television or radio as it would have a decade ago, not even on news websites as it would have two or three years ago, but through a Twitter message, a tweet, attached to a single photograph of passengers stood on the wing of a sinking plane.

> **jkrums** There's a plane in the Hudson. I'm on the ferry going to pick up the people. Crazy.
>
> *3:36 PM Jan 15th*

The message and accompanying image were forwarded to hundreds of thousands of Twitter users around the globe within seconds; it was a tourist called Janis Krums who published the world's first image of the downed plane, while journalists at *The New York Times* barely a kilometre from the Hudson were preparing stories that wouldn't be read until the following day.

My personal use of Twitter was far more mundane and usually observational, conversational or, as in this instance, cathartic. After purging my displeasure by sharing it with other Twitter users, I successfully coerced a bag of red onions into the trolley and made my way to the end of the aisle to discover a shouty mother of five, plus said five, forming a human shield around the sausages. I was stressed, she was stressed, the children weren't thrilled by their predicament either.

It was in the bread aisle where I finally snapped. There'd been some sort of multi-trolley pile-up, and there was no way through without cutting-gear or dynamite. Groups of shoppers blocked the thoroughfare, exchanging neighbourly gossip, stories of holidays abroad and their views concerning the recession, the weather, the demise of society, Cheryl Cole and any other topic that ensured I could only stare longingly at the distant French sticks beyond them.

paul_a_smith It's not a social club, people. The bread aisle is at a standstill while you reminisce how much better life used to be. Now for fuck's sake, move.

1:19 PM Jan 31st

And that's when my brain started daydreaming, leaving the rest of me to mooch about near the hot dog buns and give the plain clothes detectives cause for concern. What was I doing in that place? I wanted to abandon my trolley, set it free and skedaddle the hell out of there. But to where? Anywhere, it didn't matter. What about that idea to explore the country on a milk float? No, wait. The other idea. What was the other idea again? Twitter. Travel the world using Twitter, that was it. Why didn't I go ahead and try that? How far could I circumnavigate the globe relying on people I'd never met? Was it remotely possible? How long before I ended up a torso case in a ditch?

The anger and bile ebbed away. I'd had an idea, and a not inconsiderable one at that. I'd be the first Globe Twitterer! Globe Tweeter. A Twit Tripper. No, got it. I'd be a Twitchhiker, and I would attempt to travel as far as possible from home in thirty days, relying entirely on the kindness and goodwill of people using Twitter. It was the most ridiculous, least violent thought I'd had in the past hour, and I had absolutely no excuse not to attempt it.

Why? We all have a dozen ideas a day, and amongst them we occasionally have one that is unique and wonderful. Most of us won't act, citing our jobs, family, bank balances or other excuses, only to suffer the teeth-grinding frustration of hearing months later that somebody else had not only a similar idea, but the guts to try it. Has that ever happened to you?

I couldn't let that happen to me. I'd promised myself when I had a big idea, I'd do it – not procrastinate until I'd talked myself out of it. I'd get on and make it happen so I didn't have to live with the regret.

I was going to be a Twitchhiker, and it'd be a grand adventure, an adventure wrapped in nonsense and cocooned in daft. All I had to do was explain the idea to my wife, Jane.

The wife to whom I'd been married for four whole days.

I picked up a tub of Ben & Jerry's and a bag of Kettle Chips to assist my cause in the negotiations ahead, made a mental note to leave out the bit about becoming a torso case and speculated on whether the marriage would reach double digits.

Chapter 4

I completed the rest of the shopping on autopilot, forgetting essentials like bin liners and cat biscuits. My body belonged to Tesco, but my mind was far, far away, somewhere in the southern hemisphere where people were altogether more pleasant and spatially aware of those desperate for foreign bread products to fulfil their middle-class pretensions. The idea of twitchhiking buzzed and bolted and whirled about behind my eyes, a white-hot pinball bouncing off synapses and bits of brain.

Through the checkout, across the car park, driving home – I began painting in the detail of my outlandish folly. How would this work? How would I convince people to support me? Could I avoid driving into the Ford Sierra ahead?

I'd either failed to notice the traffic lights turn to red, or been overwhelmed at the sight of a roadworthy Ford Sierra. I suspected the latter, since I rarely paid attention to my own driving and hadn't died yet. In fact, it was an increasingly common occurrence to find myself motoring along a road and have no memory of how I'd arrived there. You first start to notice these lapses in awareness while watching the television and during conversations with customer service operators. And then that's it, game over – you're in your mid-thirties, your memory's shot, there are thickets of wiry hair sprouting out your ears and you're unable to accurately judge the age of anyone younger than twenty-five. I was thirty-three and felt I was already staring middle age square in the eye, which I imagined looked a lot like the melting face of Ronald Lacey's bald Nazi in the finale of *Raiders of the Lost Ark*. Perhaps that's why I was so enamoured with the idea of twitchhiking; I was trying to defy my age and responsibilities. None of it would matter if I died in what was becoming an inevitable collision with the Sierra.

The swift application of my foot to the brake pedal resulted in a sliding skid across the oily road, up the kerb and within a hair's girth of the B-reg jalopy. I offered the driver the response most appropriate for nearly causing serious injury through negligence – I held up the flat palm of my hand and shrugged gently while looking a little sheepish about the matter. He gave me the finger.

A near-death experience while travelling – something I'd no doubt have to prepare myself for. Did I really want to trust my life to strangers on the Internet? Maybe they'd be perfectly pleasant and normal. Maybe they'd collect live hand grenades, or own a hand-stitched suit of meat. But that was unlikely. Wasn't it?

If I were travelling for thirty days, I'd need some mechanism to keep people interested in my journey. There had to be an element of uncertainty, the possibility that I could fail at any moment and find myself at the mercy of Mister Meat. I needed rules for my world adventure like I needed toilet roll, but that was still sat on the shelves of Tesco. What I'd gained in delusions of grandeur, I'd lost in urgently required comestibles.

I unloaded the shopping from the car and realised I'd forgotten the milk too. By now my head was exploding with ideas that shouted over one another for attention. Somewhere in the muddle was the blueprint, I just needed to extract it from my head. Whenever my head was cluttered with ideas while writing, and it happened a lot, I'd put my fingertips to my temples and flick them towards the computer, as if exorcising the elusive prose from my brain onto the screen. And I wouldn't just do it once, but over and over. This brought only fleeting relief to my frustration, and in no way constituted a medical cure for writer's block. On this occasion I was stood outside my front door at the open boot of my car, violently casting my fingers from my head into the sky above. To the untrained eye of eighty-three-year-old Mrs Dorchester at number twenty-five, I was either performing a council-funded street theatre project or confirming her long-held suspicions that I was a mentalist.

I couldn't wait, the ice cream would have to sit in the kitchen and thaw to a puddle. I assumed the pose of *Le Penseur* at my desk before recommencing the crazy hand-flicking thing, trying to decide where to start. Then it occurred to me that it might be easier to decide where to finish. Travelling as far as possible in thirty days lacked a definitive finish line – a cause requiring support needed a clear goal, so I'd aim to reach the exact opposite side of the planet.

I opened up EarthTools.org, a website that identifies geographical coordinates for locations on Google Maps, and zoomed in on my address in Gateshead. There it was at 54.93 degrees north and 1.59 degrees west. After a quick scribble of maths on the back of an envelope, I traversed the globe to peer down at 54.93 degrees south and 178.41 degrees east – the point on the opposite side of the globe to where I was sat. There was no street like mine, nor was there anything to build one on – only a screen full of blue. I zoomed out. And out again. And again. And again. The southern tip of New Zealand eventually appeared to the north. I switched to the satellite view to find more blue, but it was a deep, inky blue, the colour that indicated depths where sea monsters lurked and lost cities lay undisturbed for millennia. Short of a helping hand from Doug McClure and his diving bell, I wouldn't be setting foot there.

I scoured the seas for the closest knuckle of rock I could aim for instead. At 52.54 degrees south and 169.12 degrees east there was land ahoy, or at least a good shovel's worth of grit. It was an irregular shape, like a Han character from the Chinese alphabet, and tiny – no more than 15 kilometres across. Combinations and permutations of search terms eventually revealed a name; Campbell Island was discovered two centuries ago by Frederick Hasselburgh, captain of a vessel owned by Sydney-based shipping company Campbell & Co. In the years that followed, visitors to its shores explored the island's herb fields, bemoaned the often inclement weather and slaughtered the native seal population, after which they took to sticking harpoons into nearby whales. Not content with clubbing and stabbing everything with soft brown eyes or a blowhole, the nineteenth-century adventurers introduced feral livestock to the island, as well as what would become the world's densest infestation of *Rattus norvegicus*, which decimated the indigenous wildlife and caused the extinction of several species of bird. Come the twentieth century, and upon realising what a sow's ear they'd made of it all, the feral cattle and sheep were culled, millions of dollars were spent eradicating the vermin and the island was designated a UNESCO World Heritage Site.

We had a winner. Six hundred kilometres off the southernmost tip of New Zealand and 18,847 kilometres as the crow flew – assuming it didn't die of exhaustion – from Gateshead, Campbell Island was my intended destination. As if the notion of strangers caring enough to propel me around the world wasn't improbable enough, I wanted to reach an abandoned rock where not even rats were welcome. But if Alice's Queen could believe in six impossible things before breakfast, then conjuring up a couple by mid-afternoon was surely child's play. With one part of the jigsaw firmly in place, I returned to the kitchen to find a highly irritated wife pouring a tub of ice cream down the sink.

My challenge required rules. How could I ensure people would notice my attempt and, more importantly, be so intrigued by the sheer lunacy of it that they told others? How could I hold their attention in the weeks before the event and during the thirty days I'd spend travelling? There had to be an element of risk, people had to know that nothing about the journey was a certainty and that there might come a point when their involvement would determine my fate. I considered running a bath to mull over the rules, but as it transpired I couldn't type them fast enough:

1. I can only accept offers of travel and accommodation on Twitter, from individuals or businesses.

Rather than ask people to contact friends or family and ask if they'd consider helping me, I wanted to test whether relationships built within social media had real emotional and practical value. There was another important aspect to this rule, in that others would determine when and where I travelled, with no influence from me – I couldn't ask for specific help at any time.

2. I can only spend money on food, drink and anything that might fit in my suitcase.

A bus ticket, a train fare, a lift down the road or a bed for the night – depending on a virtual community for every aspect of my travel and accommodation would certainly test their generosity and goodwill. Since I couldn't request specific help, there'd be no guarantee that an offer of transport would marry up to one of accommodation – some kind soul might offer to drive me cross-country, but would there be shelter waiting for me at the other end?

3. I can't make any plans further than three days in advance.

Unless an offer of transport or accommodation was made within seventy-two hours of it being applicable, I couldn't accept it. This would be crucial in keeping people's attention and maintaining momentum – nobody, myself included, would know what would happen next.

4. If there's more than one offer on the table, I get to choose which I take. If there's only one, I have to take it within forty-eight hours.

Twitter had to determine my fate at every step. In that context, this rule made perfect sense. In the context of having to accept an invitation from Crazy Man Withers that led to my remains being dredged up by the crew of a Spanish fishing trawler, this rule wasn't a favourite of mine.

5. If I'm unable to find a way to move on from a location within forty-eight hours, the challenge is over and I go home.

Perhaps the physical and virtual worlds people immersed themselves in every day were disparate and disconnected from one another and Twitter users wouldn't be prepared to assist me outside our online relationship, in which case I'd return to England with my tail between my legs. That would be the worst possible outcome – aside from that business with the fishing trawler, obviously.

The rules already felt like hard work. The journey would not only be unpredictable, it would be relentless. There'd be precious little time to plan my next move, even less to recuperate in between travelling. I couldn't afford to take time off from my freelance writing, so I'd have to somehow squeeze that into my itinerary too. I had a couple of solid freelance writing gigs, including one that required me to file editorial copy three to four days a week. I couldn't give that work up, not without missing payments on the mortgage, or slipping beyond the £5,000 overdraft limit. Then there was the bank loan. And the credit card payments. And the bills. Wait a minute, what the hell was I thinking? Without creating some previously unimagined branch of mathematics, there was no chance I could take this trip without causing financial ruin.

Fuck it. Fuck. It.

I couldn't let it go. I shook my head at myself for even considering giving up. I was already daring to believe it was possible; walking away from it wasn't any sort of option. Perhaps that wasn't my decision to make, at least not mine alone. Sooner or later I'd have to tell my wife what I was planning.

In recent years I'd given Jane more than enough reason to abandon me and my wide-eyed dreams. Our non-wedding in Las Vegas was the most extreme example of this, and the nadir of our relationship; we arrived in Nevada engaged and all set to wed, but returned home single. The day was without doubt the worst of my life; every minute of every hour saw the two of us sat on the hotel bed crying, the silence only broken by chokes of sobbing or the thump of Moët against the wall. Obviously Jane was aiming for my head, but fortunately her inadequate lob (who on earth throws underarm in anger?) failed to shatter the champagne bottle – allowing me to become hysterically drunk on the contents during the non-honeymoon that followed in San Francisco.

Together and apart, together and apart, yet we remained in one another's orbits and eventually recognised that each made the other whole – I suspect Jane knew it was the case many years before I did, yet I was cruel and reckless with her heart. After two proposals had come to nothing (there was another before Vegas, but that particular story lacks the tits and tinsel of the Vegas debacle), we married in Empire-Fulton Ferry State Park in New York, the view of Manhattan across the East River framed by the magnificence of the Brooklyn and Manhattan Bridges.

The date of our wedding was 27 January.

The date I dreamed up Twitchhiker was 31 January.

Of the same month.

Just four days after becoming husband and wife, I was about to tell her I was leaving her to travel to the opposite side of the planet.

'I've had an idea,' I announced, in a manner that was supposed to suggest I hadn't given it very much thought.

'Go on,' said Jane, in a tone that suggested she already knew what was coming.

'I think I might try travelling around the world using Twitter.'

'Around the world? To where?'

'New Zealand, maybe?' It was possible to hear the wince in my voice.

There was a moment's pause as her beautiful blue eyes stared into mine to ascertain whether I was serious or high on glue.

'Seriously?'

'I think so, yeah.'

'What about money? When are you going to work? And the boys? What about the boys?'

The boys? Oh yes. I was a father to twin boys, the blond-haired, blue-eyed Jack and Sam, each of them angel and demon in equal measure. As well as leaving my wife of five days, I'd be abandoning our children for a month. I was already so consumed by the idea and its trivialities that I'd given scant consideration to the boys or their needs. I'd let them down in the past, abandoning them not only on the occasions Jane and I were separated, but for the sake of my career too. Fortunately, life had moved on – we were a family, happy and together, and I'd worked hard to atone for my past failures. I reasoned that the boys were young, that they were used to me working away from home. We could buy a webcam for the home computer so we could chat online. Think about how proud the boys would be if I pulled this off, I exclaimed. In truth, I would have said anything to overcome Jane's objections, but there was no need.

'OK. Just put it on the calendar and let me know when you're going.'

I looked her in the eye, held her stare for a handful of seconds. She was serious. And she was smiling. I had her blessing and that was that. And that's why I had married her.

Chapter 5

At 139 metres tall and with a maximum speed of 206 kilometres per hour, the Kingda Ka at Six Flags Great Adventure in New Jersey is the tallest and fastest rollercoaster in the world. In 2007, the British media reported that a forty-two-year-old housewife from Bristol swallowed her own eyes, pushed down her throat by the intense acceleration. Of course, I've made this up, but the point is that, as if New Jersey isn't terrifying enough, the Kingda Ka puts its passengers through a kamikaze blur of nausea and helplessness. Once strapped in, you have no choice but to endure the twenty-eight seconds of twisting screams that follow.

But then it is only twenty-eight seconds – a doddle compared to the twenty-eight days that preceded the beginning of my journey around the world. For those four weeks I rode my own Kingda Ka, disorientated and out of control, overwhelmed by the pant-wetting terror and head-bursting excitement of it all.

It had occurred to me that mine was exactly the sort of lunatic adventure that could easily raise money for charity. At the time, Twitter was buzzing about Twestival, a worldwide series of events to raise money for '*charity: water*', a non-profit-making organisation that provides clean and safe drinking water to communities in developing nations. Awareness of the charity was so high amongst Twitter users, it made sense to continue the fundraising efforts of Twestival. The cost of drilling a freshwater well starts at $4,000; I wasn't undertaking my journey in the name of charity, but if I could raise at least that much and increase awareness of the organisation, then I wouldn't be the only person to benefit from the generosity of Twitter. I hurriedly opened an account on the Just Giving website and set a target of £3,000. It sounded too ambitious, but then I was already shooting for the stars.

I announced my idea on Twitter on Monday 2 February – just forty-eight hours after conceiving it in the supermarket – with the intention of leaving for Campbell Island on Sunday 1 March. I'd created a blog that detailed the challenge and its rules, and included my email address so I could receive electronic tickets or other travel documents once an offer was accepted. I also registered the @twitchhiker name to use on Twitter – I was more likely to be noticed if I assumed a unique identity rather than my own bland username.

paul_a_smith Alright. Here we go. Everyone, I need your help on this. Please follow @twitchhiker, RT this message and read the blog at http://twitchhiker.com.

12:25 PM Feb 2nd

I sat and stared long and hard at that tweet before sending it. Remember the last email you sent, or the last phone call you made, that you knew would have consequences? That as soon as you hit 'Send' or the words began tumbling out of your mouth, there could be no retractions, no way back? Remember how that pang of adrenalin boomed and burst in your chest, throbbing away until it choked your lungs? And once you finally fired off that mail, once you'd spat out the words and hung up, all you wanted to do was scream into a cushion?

None of this was real until I told people it was. It could have been another one of those silly ideas I filed away in the back of my brain. It was only because I sensed Jane walk up behind me that I hit the 'Enter' key. Although I'd outlined the concept of Twitchhiker to her, she wasn't convinced I'd go through with it; I'd excitedly enthused to Jane about a dozen grand schemes previously, including my plans to invent the portable toaster, and none had ever come to fruition.

> **paul_a_smith** I think I'm going to be sick.
>
> *12:33 PM Feb 2nd*

I shut my laptop down, terrified at what I'd set in motion, and retreated to the dinner table where Jane had served lunch. I cried into my ham salad, explaining what I'd done between sobs, told her I was sorry, that I didn't have to go through with it, there was still time to back out. She listened, hugged me, kissed my cheek, reassured me that it would work and we'd be all the stronger for it. Neither of us was particularly hungry.

That tweet was sent with a whisper – only 250 people followed my personal account on a daily basis. The first person to begin following my @twitchhiker persona on Twitter was Paul White (@PJ on Twitter), a friend residing some 8 kilometres from my front door. He forwarded the tweet on to his followers, and so word of Twitchhiker began to spread; others followed and they too retweeted the message to their followers. Slowly the whisper became more assured, more confident, heard first around northeast England, then the country. Within an hour, my message became the most repeated on the whole of Twitter – according to the automated Twitter accounts that monitor trends and keywords, more people were talking about Twitchhiker than anything else. The throng of electronic chatter caught the eye of Stephen Fry, who urged his tens of thousands of followers to support my cause – less than twenty minutes after Fry tweeted his support for @twitchhiker, the account had nearly 2,000 followers.

Twitchhiker had exploded into a thousand sparkling streams of craziness shooting off in all directions. I still hadn't the first clue how I'd leave the country after 1 March – I couldn't see what possible combination of events could propel me over seas and oceans – but I had no doubt it would happen. It felt as if sheer force of will would hurl me there.

arcticmatt @ambermacarthur Hey Amber, help @twitchhiker out. If you and Leo give him a shout there is no way he'll fail.

3:31 PM Feb 2nd

What? Who were Amber and Leo and why was a Twitter user in Norway asking them to give me a local radio-style 'shout'? Everything began moving at the speed of a blur. Followers asked questions I'd given not a jot of thought to. What would I do about visas if I headed towards India and China? Was I inoculated against yellow fever and typhoid? Before the day was over, the press began calling and emailing with similar questions. Within forty-eight hours the story appeared in *The Guardian* and *The New Zealand Herald*, then *The Daily Telegraph*, *Metro*, and on the BBC website. I was on page three of my local newspaper, and not just a column or two, either – the entire page, filled with words and a photo of my fat, moon-shaped face.

> **sret** It turns out that @twitchhiker only got married two weeks ago.
>
> *7:16 PM Feb 10th*

> **sret** I try not to judge people whose circumstances I don't know, but I can't look positively on his trip now. Sorry @ twitchhiker.
>
> *7:17 PM Feb 10th*

Twitter threw the occasional criticism my way, dealing a glancing blow to my confidence, but nothing could derail the Kingda Ka. I was struggling to keep my head above water, juggling work, home life and the surge of admin Twitchhiker created. The day before that first tweet, my inbox was as calm as a nun's wardrobe. Within a week there were 581 undeleted emails, 211 of which were unread – I kept digging out my inbox, but it would fill back up like a sandcastle moat too near the tide.

Dear Paul,

I'm writing to you on behalf of The One Show *[on BBC1]. We're currently preparing a piece about Twitter, and would be really keen to interview you about your Twitchhiking adventure.*

Can I ask whereabouts you are at the moment and whether this is something which might interest you?

All best

Alexis Hood

I'd watched the edition of *The One Show* featuring Twitter the previous week but the mail had been sitting in my inbox for six days before I'd opened it. The opportunity to plug Twitchhiker on national prime time television, on BBC1 no less – gone. More interviews slipped by and eventually I accepted defeat and begged my friend, also called Jane, to bail me out. Her PR company became my gatekeeper as far as the press was concerned, managing their requests and my time, with Jane barking at me whenever I forgot to talk to a radio station in Ireland or Spain. *Le Monde*, Sky News, *The Montreal Gazette* – every day brought fresh press enquiries from all corners of the globe. Yet the Jane I wasn't married to was under explicit instructions to handle incoming enquiries only, and not generate additional publicity – I wanted Twitter to be accountable for promoting the cause.

Eventually my mother learned of my plans through a news article emailed to her by a friend. If she was angry with me for not calling her myself, she certainly didn't say or reveal it in her tone, but then she never did. She always sounded delirious whenever we spoke and perhaps on this occasion she was, given the nature of the conversation that followed:

'So what are you doing now? Why are you going to New Zealand? What's a Twitter?'

'It's a website that lets you talk to new friends all over the world. They'll hopefully help me travel around the world.'

'Oh. Then you'll have to get a pomegranate phone.'

'...'

'Are you still there Paul?'

'Yes mother. I thought you said a pomegranate phone?'

'I did! It brews coffee and everything, sucks cold water right up out of your cup and spits it back out again as hot coffee! I think it might make tea too.'

'...'

'It has a shaver too. A shaver! Isn't that good? You need to get one, OK?'

'Wow. OK.'

'Sorry son, I don't know what else to say.'

That made two of us. In fact the pomegranate phone didn't exist at all – it was a nonsensical viral marketing campaign that mum had seen on the Internet. Fortunately, Twitter provided a more reliable source of information for my trip. Two weeks into February and with the help of my followers, I finally stole the time to compile an exhaustive list of items to pack and tasks to complete:

- passport / driver's licence
- photocopies of documents, to avoid having to surrender the originals to crooked officials
- US currency, to bribe the crooked officials if the situation turned grim and I wanted to avoid being tied to a chair in a cell
- MacBook, power leads and adaptors for all occasions (except, I suspected, the occasion I really needed the wires and adaptors for)
- solar charger for my mobile (a PR agency had donated it, and it seemed like the sort of pointless gizmo I'd find a use for)
- camera
- mobile phone for tweeting / photos / video uploading shenanigans
- tent / sleeping bag / ground mat
- rucksack
- suntan lotion
- earplugs
- devise a back-up plan in case something goes horribly wrong (no idea)
- arrange an appointment with the sadistic bastard that is my dentist (to ensure I wasn't going to suffer toothache while travelling)
- call the nurse about vaccinations, sooner rather than later

Now it was one thing to have a comprehensive list, pooled from the collective knowledge of experienced travellers and people far wiser than you; finding the time or the inclination to bother actioning any of it was quite another matter. For example, I was looking to Twitter to see me stay warm and dry, and dragging a tent around with me sounded like a pain in the backside, so immediately I crossed it off the list. I didn't own a rucksack, I had little love for dentists and what possible need would I have for earplugs? I wasn't intending to share a bed with anyone.

> **twitchhiker** I'm neither nervous nor excited right now. Both sensations hit me in waves, like... well, waves. Sure I'll be nervously excited soon.
>
> *2:38 PM Feb 16th*

With six days to go, my @twitchhiker account reached 4,000 followers. That was about my only achievement, since I was yet to receive any vaccinations against the more unpleasant forms of death I might encounter, nor had I started any packing. The list of tasks I absolutely had to complete remained ignored to the letter. There was a disparity between my furious activity online and the physical preparation required to undertake the trip.

And there were consequences – reasonably serious ones at that – when I eventually bothered to have my much-discussed and long-avoided shots. Let me offer this advice as a result; if you require inoculating before you travel, don't turn up less than a week before setting off having had no consultation regarding what vaccinations you might need, because some require more than one course over several weeks. The nurse at the clinic, a stout Chinese lady in no mood for nonsense, was firm but fair in her assessment of the disorganised fool before her – I was going to die in an excruciating manner due to my own blind stupidity – and proceeded to repeatedly stab vials of poison into my right arm with a sense of satisfaction that the situation didn't call for. While the media continued to squeeze the breath from my lungs, Irish bookmakers Paddy Power offered odds on the likelihood of my success or failure, the odds on the latter being shorter than the shortest of Tom Thumb's thumbs:

7/2 – Twitchhiker to reach Campbell Island within 30 days

10/1 – Twitchhiker to reach Campbell Island within a week

7/4 – Twitchhiker not to get out of Britain

5/4 – Twitchhiker not to get out of Europe

2/1 – Twitchhiker to have to abandon his mission due to lack of support from tweeps

Finally the time arrived. The rules stated I could only accept offers of transport and accommodation within a three-day window of travelling. That meant that 26 February was the first day I could seek help for the start of the journey on 1 March. Once that process was set in motion, it wouldn't pause for a whole month – every day would mean trying to plan ahead as far as those rules allowed. The prospect of it turned my guts inside out. Had I done enough to galvanise support and encourage the world to participate, or would

Twitchhiker be a spectator sport with plenty of noise from the terraces but sweet little action on the field? Would my journey begin at all?

paul_a_smith Tomorrow makes or breaks @twitchhiker. What if everyone turns up at midday just to point and laugh at the silly man? Twatsticks. Terrified.

11:45 PM Feb 25th

Chapter 6

twitchhiker Well this is the day, folks. This is when we see whether you're there, ready and willing. See you at midday.

8:19 AM Feb 26th

On the morning of 26 February, confidence was low; my sleep had been light and restless and I'd considered having the toilet seat heated and upholstered. I couldn't face breakfast and was becoming increasingly crotchety with new followers. Despite my going to painstaking lengths to spell out the idea and associated rules, dozens of new voices were appearing every hour and demanding to know where I was and was I there yet and would I be stopping by Sweden after lunch? News of Twitchhiker radiated across cities and continents, and each passing moment increased the momentum, amplified the signal, pushed the message further and further. There was a palpable sense of excitement from these strangers, and their giddiness and enthusiasm was as reassuring as it was incapacitating – at my desk, in the undecorated dining room of a terraced house in Gateshead, I sat still wearing my dressing gown, unable to peel my eyes away from the computer screen and my bare legs away from the faux leather upholstery of my chair.

twitchhiker 60 seconds. Oh God.

11:59 AM Feb 26th

Barely a month before, I was standing in the shadow of the Brooklyn Bridge reciting my vows. Five days later, an incident involving a supermarket and a bad mood revived a passing thought that had bloomed into something magnificently silly. And then it was time, the crescendo, the big reveal. Do or die.

twitchhiker Well. I'm all yours folks. I start in Newcastle on Sunday. Can you help me get anywhere else? Can you offer me a bed for the night?

12:01 PM Feb 26th

And... nothing. Nothing at all. Two or three excruciating minutes passed where all the tweets stopped, like animals sensing an imminent earthquake. Nobody would step forward. Where once there was an aviary of activity, there was silence. Hardly time to quit, but perhaps time to put some underwear on. Jane had thoughtfully left clean boxer shorts and red socks on my desk before going to work, a gentle reminder that while I didn't have a proper job that was no excuse to stay in a state of undress until bedtime. The boxer shorts were mid-thigh when the first tweet appeared, piggy-backed immediately by another:

kierondonoghue @twitchhiker I can give you a first-class ticket to London, if that's any use?

12:03 PM Feb 26th

minxlj @twitchhiker Have you been to Amsterdam? I have an overnight ferry trip to Amsterdam for you, leaving Sunday afternoon.

12:03 PM Feb 26th

Two offers appeared near-simultaneously and the crowds went wild. We were back and ready to take on the world. From the depths of despair to unwavering faith in a tweet or two. Screw Campbell Island, let's go to the moon! Tweeps found their voices and suddenly everyone had a sofa I could crash on, a porch I could shelter under, a floor or a spare room. Offers of accommodation burst into view every few seconds – Denmark, South Africa, New Mexico, Florida – but no other tweets provided the means to reach them. It didn't matter, there were people who wanted to help me and the prospect warmed my heart.

Where to first? I'd lived in London for a year while working at the BBC, but it was shortly after the Las Vegas incident – I spent most of my time in a boozy haze of manic highs and suicidal lows and as a result had little love for the place. I'd never visited Amsterdam, though I was entirely happy to visit a city I knew only by its reputation for soft drugs and pretty girls in shop windows. Then a third offer punched through the noise:

flycheapo @twitchhiker Would you like to visit Paris? To get you started, how about getting on the flight from Newcastle at 1545 on Sunday?

12:15 PM Feb 26th

The thought of Paris petrified me. I last visited while at secondary school, and it rained a miserable, oily rain every day. We wanted to go up the Eiffel Tower, but our French teacher, Mrs Perkins, insisted we visit the Pompidou Centre. 'The streets will be full of theatre, magic and dancers!' she yapped, with that dribbly enthusiasm of all French teachers. In fact, the streets proved to be full only of water and piss-wet twelve-year-olds wondering why they hadn't visited the most famous building in Paris. I still have a photograph of my best friend Stuart McGhee and me taken that afternoon – the two of us sat outside the Pompidou Centre, soaked to the skin and looking as happy as two children who have just learned that their parents have died in a Victorian threshing machine.

nuniwagner @twitchhiker If you want to go to Brazil I will offer you somewhere to stay!! Pick a city!!

12:35 PM Feb 26th

Offers from strangers around the world continued to appear. And in amongst the tweets and the retweets, strangers were becoming friends and began pooling their resources. Could the Parisians find accommodation in the city to secure my interest? How much free booze would it take to nail

London? It was my choice to make, but since this was the first leg of my journey, there was a need for a third party to keep me honest. I handed the choice back to Twitter and presented them with the three strongest offers – London, Amsterdam and Paris – and left the decision to an online poll.

After ten minutes and 300 votes, it was obvious the Twitter community were mad keen for me to live out their drug-addled fantasies of sexual deviance – Amsterdam won by a country mile with nearly two-thirds of the vote. I would set sail for mainland Europe in three days' time on 1 March, and as the crossing was on an overnight ferry I had no need to worry about accommodation for that first night. More importantly, I'd proved I wasn't a crank. A silly, solitary cause had united a global community and they were beginning to believe. I was already a believer, it was going to work, I was going to Campbell Island – *we* were going to Campbell Island – but not before I pulled up my boxers and set about boiling the kettle.

Chapter 7

Day One – Sunday 1 March

'When are you going to start packing?' Jane enquired as I finished burning the Yorkshire puddings. 'Just so I know if you need anything else ironing.'

Asking anything of me while I'm trying to make Sunday dinner usually ends in unpleasantness or, at the very least, a serving of undercooked cauliflower. The distraction meant I lost my place in the mental running order of turning off the gas and preparing the gravy and carving the chicken and draining the sprouts. 'I don't know, when it's time to leave,' I hissed back grumpily before burning my thumb on the stuffing tin.

In fact, I was due to leave for Amsterdam in less than three hours, and aside from dumping a pile of T-shirts and underwear on the dining room table I hadn't done anything to prepare for a month away from home. I'd decided to forgo a rucksack, which I didn't own and would have had to buy, and rejected my cabin-sized suitcase, because that made me look like a tourist. If I found myself lost on the dark side of town, nothing screamed fresh meat like a confused stranger wheeling his possessions down an unnamed alley. Instead, I'd settled on two messenger bags to sling over my shoulders – one packed with clothes, the other containing my laptop, camera, power leads, notebooks and all the crapola I'd no doubt accumulate throughout the month. The larger of the two was a bulky black sports bag that had accompanied me abroad before, the other was a present from Jane several years previous – a hessian satchel modelled on Jack Bauer's manbag of choice. It even had a metallic CTU crest – presumably Bauer's didn't have one of those, since that sort of thing would give the game away while on secret missions.

Packing my bags hadn't registered as a priority in the three days since 26 February and the pandemonium that saw Twitter send me to Amsterdam. For one, there was the continuing matter of twitchhiking to contend with; my three-day rule meant that on 27 February Twitter users could offer help for the second day of my journey. And indeed, I'd awoken early that morning expecting a glut of offers to move me on from Holland. Instead there wasn't a single offer.

Slowly, the tweets appeared – I had the choice of transport from Amsterdam to The Hague and a night at the sumptuous Haagsche Suites courtesy of its landlord; train tickets to and a hotel in Berlin; train travel to Paris from a Frenchman and board in a Parisian hostel.

The Hague barely moved me on from Amsterdam, so the choice came down to Berlin and Paris. My concern with Berlin, despite it clearly being more popular with tweeps than Paris, was that Twitter would look to push me further in that direction. Heading east meant issues with visas if my path strayed into Russia, China or India, as well as potential exposure to diseases I was too late to be immunised against. More importantly, Twitter activity in eastern Europe had been next to non-existent compared to the West. The rules allowed me to choose when more than one offer was available, so I accepted the train ticket to Paris, offered by a Frenchman called Chris Carriero (@ikangaroo on Twitter). At least I assumed he was a Frenchman – his name certainly sounded foreign to me and he did live in Paris. Case closed.

I also accepted a ride in a stranger's car, despite what my mother used to tell me. The official starting point of my journey on 1 March was to be Central Station in Newcastle, instead of my anonymous end terrace with its broken gate and garage too narrow to park a car in (I didn't build it, might I add). I hadn't considered how I'd travel from the station to the Port of Tyne in North Shields to catch my ferry to Amsterdam. Fortunately, a Newcastle tweep called Lindsay with the curious Twitter handle @rivets had spotted the discrepancy and offered his services to taxi me between the two.

twitchhiker Right then. Here we go. MacBook off. Goodbye desk. See you in 30 days! Next stop – Central Station, Newcastle...

1:18 PM Mar 1st

My final hour at home saw me running about like a man on fire, in a vain attempt to complete all the last-minute chores I'd had four weeks to finish. In any given moment I was both delirious at the scale of the adventure ahead and desperately fighting the urge to go to the toilet again. As expected, packing my bags required little preparation – that particular task had kept me awake many an hour as the sky had lightened and I'd committed my lists to memory, a little like the films where the soldiers assemble their guns blindfolded. I'm not saying I wore a blindfold to pack, I'm just saying I could have. Everything else conspired to rob me of what little composure remained. My polythene wallet of foreign notes and coins that always sat in the top drawer of my desk had been purloined by the desk pixies, so I was heading to Amsterdam without any currency. Somebody had moved my trainers to the bathroom of all places. Admittedly, that may have been me. And I'd planned to photocopy all my documents on the way to the station, but the one newsagent I knew to have a photocopier was shut.

When we arrived at Central Station and it was time to leave Jane, the tears were all mine. Every time I'd doubted myself over the past four weeks, every time the situation overwhelmed me, Jane had picked me up and dusted me down, held my hand and stroked my cheek. As independent as I thought I was, I was going to struggle without her. Promises were made, crushing hugs were exchanged, children were embraced and kissed hard on the crowns of their heads. I hadn't given much thought to the impact my departure might have on Jack and Sam, how much they depended on my presence in their lives, but for now they were delightfully giddy, teeming with the same child-like curiosity for the journey ahead as I was. Jack asked if I'd travel as far as the moon. I promised him his very own piece of moon rock if I did. He smiled, then giggled, swelling my heart with happiness and crushing it just as quickly. As the family drove away I turned and wiped my face, and headed into Central Station alone. The day was bright, the sun beamed down at trains and passengers from the glaze of the Victorian spanned roof high above. The station was lively for a Sunday, with shrieks of hen night refugees and ruts of stags shaking off hangovers.

The story goes that many years ago, Newcastle was declared eighth best party city on the planet. Not unexpectedly, Newcastle proceeded to celebrate its accolade by drinking until it threw up. The liberated nature of the locals, the countless bars and clubs, the altogether more reasonable bar prices compared to the south: Newcastle offered a majestic night out for tourists and stag parties alike. For too long that inebriated persona threatened to overshadow the gradual transformation of the city beyond its monochromatic ship-building roots. Fortunately, the years that followed saw both Newcastle and Gateshead achieve sobriety, to become one of the most effervescent places in the country. There's still no better place to party and end up in the gutter ruined by booze, but now you can see some smashing abstract art while hungover the next day.

There'd been chatter over the weekend about a send-off from local tweeps, and a dozen or so Twitter users appeared and swarmed around to wish me well; some faces I considered friends, others I knew only by their profile photo on Twitter. It wasn't quite Beatlemania but far grander than a whimsical globetrotter had any right to. Amongst them was my friend and former radio colleague Kelly, who I'd known since my BBC days in Manchester. Like my friend Jon, she was able to raise my spirits whenever they sank, and the unexpected presence of this slim blonde bundle of chaos buoyed me up no end. She'd brought along a carrier bag of what could loosely be described as 'gifts' for my trip, including:

- a copy of *Good Old-fashioned Advice* by Michael Powell
- a magic set
- earplugs and eye mask
- a battery-powered pocket casino

All of which I didn't need nor had room to carry, but to dump it in the bin while Kelly watched would have been rude. Fortunately, Kelly was bearing a more useful gift from my other best friend – specifically, a bottle of Moët from Jon, who was tied up presenting a radio show. It wouldn't last the night, I thought – there was no point dragging the extra weight around Amsterdam with me.

Also amongst the crowd of well-wishers were Leanne (@minxlj on Twitter) and Lindsay (@rivets), the two Twitter folk seeing me on my way from Newcastle. Leanne, who had offered the ferry ticket to Amsterdam, was a cute thirty-year-old designer with snow-white blonde hair and green eyes, piercings here, there and everywhere and aquamarine tattoos wrapped around both arms. She gave me a big grin and a hug, and more importantly a one-way ticket to Amsterdam. By contrast, Lindsay was a middle-aged university lecturer with a face worn through thick and thin, full of mischief, with a wild grey beard and frazzled ponytail to match.

I'd suggested a gift exchange in the days leading up to the trip, where I would swap presents with people who helped me complete each stage of my journey. I began by presenting Leanne, the first Twitter user to help me, with the first gift – my dog-eared and flood-damaged copy of *McCarthy's Bar* (tip – never store your precious books in a cardboard box under a water boiler which sounds like it's gargling spanners every time you switch it on). In return, Leanne handed to me a small dog-faced clay figurine of a pig (although it may have been a mouse – I wasn't sure and didn't like to ask), which held a plaque reading *Bon Voyage*. I then presented the mongrel figurine to Lindsay, the second person to offer help, who swapped it for a small orange metal tin bearing the name BIFURCATED RIVETS. Lindsay had collected dozens of them; it was a small and pretty thing, pleasing to the eye, and would make a fine gift to exchange with my new French friends in Paris.

With the ferry ticket from Leanne safely in my possession, I said my farewells to Kelly and the crowd, jubilant at the support I was leaving behind, and departed for North Shields with Lindsay in his comfortable and anonymous brand of people carrier. We discussed summer holidays and the behaviour of the English abroad, and my chances of making it to Campbell Island. Lindsay confirmed what I already knew; it'd be impossible to travel the majority of the distance by land in such a short period of time. I could only agree, and hope to be offered a long-haul flight. As we hurried along the coast road, missing our exit and doubling back, what might or might not happen next wasn't worrying me. I was off and away! I was so excitable, like a child on a school trip who'd snuck into his packed lunch while still on the coach going there. I was now the Twitchhiker! I was twitchhiking! My fate lay in the hands of strangers scattered across the face of the planet, and I was about to step into the fantastic.

@

It's unlikely mine was the first adventure of a lifetime to begin at North Shields ferry terminal. That said, there can't have been that many. This was certainly the starting point for many a tale of depravity and sexual deviance, as hoards of beery men in Newcastle United shirts sailed the seas to Amsterdam, in search of leather-clad ladies who'd do everything the wife wouldn't.

I saluted Lindsay farewell as he drove off, slung my messenger bags over my shoulder, picked up the Moët and stepped into 1989. The contemporary stone facade of the terminal betrayed an interior upholstered in every conceivable shade of blue and grey, but mostly grey. Not only did the terminal appear to be suspended in time, but so did the smell, a stale odour not unlike a nightclub the morning after the night before.

From the terminal, the *Princess of Norway* was a beast of a boat, blue and white and unnervingly tall and angular, almost cuboid in shape and lacking any sleek lines one might expect of a sailing vessel. This princess wasn't built for speed or style – she was as capacious as an elephant's intestinal tract and about as easy on the eye. The interior was only slightly more colourful than the terminal – patterned carpets and aged fittings, cabin suites available in any colour so long as it was sky grey, not a calming sky grey, but the sky grey that makes you re-evaluate putting the washing out to dry. It was an internal cabin, so with no sea views to distract me I wasted no time in availing myself of the shrink-wrapped beaker in the bathroom closet, cracking open the Moët and chugging it down as fast as my neck could swallow. After a good pull on the bubbles, I paused long enough to weave my way outside and up to the top deck, as the rich red sun descended over Newcastle. The seas ahead were grey but calm, the skies were warm and clear, and in our wake the defiant north and south piers harbouring the mouth of the Tyne slowly trailed into the background.

A further generous serving of champagne later and I was ready to explore the boat. Was it a boat? Or a ship? Did it matter? It didn't matter; I'd knocked back nearly two-thirds of a bottle of champagne and could have been adrift in a pedalo for all I knew. The main bar area had renounced the grey colour scheme found elsewhere and plumped for a more seductive black. A large stage was the centrepiece, where passengers were treated to the sounds of the ageing house band performing songs fractionally beyond their musical ability, such as AC/DC's 'Back In Black' neatly segued – in a manner that defied the traditional definition of the word 'neatly' – with The Proclaimers' 'I'm Gonna Be (500 Miles)'. But wait, there was more. Oh God, there was more. The Sugarbabies were introduced to the stage, where they attempted to possess the male audience with their asexual dance routines. They were followed by an act that could only be described as a magic routine performed by overweight strippers, which couldn't have been less erotic if they'd stopped to conduct smear tests.

The band returned and launched into 'Black Velvet' by Alannah Myles, and together with the company I was keeping – middle-aged alcoholics, sex tourists, stag parties and Belgian HGV drivers – the experience quickly lost its allure. Short of a meat raffle, I was trapped on board a seafaring working men's club. I lurched back outside, unable to convincingly coordinate my drunken stagger with the sway of the ship, called Jane to let her know I was safe and well, and then Jon to thank him for the Moët which had proved a worthy first mate on my maiden voyage.

The mobile crackled and died as the ship slipped into the dark waters between England and the European mainland, and I weaved my way back to my cabin, attempted to open somebody else's door, apologised profusely and eventually located my cabin two decks above, where I polished off the last of the champagne and was gently rocked to sleep by the North Sea.

Chapter 8

Day Two – Monday 2 March

Previous to my grand Twitter adventure, the longest I'd ever travelled for without interruption was during the heady days of my school summer holidays, when the Smith family took the Siesta coach from Darlington to L'Estartit, a small resort nestled on Spain's north-eastern coast. At a time when holidays abroad meant expensive short-haul flights – over a decade before budget airlines became commonplace – booking four seats on board a coach must have seemed a perfectly sane alternative, at least until boredom and additive-rich supermarket brand cola kicked in with twenty-three hours to go.

European geography being what it is obviously meant the coach couldn't drive non-stop to Spain. Construction work had barely begun on the Channel Tunnel at that time, so even cars had to travel to France on the ferry. We'd clamber on deck and bask in the watery British sunshine as we sailed from Dover, my brother and I feigning a moment's interest in the white cliffs before racing one another inside to watch moody French teenagers with pretty girlfriends playing *After*

Burner and other arcade games. What I remember most about those childhood voyages across the sea is spewing into paper bags, my mother's handbag, my own hands and once into my brother's lap. He was four years younger than me and didn't stop sobbing until Calais. The waves hardly had to breach the hull to see my stomach pulled inside out and my throat full of bile.

And so as my eyes rolled open on board the ferry that time forgot, I felt my chest heave into my mouth and feared the worst. However, other than the immediate urge to sick up a jeroboam's worth of Moët, gastric acid and other stringy fluids, there were no other symptoms of the motion sickness I'd suffered while seeking a taste of Spanish sun as a child. Until that moment I'd forgotten how ill even a short ferry crossing made me as a teenager. That's not to say I felt invigorated after a night's rest on the ferry – my head was as heavy as a wet shoe, the victim of my decision to pursue a purely liquid diet the previous evening. I swung my legs out of my bunk and patted the walls down for a light switch, successfully locating it on the fourth attempt. As I blinked in the light and my soulless grey box came into focus, a quiet grin broke across my face. Perhaps drinking alone wasn't the best idea but then I remembered why I was there – I was twitchhiking my way to mainland Europe and that had most certainly been worth celebrating.

In need of a toothbrush and paracetamol, I picked through the tightly rolled clothing in my messenger bag and noticed a flash of yellow. It wasn't something I recognised, tucked away in a separate pocket at the back. It was an envelope, banana yellow, with a card inside – Jane had squirreled it away before we'd left the house. The card was ocean blue, and a large star swung across its face on a length of ribbon. Inside was a message from my new wife:

Every time you see a bright star in the sky, that will be Jack, Sam and I thinking of you and watching over you. The other stars in the sky are your friends and all your family thinking about you too. Remember – even if you can't see a star in the sky, the one on the front of this card is just for you, and you are my star.

Jane x

The tears welled up and streamed down my face. Such a beautifully tender and heartfelt message from my sweet and loving wife. She must have copied it off the Internet. The printed text inside read 'Have a great day!' – Jane had crossed out 'day!' and replaced it with 'trip!!'. On the reverse of the card was the warning 'made in China – not suitable for children under 36 months due to small parts' which Jane hadn't crossed out – presumably she felt this was relevant and that I might try to eat the card in a vulnerable moment.

Ablutions completed and less than an hour away from port, I switched my mobile on, figuring I'd be within range of a cell tower once more. Except the pay-as-you-go handset that had been given to me by a phone company for the trip was stubbornly refusing to make calls or connect to the Internet, and instead insisted that there wasn't enough credit available. Bollocks, I informed it in no uncertain terms – there had been £20 credit on the handset the previous day. I whipped out my wallet, plucked out the credit card and was soon back in business. I was able to browse Twitter once more, and the mystery of the missing credit was quickly solved by knowledgeable followers – my late-night calls had most likely been routed through the ferry's own satellite mobile network at a shockingly high cost per minute. I continued to scan through the messages, looking for another offer to take me beyond Paris – I was meeting Chris the Frenchman at Gare du Nord later that afternoon and would then have just two days to move on somewhere new.

Holland slowly rolled into view through fog and spitting rain. Naively, I'd expected to sail straight into the heart of Amsterdam and see tulip-lined canals and pretty townhouses from the deck. Instead, through the mist were smoking towers and blackened steelworks, metal islands scarred by rusting hulls. This was IJmuiden, Holland's gateway to the North Sea and as welcoming to visitors as a punch in the crotch.

Once docked, the crew quickly herded the human cattle off the boat to the terminus where buses waited to transfer passengers to Amsterdam. As is standard for continental coaches, there was just enough legroom between the rows of seats to ensure they didn't quite touch one another – ideal for children under the age of four but less so for everyone else. I squeezed into the toddler-sized space and waited with my knees tucked under my chin, scowling at the other passengers who dawdled outside chatting and laughing as if they were on some sort of holiday. I still had three hours before I was due to catch my train to Paris from Amsterdam's Centraal Station but I didn't know how long the transfer would take or where the coach would stop relative to the station. And I didn't have my ticket for the train yet – the Frenchman had sent an email the previous day, full of the pass codes and pin numbers required to retrieve my ticket once I arrived at the station.

twitchhiker The coach from the ferry terminal in Amsterdam is playing The Final Countdown by Europe. I bet it's still #1 here.

9:25 AM Mar 2nd

The coach terminated in full view of Centraal Station. I still needed to check emails, locate train tickets, sniff out lunch and hunt down the train platform, all of which left roughly thirty minutes for casual meandering to form my first and indeed only impressions of Amsterdam. If the Dutch capital was teeming with pot-addled cafes and ladies in windows teasing leery strangers with their tits and tuppence, they were all hiding from me. Not that I went in search of them, obviously – I'm not that sort of leery stranger. Even if I were, I'd have been hard-pressed to get my money's worth before boarding the 12.26 train for Paris. Amsterdam in summary, then – flat, cloudy with occasional drizzle, and likely to see many a foreigner die under the wheels of a car, tram, bicycle or combination of all three. The roads girdling the station had pairs of lanes for each, so negotiating my way from one side of the street to the other meant traversing not two lanes of traffic, but six. It was a real-life game of Frogger.

The platforms of Centraal Station were covered by decadent arches of steel, while underneath a dark concrete concourse lurked a soulless bunker illuminated by storefronts and shafts of grey light from the platforms above. In the customer service hall near the entrance I retrieved my ticket using the details sent by Chris, but before tucking it away in my wallet I noticed the price. EUR 83,00, it read. I realised my theory about how I might travel was already out of kilter with reality; I'd envisioned people giving up tickets already booked or offering a lift further down the road as part of a journey they already intended to make. Why would a stranger, a Frenchman, dip into his own pocket and pay the best part of £100 for another stranger, an Englishman, to catch a train from Holland? It wouldn't last, I suspected.

Ticket secured, I proceeded through to a brightly lit reception area offering plump red sofas and the promise of Wi-Fi, and my laptop was out before my backside sank into the seat. I'd been lost at sea for seventeen hours, so I needed to play catch-up with Twitter and begin forming plans beyond Paris. Twitter had one or two suggestions for me, not least from Owen Watkins of Chester. Who? Two days into my journey, a man, known to a handful of people on Twitter as @clocsen, had offered me a flight.

Across the Atlantic.

It must have been a wind-up. I couldn't possibly be having such an easy time. What idiot was going to fly me to the States? I logged into my email and already there was a message waiting for me:

Morning Paul – I hope you slept well.

As I mentioned on Twitter, I am happy to provide a single ticket to the US or Canada, however the requirement for an onward/return ticket could be a stumbling block. If you have not already given some thought to this, I would strongly recommend you discuss with consular staff in Paris/London/Amsterdam before getting on an aeroplane. I'm happy to give you a ticket so long as I'm reasonably persuaded they're not going to put you on the first flight back, which would be a waste of your time and my money.

I can fly you from most major airports – Frankfurt, for example. For some reason I can't seem to get US flights out of Paris. As for destinations, New York and Washington are probable and other destinations depend on availability.

Regards

Owen Watkins
@clocsen

The unexpected glee that had splashed a grin across my face was beaten to the ground and substituted with blind, raging panic. I hadn't stopped to consider how I'd handle immigration control in foreign countries. Assuming the airline would even let me board the flight, if the likes of US Border Control learned I'd entered the country with no clue of how or when I would depart, I'd likely be led into a windowless room, hear the sickening snap of latex and be thoroughly fingered before being sent back the way I came. There was no way around it. Flying west wasn't going to be possible; I'd have to look at travelling by land to the east or south, a prospect I wasn't relishing because there'd been so little support from either Africa or Asia.

Then a dormant thought sparked into life; I *did* have a return ticket. Three months beforehand, Virgin Atlantic had promoted a sale for flights to New York for £249 return. Any excuse to go back there, I was front of the queue and had booked up immediately. I raced to find the email itinerary and checked the dates – I was due to fly from London Heathrow on May 6th and return on May 25th. US Immigration allowed travellers without visas to stay up to 90 days. Assuming I reached Frankfurt in the next three days, the duration between my inbound flight and previously booked return flight was 81 days. I could take up @clocsen on his offer of a flight to the US, and provide my previously booked flight as proof I intended to return. There was still the issue of reaching a major airport beyond Paris. How likely was that?

Very, as it turned out.

After the dozens of offers of help the previous week, barely any had been tweeted since. One of the few had been sent by a German lady called Andrea:

pluripotent @twitchhiker could send you a ticket for TGV from Paris to Saarbruck and accommodation. And a lift to Frankfurt to leave for the whole world.

8:02 AM Mar 2nd

If I'd been an outsider looking in, I'd have denounced the whole affair as some outrageously contrived bollocks that had so far fooled nearly 6,000 people on Twitter and countless media outlets around the world. Without realising what one another had offered, two Twitter users had provided me with the opportunity to reach North America within my first week. I squealed uncontrollably in excitement, and possibly too loudly, judging by the look from the woman in the brown crushed velvet tracksuit sat opposite. By hook or by crook, it was working.

> **twitchhiker** @pluripotent hello! Would the offer of a ticket to Saarbruck and a lift to Frankfurt still be available? For Wednesday, maybe?
>
> *10:43 AM Mar 2nd*

As my departure time ticked into view, I packed up and stuffed my debit card into a cash machine for a fistful of euros, bought a distressed-looking BLT sandwich and bottle of fresh orange from a supermarket in the underground bunker, before emerging on what I hoped was the correct platform – I couldn't understand a syllable of the Dutch Tourette's pouring out of the loudspeaker system. As the escalator carried my eye level into view of the tracks, I spotted a thing of beauty and wonder to my right. Let it be stated for the record I have as much love for trains as I have for stapling my eyes shut, but that was before I saw a *double-decker* train. Two floors, one on top of the other, like a house! A long, bold, yellow bullet, with passengers upstairs and passengers downstairs, an elegant train for a more civilised age. It was without doubt the most wonderful thing I'd seen that day.

It goes without saying, of course, that this was not my train.

The journey to Paris passed without incident or concern, save for the French gentleman sat across the table, who dropped his phone on my foot. He apologised profusely in his native tongue, and feeling my E grade in GCSE French might be stretched by any attempt to enter a conversation, I responded by smiling inanely and pretending I'd noticed something far more interesting out the window. It could easily have been the train station at Antwerp, an underground lair of sculptures and shapes illuminated by curtains of neon blue light. It certainly wasn't Brussel-Zuid because that particular train station was a shithole, seemingly the victim of a catastrophic disaster that had decimated both customer demand and the maintenance budget. It was a pleasant enough journey that could have been one through the British countryside on a bright spring day, through toiled fields and green pastures, huddled villages and stray farmhouses.

After Antwerp and Brussel-Zuid, the train panted into Paris Gare du Nord, the third busiest train station in the world. It was rammed with lackadaisical tourists and frustrated locals, dozens of people sliding past one another onto the platforms, and hundreds more milling about the concourse under the distant cream roof of the vast train shed. I had no idea how I would find Chris amongst the throng – it was impossible to see any distance through the bodies packed on the concourse, and the photo on his Twitter page was small and difficult to make out. If he was wearing the same brown tracksuit then I was sure to have no problem, otherwise another gaping void in my preparations would be exposed. Fortunately, Chris recognised me, and so moments later we met and exchanged firm handshakes and broad smiles and, to my surprise and immediate embarrassment, effortless conversation. The tall, dark, well-groomed, designer-stubbled Frenchman wasn't French at all, and had a gruff American accent – while he had lived around the world, Chris hailed from upstate New York and arrived in Paris only the year before.

twitchhiker Thanks to @ikangaroo for getting me here from Amsterdam by train. He scared me by not being French.

4:09 PM Mar 2nd

Chris bought a Metro ticket for each of us and together we descended into the labyrinth of the Parisian underground. We re-emerged three stops north along line 5, at a station called Laumière in the 19th arrondissement, or district, far to the north of the city centre. Ascending the steps into bright sunlight, the scene was one of colour and bustle; thick accents spilled out of the local boulangerie, gesticulating Frenchmen bellowed angrily into mobile phones and traffic stop-started along Avenue Jean Jaurès. Everyone was eager to go about his or her day, or happily watch others do so from their cafe table. I was off the radar in a neighbourhood far from the tourist traps, lost amongst real life – it was brash, it was loud and, in the glare of the Parisian sunshine, it was exhilarating.

We picked a path through the meandering side streets to the bridge over Bassin de la Villette, a lozenge-shaped canal, and arrived at St Christopher's Inn, the hostel that had offered me free board for the following two nights. I'm always wary of hostels, having spent many an uncomfortable night on a dishevelled mattress in a room starved of warmth or matching furniture. I usually travel for the experience of the city I'm visiting rather than the accommodation where I'll snatch a few hours' sleep, so I'm happy to eschew the complimentary shortbread biscuits and extensive selection of pay-per-view pornography. My propensity to save a few hundred pounds has exposed me to the gamut of hostelries available, from delightfully adequate to unfit for rat infestation, to the shared bathroom in Prague where the national rugby team had seemingly shaved their genitals in succession and left the resulting short and curlies strewn across the floor, the toilet seat, the sink and every other tiled surface within sight. St Christopher's Inn was unlike any of these places. It was a vast cuboid building decorated in subtle strips of wood and metal, bordered by a broad, tree-lined square to the north and the canal to the south, striking the perfect tone for the facilities within; a modern, clean hostel and a bar bubbling with life, with bright spotless dorms, near-new mattresses and, joy of joys, free Wi-Fi.

Chris and I sat outside the hostel in the late afternoon sun and slowly sank a pint; I was still a little tender after my solo champagne bender but there was an obligation to celebrate my arrival.

'The price of beer's expensive here, isn't it?' I exclaimed.

'Five euros a pint!'

'That's cheap for Paris,' deadpanned Chris.

'Really? You must be drinking in the finest Parisian bars,' I grinned.

'Not really,' was the eventual response.

Initially our conversation was stilted and littered with awkward pauses, two strangers with little in common beyond a few syllables of dialogue shared online. The likelihood of such a scenario had nagged at me for several days – at some point I was bound to meet a tweep who had been generous in their assistance but proved so excruciatingly tedious in real life that I'd prefer to set my own head in cement. It would be a succession of blind dates, where I'd have to put out and be as dirty as they wanted, in a manner of speaking. That wasn't the case in this instance – Chris was perfectly polite and his wit was samurai sharp, but he wasted few words when replying to questions. By the second pint we'd warmed to one another and found ourselves discussing Twitter, the French and the events that had brought Chris to Paris. He had arrived the previous August with his American wife Sarah who worked in the city, and he kept himself busy with his travel website, iKangaroo. He had travelled extensively in the past and relied on the charity of others to shelter him from harm's way while far from home. Chris was passing that global karma forward, and I made a mental note to do the same wherever I could.

As dusk settled over northern Paris we were joined by Sarah who immediately punctured the cool exterior of her husband and yanked out smiles and laughter; his broody exterior melted away in the presence of his lovely wife who popped with vim and vigour. The hostel staff were taking the three of us out for dinner at a local restaurant; amongst them was Duncan, the tweep who had offered the room to me, an energetic twenty-something-year-old South African, fresh-faced and brimming with enthusiasm for my trip. Together with Geneviève, the hostel manager, and Romain, the managing director, we strode along the canal, the tip of the Eiffel Tower breaking through the skyline several kilometres in the distance. Geneviève explained that up until a few years ago, the 19th arrondissement was strictly off-limits to tourists, an unsavoury neighbourhood with a reputation for squalor and crime, home to impoverished students and immigrants. Over the past five years regeneration money had been pumped into the area, the canals cleaned up and the parks restored. Even the hostel played its own small but influential role, providing employment and a focal point for the community.

Le Jaurès Café was hectic, tables and customers piled on top of one another, the waiters weaving in between with impossible grace, their forearms laden with platters. It was a dimly lit nub of a venue on the delta of two streets, tightly packed and noisy but exuding charm and warmth. I embraced the cuisine as any hungover Englishman who hadn't eaten properly for thirty-six hours would do – I wasn't overly desperate to indulge French stereotypes but keen to try everything once. When others offered escargots or a taste of foie gras, I scoffed the lot, taken aback by how rich and flavoursome snails and unnaturally fattened goose liver were. My own starter was French onion soup with a cheese crust as thick as my wrist. It was ambrosial.

I can remember with pinpoint accuracy where and when I've enjoyed my favourite meals. The third best was fresh quattro stagioni pizza in Sorrento in March 2001. Second was a meal during my non-honeymoon in San Francisco in October 2004; Izzy's in Steiner Street served up a decadent New York sirloin steak with potato gratin and creamed spinach. My favourite meal was undisputedly my Nana's chicken dinner, although there were so many of them the dates and times are irrelevant, but most were enjoyed around her dining table at home in Barnard Castle. It was not unlike a medieval feast; countless pieces of matching green crockery blanketed the table, stacked high with hand-carved chicken, Yorkshire puddings the size of hubcaps, an Everest of mashed potato, roast potatoes and carrots and broad beans, parsnips and turnip and peas and sprouts, apple sauce and bread sauce and gravy of course. My stomach has never ached so much with satisfaction.

The main course served up at Le Jaurès took no prisoners and muscled its way straight into my third favourite meal of all time. Gratin dauphinois and 'Recipe Medallions' of pork have never tasted so rudely moreish and were it not for the sake of keeping up appearances, I'd have ordered a second helping. Or perhaps not, since a considerable amount of red wine had washed down my neck and bloated my stomach.

I told my story to those who had yet to hear it and shared photos of the evening with Twitter, indulged in a further glass or three of obscenely rich Merlot before we weaved our way back to the hostel in the crisp Parisian night. Chris and Sarah departed to catch their Metro home, but not before I thanked them repeatedly, not only for believing in my journey but for re-introducing me to a city I'd felt unreasonably sour towards since I was twelve years old.

twitchhiker Thanks to Klive Humberstone whose donation means we've reached £2,000! Thanks to everyone, let's keep going.

11:14 PM Mar 2nd

Since the setting up of the charity appeal at the beginning of February, donations had trickled in in fits and starts, and after four weeks a milestone had been reached for *charity: water*. It provided one final reason to smile before I turned the lights out in my lonely dorm room and reflected on my first full day of adventure, while quietly digesting fresh pig and red wine. If every day ahead was as full and rich, I thought, I'd be the luckiest man alive. And possibly the fattest.

Chapter 9

Day Three – Tuesday 3 March

I'd decided to stay over in Paris for two nights to knuckle down and do some work – apparently bank managers didn't look kindly upon gallivanting around the world in lieu of a month's mortgage payment. Duncan and Geneviève had provided me with Metro tickets to oh la la my way around the spectacles of the French capital, but instead I sat chained to my laptop for ten hours, rattling off words of whimsy for editors in London. *Au revoir*, Arc de Triomphe! Jardin du Luxembourg, *à bientôt*! Weep not Paris, but celebrate in the knowledge that I wrote beautiful features about budget airline baggage limits and council tax property bands. *Sacré bleu* indeed.

Still, it was a brilliant day as far as twitchhiking was concerned, so long as you ignored the fact that I sat on my fat arse in the hostel bar and went nowhere. My travel arrangements from Paris to the US had come together, and better yet my destination was New York City. A train ticket from Paris Gare de l'Est to Saarbrücken in Germany would arrive the next morning, sent by German Twitter user Andrea Juchem (@pluripotent). The oppressive online booking system in Germany wouldn't allow Andrea to email the ticket, so she'd driven to the station to collect it and send it by registered post. Andrea would meet me in Saarbrücken and I would spend the night at her home in Eppelborn, a village 20 kilometres from the French border, before returning to the station the following morning to board a train bound for Frankfurt, again paid for by Andrea. So much expense and effort to assist a perfect stranger.

Then we had the Twitter user in Chester willing to spend his money and air miles to fly me from Frankfurt to North America. Owen had reserved a booking on a flight from Frankfurt to New York, via Amsterdam's Schiphol airport – I'd be passing through Amsterdam again, even faster than I had done previously. I sensed Owen was still uneasy about how Immigration Control would receive me stateside. Everything would be fine, I assured him, because I had a return trip to New York booked in three months' time – the return leg of that ticket would provide all the reassurance the stony-faced officials and their holstered guns would need. Nothing to worry about, I said, nothing to worry about whatsoever. It was true – I could breeze through border control at JFK without officials glancing twice at me, but then if they asked me why I had two messenger bags of luggage for a three-month visit, I'd be screwed. I wasn't entirely confident of my chances. In fact I was bricking it. I tried to keep calm and carry on, not panic or rush to the toilet; everything would be fine, just as I'd insisted to Owen it would be. Focus on the good, I told myself. I was twitchhiking, there was good and love and hope in the world and it was carrying me to New York once more, my second visit in five weeks and yes, I truly was a lucky, lucky bastard. I sent Owen the personal details required to book the ticket, including a fictional place of residence for my first night in the city – a security requirement I couldn't satisfy since I hadn't tweeted the news and received an offer of accommodation. As soon as Owen confirmed the ticket, however, Twitter certainly heard all about it:

> **twitchhiker** @clocsen Brilliant, thank you so much! New York, I'm coming to you on Thursday!
>
> *4:51 PM Mar 3rd*

And then a funny thing happened. Admittedly, it was less funny and more pant-wettingly, run-around-in-circles-clucking-like-a-chicken amazing:

> **M4RKM** @twitchhiker I'll fly you to Los Angeles the next day! Let me know when you want it booking for!
>
> *4:52 PM Mar 3rd*

Whoa there, cowboy. LA? In less than a week? That wasn't what I'd been expecting at all; the words alone caught my breath. How exhilarating to be catapulted to the Pacific so quickly! How unexpected, how mind-blowing! How wrong. It felt like cheating, to hop off one long-haul flight straight onto another. What would I prove by flying over 5,000 kilometres of potential goodwill and generosity?

I asked the Twittersphere what it thought of the news. The Twittersphere went horseshit crazy. There was a deafening chorus of individuals who wanted to see me on that flight and suffering deep-vein thrombosis. I began by replying to individuals, putting across my point of view in 140 characters or less. It didn't matter, because the majority of followers wanted me on that plane. 'You don't understand the scale of the US, it's huge!' and 'Isn't the point to travel as far as you can in thirty days? Take it!' followed by 'It's been offered by Twitter, so why is it cheating?' and so on and so forth. And they kept coming. Like a rake-thin mongrel with a fat girl's thigh clamped between its teeth, Twitter wasn't going to let me walk away from this offer:

> **tammisutton** @twitchhiker I'd love to put you in my next feature film as a hitchhiker. I'll put you on a train or plane across America!
>
> *5:13 PM Mar 3rd*

In the words of Graham Chapman, it was all getting far too silly. What paying member of the public would derive any pleasure from visiting the local multiplex to view a fat-faced giant with more hair on his shoulders than his head? Who on earth and indeed, Twitter, was Tammi Sutton?

My wildest expectations were exceeded when I searched the IMDB.com movie database for a listing and one appeared. Tammi Sutton was real – a petite, peroxide blonde with a substantial girth of credits to her name. There was the role of a street vendor in *Spiderman*, while in straight-to-TV smash *Getting Away with Murder: The JonBenet Ramsey Mystery*, she played the diner waitress, and in 2001's *Horror Vision*, Tammi Sutton played a crack whore. The acting roles were modest but clearly Ms Sutton was an experienced producer and director, even if her projects were ultra low-budget horror movies with story elements concerning murderous clowns and gruesome slaughter.

Tammi Sutton wanted me in Los Angeles, and so did everyone else. But the more Twitter bullied me into accepting the offers, the more I resisted. It wasn't right. My rules didn't restrict my means of transport, but accepting long-haul flights at every step didn't sit easy with the spirit of my challenge. I'd expressed my concerns about heading east out of Europe, in that my greatest fear was the lack of Twitter activity in that direction. I couldn't traverse 9,000 kilometres by land in three weeks unless there were plenty of options, but I didn't have that excuse on the North American continent. Both the United States and Canada were teeming with Twitter users. I wanted to experience the hospitality of strangers and embrace the spirit of Twitter, rather than fly 9 kilometres above it at 900 kilometres per hour. Besides which, if I was going to reach New Zealand, I had to find my way across the Pacific and that was a mammoth ask of Twitter. I needed to build up considerable awareness of my journey before I arrived on the West Coast.

twitchhiker Thanks for the replies. Friday will be just day 6 of 30. Heart says to travel US by land. I'll sleep on it, I think.

5:33 PM Mar 3rd

Do you remember *Choose Your Own Adventure* books? I collected them as a kid. You probably did too. I adored them. They. Were. Brilliant. It was a range of children's stories that asked the reader to determine the narrative. You would read several pages and then be asked to choose what your character should do next from a list of options. Should you take the left path into the temple, the right path that led to the waterfall or turn around and retrace your steps back through the jungle? Each choice meant flicking forwards or back to a different page of the book, to continue the story and then choose once more. You could enjoy the books again and again and experience a different adventure every time. Magical.

Twenty-five years on, I was the protagonist in my own *Choose Your Own Adventure* novel. Thousands were reading to see where their choices would lead me. Every turn of the page presented new paths and while I couldn't dispute the options presented to me, the choice was mine to make. I wasn't travelling alone, I had a duty of care to my Twitter followers, my vicarious travel companions. And neither they nor I would experience a great adventure spending hours vacuum-packed into an economy-class seat watching *Two and a Half Men* on the entertainment system somewhere over Utah.

Screw the flight from New York to Los Angeles; there were far more interesting ways to cross America, and hopefully I'd be offered them. After all, I was still only in Paris.

Save for the toilet breaks and occasionally escaping into the cool Parisian sun, I sat in the bar of St Christopher's and typed for ten hours. Work, blog. Work, work, blog. Work, Twitter, work, Twitter, work, Twitter, blog. And so on. A toasted ham and cheese sandwich and bottomless cup of coffee saw me through the daylight hours, while a single beer was unlovingly nursed through the early evening. Twitter talked of parties elsewhere in the city but as perverse as it sounded, I was petrified of stepping out into the unknown. Provide me with an introduction to people, virtual or real, and I was confident and at ease; maroon me in a hostel full of cheerful strangers hoping to share stories of travelling the globe and I was self-effacing, so desperately shy – the guy you always promise you'll get back to after you've been to the bar but never do.

I retired to my room early that night, tired and weary of my own company. The five beds that lay empty the previous night were now full of snoring backpackers, save for the bunk below mine, whose occupant spent several minutes throwing up in his mouth then vaulting out of his bunk to puke in the sink, before climbing back into bed and repeating the process. The bunk alongside mine was stuffed from top to bottom with a hulk of Dutchman, who was snoring like a pneumatic hammer trapped in a washing machine locked in a filing cabinet being kicked down a hill. It was very funny for the first five minutes, less so for the hour that followed.

Fuck, I cursed in the privacy of my own head, if only I had earplugs. Oh I have, I remembered – Kelly had given me a pair in Newcastle and I'd shown rare sense in keeping hold of them.

twitchhiker Earplugs in. Can still hear him. Either he's very, very loud or I also have ears in my knees, like a cricket. In which case, I've not enough earplugs.

10:18 PM Mar 3rd

Eventually the Dutchman turned over and stopped snoring, or died quietly in his sleep and did everyone a favour – either way there was peace in the dorm, save for the occasional gagging sound from my bunkmate below. It was an early night, hardly the stuff of epic adventures, but there would be plenty more in the days to come. I could sleep soundly that night, content in the knowledge that my itinerary for the next three days at least was set in stone and problem-free.

'Paul, I'm sorry to wake you but there is a problem you should know about,' whispered Geneviève into my bunk, just moments after I'd nodded off and begun a peculiar dream about owls. Late-night visits from girls in dorms, eh? That hadn't happened since... that had never happened. I'd once visited a girl's dorm late at night, but I was twelve and it was for the altogether serious business of a pillow fight.

'I have received an email from... Andrea in Germany?'

'Yes, she's my host for tomorrow night,' I whispered back matter-of-factly, unsure why it was worth interrupting the business with the owls. 'She's the lady who posted the train ticket to me.'

'Yes, that's what she said in her email,' continued Gen. 'Unfortunately she has posted it to the wrong address.'

Geneviève had my complete attention.

'I don't think we'll receive it tomorrow,' she explained, unnecessarily.

Obviously. Oh God. My brain raced to consider the implications and how I could rectify the situation. It was Tuesday evening and I still had until Thursday dinnertime – some 36 hours – to reach Frankfurt Airport from Paris, but there was the considerable matter of the two being 900 kilometres apart.

'Thanks for letting me know Gen, I'll sort it out in the morning.'

Geneviève left me alone to stare at the ceiling, shortly before the resurrection of the Dutchman and the accompanying cacophony of the Devil.

Chapter 10

Day Four – Wednesday 4 March

Wednesday morning arrived at St Christopher's Inn in Paris. It was the Wednesday before the Thursday I was meant to board a flight in Frankfurt. A well-intentioned Twitter user had spent their hard-earned money on my train ticket, and then unwittingly sent it to a made-up address. It was a setback to be sure, but before setting about inventing molecular transport or some other solution to my dilemma, there was the complimentary breakfast to tackle. The bar area of the hostel, cleared of dead bottles of lager and amorous backpackers, was now heaving with the same shabby-haired guests wearing their pyjamas. The larger tables were adorned with rolls and preserves, cereals and brimming jugs of juice and milk, surrounded by these swarms of travellers, locusts each and every one of them, devouring their body weight in prunes and pastries to avoid spending a cent more than necessary before suppertime.

I've never been terribly regimented in my breakfast routine. If there's a restaurant buffet offering as much streaky bacon, oily sausage, charred black pudding and overcooked scrambled egg as I can push down my gullet, game on. If it's a solitary slice of marmalade on toast, that'll do nicely also. Since I'd begun working freelance from home, the proximity of the kitchen had seen my sphere of breakfasting opportunities expand to include cheese-on-toast, prawn sandwiches, noodles, Worcester Sauce-flavoured crisps and raw cabbage dipped in mango chutney. I therefore surprised myself when I recoiled in horror at the petite Danish girl ahead of me – blue of eye and wide of smile and barely wearing her ash-grey pyjamas – who added cornflakes to her bowl of Coco Pops. Despite the childhood highs of Kellogg's variety packs whenever my brother and I stayed over at Nana's, it had never occurred to me to mix two boxes in one bowl. Ever.

twitchhiker Don't cross the streams; it's always good advice and applies equally to Ghostbusting and breakfast cereals.

8:11 AM Mar 4th

I spotted Geneviève at the opposite end of the bar. The dark-haired, brown-eyed, half-French, half-English hostel manager was walking towards me. Actually, she was bouncing, a giddy little skip in her step and a grin on her face as she sat down opposite and thrust out her fist, in which was a fistful of euros.

'I've talked to Andrea in Germany. The hostel will give you the money for your train ticket to Germany.'

Thank you, global karma. I never doubted you for a second. Apart from a fleeting thought the previous night when I thought you were a prize cocksocket.

'As long as your rules allow me to give you the money,' added Gen.

Ah. Andrea had offered the train ticket to me on Twitter, but hadn't provided it. It was now a third party providing the means outside Twitter, although the hostel was on Twitter and it wasn't as if Andrea hadn't already paid for a ticket.

'That's lovely of you Gen, but I need to have a think about this,' I replied. 'I don't know if I can take money for a ticket. The help has to be provided by the Twitter user, I think. I'm not sure, my rules don't really cover this sort of thing.'

'I could come to the train station and buy it for you,' offered Gen. 'And it's not the hostel's money, if that helps? Andrea has given me her VISA details so I can charge her for the cost of the ticket.'

My German Twitter friend was prepared to pay for a second ticket to see me succeed. I assumed she'd shrug her shoulders and pass the baton back to Twitter, let someone else figure it out. How hard was I making it for myself? The woman had already bought me one ticket that had gone astray, and she had paid for the replacement. I was barely bending the rules by accepting Gen's offer, so I humbly accepted the money – three crumpled blue 20 euro notes and four one euro coins – and celebrated with a second bowl of cereal. Just the one type in there, mind – I wasn't getting too carried away.

I returned to my room and crammed my possessions back into my messenger bags. Either the bags had shrunk over the past two days or I'd acquired more belongings, because neither would close properly. I was already carrying less than the bare minimum required for a month's travelling but there were socks and pants and cables spilling everywhere. After a considerable amount of patience, unpacking, repacking, loud swearing and the traditional sitting on the bag while stretching the straps to the absolute maximum, everything was eventually thumped, kicked and squeezed into place.

The train to Saarbrücken didn't depart Gare de l'Est until late afternoon, meaning plenty of time to work and ensure I didn't return home to red letters and hungry, feral children feasting on the kitten we'd bought them before Christmas. It seemed my fear of struggling to balance work and travel was unfounded, but then I'd deliberately stayed on in Paris for two nights for that reason.

While I tapped away at the laptop, Twitter presented new offers of assistance concerning my arrival in the US, although none provided a bed or a porch in New York. As it stood, I was flying into the Big Apple the following evening and sleeping on subway vents unless whispers of my arrival reached a sympathetic ear. They had been heard in Washington DC, however, where one tweep had offered to buy me a bus ticket to the American capital from NYC, and another had offered a sofa on Saturday evening. Independent of one another, Katy from York, Pennsylvania and Allison in DC – @katyhaltertop and @ateedub were their respective Twitter names – had provided my second destination stateside. The mystery of where I'd spend my time between arriving in NYC on Thursday and departing for Washington on Saturday would remain unsolved for the time being.

The gift I'd received from Lindsay in Newcastle – the ornamental tin for bifurcated rivets – had been offered to Chris and his wife Sarah on Monday evening during our meal in the restaurant. I'd squeezed the topic into our conversation as gently as I could after sensing Chris was unaware of the gift exchange, despite emailing him to explain it. A pat-down of Chris's pockets had failed to reveal an impromptu present, at which point Sarah had thrown open her handbag, emptied the contents onto and across the breadth of the table, rummaged through the minutiae to eventually identify and hand over a French postcard, plus a stamp. All that random crap, forgotten about and lost to the light-deprived depths of a woman's handbag, does come in useful on occasion.

It was this French postcard with its French stamp that I sheepishly offered to the manager of the French hostel. Gen feigned delight with impressive ease and handed over a generic hostel T-shirt for me to exchange with Andrea in Germany. What it lacked in thought or sentimental value, it more than made up for in garishness. There was one final outburst of profanity as I attempted to stuff the T-shirt into my tiny bag, before thanking Gen for her hospitality and turning to the door. I was pleased to be moving on; I had no qualms with the hostel but I'd seen nothing of the city except my immediate locale, and two days of occupying the bar with my nose buried in a laptop had left me lonely and homesick. Time to move on.

I made my way back over the canal, onto Avenue Jean Jaurès and towards Laumière station, where once more the sun broke through an otherwise washed-out sky to wish me well on my way. My train was due to depart Gare de l'Est in a little under an hour and Gen had assured me the station was only one stop further along the Metro line from Laumière. After descending the steps into the station, I made the mistake of double-checking the route map for myself, rather than accept Gen's advice in good faith. Maps for underground networks across the world share many commonalities – a rhumba of snaking lines differentiated by colour with station names and positions clearly marked. Compared to that of the London Underground, however, the map of the Parisian Metro was desperately unclear, insanely cluttered and, significantly, in French. It was of little assistance to the untrained eye of the fretful foreigner in a hurry and made as much sense as a bearded horse.

Despite being told I could reach Gare de l'Est direct on Line 5, it appeared I might have to change once, maybe twice, by taking Line 5 then Line 7. And there wasn't just one Line 7, there was a pink Line 7 and a turquoise Line 7. I could see both Laumière and Gare de l'Est, but my eye couldn't follow which line led where. Commuters brushed by as I tried to make sense of my journey. The longer I stared, the more I panicked about missing the train I didn't yet have a ticket for. And then I saw it. The orange Line 5 from Laumière turned north before turning south again to Gare de l'Est. My eye hadn't properly followed the route because there were another five lines crossing the same space. Idiot boy.

Once at Gare de l'Est, I made the schoolboy error of attempting to engage the sales assistant in a language I hadn't learned properly some two decades earlier, at which point the lady replied in near perfect English to save me further embarrassment. There's nowhere to run at that point, is there? You're an imbecile, an ignoramus; your lack of education has been laid bare. Oh, how you wish you'd done the world a favour by not spending second-year French scrawling giant knobs in foreign textbooks.

Once I discovered where the sneaky French had hidden the platform, I found my train to be a revelation in terms of style and comfort. Having spent a lifetime travelling on the UK's railways – either with my Nana to Whitley Bay for a day at the seaside at the weekend (even when it meant missing *Swap Shop*) or back and forth to London while I worked there – my expectations of what Europe might offer were subterranean. Once again, I was so far off the mark, the distance could be measured in light years. My ticket clearly stated it was a second-class carriage, yet it was light and clean, smothered in oak panelling and extravagant fittings. And I had legroom, sweet merciful legroom – my knees enjoyed a full six inches of fresh air with no fear of being crushed by the ignorant bastard in front who dropped into his seat as hard as possible. First class, I concluded, must have been chock-full of all-you-can-eat steak-based buffets and fluffers. The cluttered suburbs of eastern Paris slowly thinned out and allowed rural France into view, a patchwork quilt of farmed land with a handful of towns scattered here and there.

The journey slipped into darkness before the train crossed the German border and reached Saarbrücken. Andrea was waiting for me on the platform – blue-eyed with cropped blonde hair, wrapped up in waterproofs and apprehensive, obviously nervous about my arrival. She was accompanied by a German television crew who filmed our meeting for the local news, and who planned to follow us back to Andrea's home for further interviews. Before taking up twitchhiking I hadn't thought much about the type of person I might forge these physical connections with. I certainly didn't picture it to be the likes of Andrea Juchem; a middle-aged, middle-class lady with two teenage children, running a successful family business founded by her grandfather. And it wasn't some small, twee business, either; the Juchem Group based in Eppelborn provided fat, cereal and egg processing services to the biggest food brands in Germany.

Outside the glass and metal facade of Saarbrücken station, the weather was grim and moist. Eppelborn was half an hour away by autobahn, and Andrea was to drive us there in her car. The reporter asked if his cameraman could accompany us in the rear seat and film the journey, which seemed a reasonable, if slightly odd, request – what would he possibly film while we all sat in darkness? It was only once we left the sodium of Saarbrücken and sped through the oil-black night on the autobahn that he spoke up. There was a brief exchange with Andrea in the German tongue, an unnerving matter-of-fact conversation of which I didn't understand a syllable.

'Where shall we dump his body,' the cameraman had perhaps enquired of his accomplice.

'I don't care,' replied Andrea. 'We mustn't disembowel him in the car, I've just had it valeted.'

'That's fine by me,' agreed her conspirator. 'As long as I can keep his lower intestine for a nice scarf.'

The moment punctured my conscience – I'd abandoned a new wife and two beautiful children I didn't spend nearly enough time with, a family who completely relied on my love and well-being, and I was taking an extraordinary and unnecessary risk by blindly accepting charity from whoever happened to offer it. My intention had been to email my host's contact details and address to both Jane and Jon, to ensure my safety and their peace of mind. It hadn't happened because I didn't perceive any risk. Regular tweets meant thousands of people already knew my location; should my messages suddenly stop, somebody was sure to notice. Of murderers and rapists and evil-doers there were plenty, but I'd chosen to believe I was somehow immune from that world – a belief perhaps at odds with my situation as I was escorted through the German countryside.

'Sorry Paul, it is perhaps rude to speak in German while you are our guest,' offered Andrea.

Well yes, yes it was, I thought.

'The cameraman has asked me to switch on the internal lights so we can be seen by the camera,' continued Andrea.

He didn't want my intestines for a scarf, then? Thank fuck for that.

Switches were flicked and the interior of the car was bathed in a dull light. The laws of contrast, being what they are, saw that our scope of vision through the windscreen was immediately reduced, the granular detail granted to the eye by darkness had vanished.

'He would also like us to talk to one another,' she continued.

Fine, so long as Andrea could concentrate on the road ahead, a road along which she was accelerating at trouser-browning speeds. No reason to panic, I told myself – it was a solid, well-manufactured German car and Andrea appeared to be a more-than-capable driver. Then Andrea began turning her head towards me every time she spoke, in a polite and obvious way for the sake of the camera. To summarise; I was sat on the wrong side of the car driving on the wrong side of the road, with the interior lights and pouring rain reducing visibility to near-zero, the speedometer creeping past 140 kph, and the driver was keen to look me in the eye. My sphincter couldn't have been any tighter.

Andrea's home in the village of Eppelborn was magnificent and welcoming, a grand labyrinth over four floors. One room on the ground floor was dedicated to the building's history; a glass panel depicted a timeline of the buildings that had stood there over several hundred years. A tall glass case displayed artefacts found buried beneath the land during renovations, some pieces dating back to the Napoleonic Wars. It was a home of character and warmth, qualities it shared with my host who had gone to extraordinary lengths to see me arrive there.

The reporter had completed the journey in a similarly buttock-clenching time in his own car, and together with his colleague interviewed Andrea and me for German television. I heard for the first time why this successful businesswoman and mother of two had invested time, effort and expense in me. The story of the Twitchhiker was an extraordinary one, she explained, and for Eppelborn to be part of that story was a remarkable opportunity – the role played by the town would always be remembered and people around the world would learn of this small town tucked away in western Germany. Humbled wasn't the word.

The television crew didn't conclude filming for nearly another hour, which took its toll on the vegetarian curry prepared by Andrea's daughter Johanna and her boyfriend – rice is rarely better for reheating and Johanna's had dried out in the pan. Having never perfected the art of home-cooked rice myself I was perfectly prepared to indulge, but Andrea would have none of it. She was anxious, determined that my time spent in Eppelborn pass without complaint, and ordered three portions of boiled white rice for collection from the local takeaway. I had no complaints whatsoever, except with myself and my inability to speak any language other than my own. Johanna had studied A Levels at Framlingham College in Suffolk, and her English was pristine. Save for the occasional clipped syllable, her vocabulary and intonation were flawless. Andrea's grasp of my mother tongue was also impressive, despite her assurances to the contrary. Few situations stir such feelings of inadequacy like the company of others who speak more languages than you do.

'I really would have been happy to eat your rice,' I reassured Johanna as we waited for Andrea to return from the takeaway.

'She's not normally like this,' said Johanna. 'I think she's very keen that you have nothing to complain about when you leave.'

'But I haven't, really I haven't,' I replied. 'I didn't come for the rice, I came to meet you all.'

'I know, she's just…' Johanna paused. 'She likes to be in control. And besides, the rice was terrible. I wouldn't have fed it to the dog.'

Clearly Johanna hadn't sampled my cooking before. After two plates full of fresh rice and vegetable curry, I retired to Andrea's bed for the evening – my host had insisted I take her room and that she sleep in the guest bedroom on account of it being littered with un-ironed laundry. It was a sweet and thoughtful gesture, but entirely unnecessary – as keen as I might have been to sift my way through the family underwear or feed my insatiable desire for late-night ironing, I was too tired. Snuggled beneath a duvet as thick as the mattress, I logged onto Twitter to see what, if anything, awaited me beyond my flight from Frankfurt. I was due to arrive in New York the following night and depart for Washington two days later on Saturday morning, and my itinerary showed white space in between the two.

M4RKM @twitchhiker I can put you up for two nights in the spare bed at my hotel!

7:56 PM March 4th

He was one of the two people who had previously offered to fly me from New York to Los Angeles, and having failed to do so, he was prepared to host me for two nights in Manhattan. His enthusiasm and insistence set alarm bells ringing behind my tired eyes. I opened Mark's Twitter page and scanned through his history of tweets – reading through the spontaneously published messages provided a useful window into the personality of the user.

M4RKM I hope the traveller accepts my gracious offer. Can't wait to smear myself with his cooling blood and wear his face to dinner.

8:12 PM March 4th

Fortunately there was nothing of the sort. Mark Milaszkiewicz was a serial tweeter, disseminating many matters of little consequence to everyone, a constant hyperactive bundle of noise. His intentions appeared honest and without agenda, besides which it was less than eighteen hours before I boarded my flight for New York.

> **twitchhiker** @M4RKM hey Mark – could I take up your offer of transport from JFK and a place to stay tomorrow night? I'll buy the beers :)
>
> *10:49 PM Mar 4th*

The deal was sealed in just two tweets; Mark would meet me off my flight at JFK and away we'd go. I had an itinerary that stretched a full three days in front of me – from Frankfurt to Schiphol, to the Big Apple and the White House beyond that. Campbell Island was only a matter of time, surely? Only the expanse of the North American continent and the Pacific Ocean could stop me. There was nobody to celebrate the good news with in the Juchem house and no time either – I'd be unable to work the following day so I knuckled down to my writing. When the bedside clock struck two and my eyes refused to focus on the screen, enough was enough. A few hours' sleep were critical for the day ahead – the day Twitchhiker turned transatlantic.

Chapter 11

Day Five – Thursday 5 March

By daylight, Eppelborn was drab and moist, the sky too lazy to dispense proper rain, so instead the air propagated a miserable drizzle that could barely be bothered to fall down towards the ground. Whatever the day held for the town's 18,000 inhabitants, it would involve being uncomfortably damp.

Breakfast in the Juchem household was served at seven o'clock; not my favourite hour of the day and certainly not after five hours' sleep. But what a breakfast. The legs of the kitchen table buckled from the quantity of food laid out across it. There were your standard cereals – frosted and plain alternatives – but then there were otherworldly cereals in tubes, and yoghurts, jams and preserves, salami, hams and cheeses, a tub of Nutella and a landslide of bread rolls.

'Is there anything I can cook for you?' enquired Andrea, hovering near the oven with a carton of eggs at the ready. I politely declined, opting instead for the continental option of meats and cheese accompanied by a brace of fresh rolls.

'It's no trouble,' Andrea pushed. 'I'm having these eggs, I might have something else you'd prefer?'

'Really Andrea, you've done more than enough. I can't thank you enough for what you've done.'

'It's no trouble,' she repeated.

Andrea had to leave early for a meeting, so her daughter Johanna would drive me to Saarbrücken. As a timeless reminder of my visit and the hundreds of euros she had spent on my transport and lodgings, I presented Andrea with my polythene-sealed hostel T-shirt and immediately felt ashamed. Andrea said she'd chosen the perfect gift for me to later exchange with Mark in New York, but changed her mind at the last moment. It was originally going to be a product that her family's company milled the flour for – a kit for baking biscuits, complete with an oven tin for cooking anatomically correct gingerbread men. The lewd nature of the gift wasn't the concern, rather more the fact I couldn't pass through JFK with flour and yeast. Not that a cock-shaped metal tin would do me any favours either. A stand-in gift for my US host was called up in its place, and so I shook Andrea's hand as she passed me a bottle of shower gel. Perhaps there was some significance or hidden relevance, or perhaps the explanation was lost in translation. It didn't matter – my Twitter acquaintance had gone above and beyond to make me welcome in Germany. She had been gloriously successful.

Johanna accompanied me onto the station concourse to buy my single ticket to Frankfurt, kissed me on the cheek and wished me luck. I was leaving Saarbrücken barely fifteen hours after first arriving there, tired but warmed to the bones by the generosity I'd been shown. I was a train ride away from Frankfurt, two flights away from New York, losing a day's work to travel but otherwise life was good. Every day, more and more people were hearing of Twitchhiker and following the cause. I wasn't necessarily receiving more offers of help as a result, instead playing out my role to thousands of voyeurs in the shadows who preferred to observe rather than partake.

The train to Frankfurt Airport was lacking compared to the relative luxury of the previous day; it was an elderly carriage that rattled along its rails, stark and devoid of warmth, no decorative fixtures and fittings, with hard seating and scarred linoleum. There were no blue skies to brighten the occasion. The view was dull, monochromatic countryside. The handful of passengers in the carriage offered little relief, instead content to keep their own company or make quiet conversation in hushed tones of German. I may have been deep in West Germany, but the scene was more reminiscent of the Eastern Bloc; grey, dispirited and no trolley service.

twitchhiker On a local train from Saarbrücken to Frankfurt. Anxious for the first time – don't speak the language and there's nobody to help me at the other end.

9:50 AM Mar 5th

There had been tiny flickers of fear throughout the trip so far, but a giddy roar of adrenalin in my chest usually overwhelmed them. There was no real justification for

107

being afraid, yet within minutes of leaving Saarbrücken I was terrified by my inability to speak German should something go awry. My chest boomed and my eyes welled up. I couldn't explain it. Perhaps I was tired, maybe the realisation of what this journey involved was dawning on me – it was unlikely to be friendly faces and continental breakfasts all the way to Campbell Island. There was still the uncertainty of whether I'd be caught out bluffing my way through US customs – the journey could be over by the day's end. But in the main, it was my own ignorance that frightened me, an absolute lack of understanding of what the couple sat opposite were discussing or the small talk the ticket inspector had attempted to engage me with. I was paranoid.

> **twitchhiker** Only now I realise the sum total of my German vocabulary was learnt from Indiana Jones and the Last Crusade.
>
> *10:13 AM Mar 5th*

> **flashboy** @twitchhiker If they give you any trouble, just punch someone, throw them out the window, and say 'no ticket'.
>
> *10:19 AM Mar 5th*

Twitter users flocked to talk me down off the ledge I'd stepped out onto, eager to reassure me. I was assured the majority of Germans under thirty were likely to speak English as their second language. My aunt lives in Frankfurt if you have trouble, said one; if you're stuck you can always call me in Berlin, said another. Perhaps I'd been too honest in exposing my fears to Twitter – nobody wanted to follow somebody whinging their way around the world.

The train grated its way into Frankfurt Airport and the anxiety quickly ebbed away. Airports are a comforting constant in the universe; you can employ the greatest architects in the world to design them, but the end result will still appear, to all intents and purposes, grey. Award-winning structures of unrivalled form, the juxtaposition of glass and metal, cathedrals that praise the sky – they'll still be grey. Yet however impersonal and duller-than-Doncaster they may be, airports rarely fail to raise the spirits; arriving at one means before too long you'll be setting out on a new adventure and leaving it far behind. So there was that. And the fact that all the signs at Frankfurt Airport were translated into English.

The hour-long flight to Amsterdam was effortless, and barely 90 minutes later I boarded my flight to New York. Accompanying me on my flight were several hundred passengers and their cacophony of broad accents from across the EU, suitcases, holdalls, backpacks and handbags plus one white Lamborghini I'd spotted from the terminal building. It was secured to a vast pallet that a forklift truck driver nervously manoeuvred into the hold of the waiting 747. A white Lamborghini. Who had so much money they could take their car with them on a jumbo jet? Was that even covered in the rules on additional baggage?

Sat down, strapped in, my second safety demonstration of the day half-heartedly paid attention to, we were away. Thanks to @clocsen, the compliance manager from Chester I'd never met, I was being catapulted over the Atlantic towards New York City in a pressurised steel cylinder. I was thrilled, wild, breathless with wonder that I'd made it so far, my bleakest fears defied. Yet my mood soured the moment I dared to congratulate myself, and the prospect of what awaited me in New York caused my gut to implode. Somebody had put both their faith and money in my journey, but there was still that nagging doubt as to whether I'd be allowed through US Immigration.

As the flight passed over the UK, I glanced at the flight map displayed on the video screens. For the UK, just four city names were displayed – Cardiff, Glasgow, Birmingham and Newcastle – and our route was painted straight over my home. And I cried, just a little; I was tired and anxious and missing my home, my mattress, my pillow; I was missing a lot of really good television, and how much I missed my wife of barely a month and my boys was overwhelming me. I missed them so much it caused physical pain. I knew I had to shake myself out of my melancholy funk, a mood not improved by the in-flight entertainment screening *Four Christmases*, or the lardarse in the seat ahead who reclined his seat at knee-shattering speed, oblivious to my 6' 4" frame. The seats behind me were pressed up against a bulkhead, so I graciously refrained from reclining my chair, for which I was rewarded with having my headrest punched and pulled for eight hours straight.

@

After visiting New York the first time, you realise the importance of marching with purpose upon leaving the aircraft and entering the terminal. How long it takes to clear US Immigration at JFK varies between five minutes on a good day, and ninety minutes on the day you needed to be somewhere in a hurry. The situation has improved substantially in recent years, but if there are only a handful of desks open and other flights arriving, your will to live will ooze from your ears. So I marched and I took no prisoners, weaving between weary couples and doddering old ladies, and despite being one of the last to leave the plane I was amongst the first two dozen into the immigration hall, just in time to see another planeload of passengers arrive and doom my tardier companions to an hour's slow shuffling.

Had the lamb skipped merrily to its slaughter? Had I simply hastened my own demise and that of Twitchhiker? In a word, no. After those eight hours of stomach-scrunching anxiety, I waltzed through immigration without a whiff of suspicion. Admittedly, I had the European couple ahead of me to thank for the smooth ride; their poor grasp of English meant they'd made a sow's ear of their visa waiver documents, and they were banished to the rear of the immigration hall to fill in fresh forms. When I stepped forward in their place, the pretty Hispanic officer already had her opening line:

'Well, you don't seem to have a problem with filling in the paperwork.'

'Thank you! I was here in January to get married and I visit whenever I can. Plus I'm back here in May, so I've had plenty of practice!'

'You got married here? Is your wife American?'

'No, she's English but I wanted to bring her here to get married, because I love your city sooooo much!'

'Wow, that's so romantic! Did you bring your family over with you?'

'No! We didn't tell a soul until we went home! It was all a secret!'

'That's how I want my marriage to be! No fuss, no hassle. Have a great time in New York!'

'Thanks! I will!'

All lies. For one thing, Jon and Kelly knew about the wedding beforehand, as did everyone who attended Richard Spencer's birthday party, during which I was so riddled with booze I blurted it out. No matter, my white lie had passed unnoticed and even if it hadn't, it was hardly grounds for refusing entry to the country. The carefree exchange with Little Miss Sunshine brightened my mood immediately; I was in my favourite place in the world, a city I wore like a second skin, and I could allow myself a moment to relax and stop being so wet.

I arrived in Terminal 4's arrival hall ahead of my host and so pottered about for several minutes, trying not to look too guilty in front of the armed police officers as I restored circulation to my legs and dodged the drivers offering illegal cabs to the city. Mark was easy to spot when he finally bounded over towards me a few minutes later. He was waving an A4 sheet of paper with @twitchhiker scrawled across it, which was my first clue. Physically he was a big guy, as tall as me but bigger-boned, his hair an explosion of unkempt spikes and curls. I'd got to know a little about Mark after he'd confirmed his offer to help me in New York; he was a Yorkshireman from Wakefield who'd attended university at Sunderland, and we shared mutual friends from there and elsewhere. He was in New York to celebrate his thirtieth birthday, although that was more of an excuse since he harboured a similar affection for the city and visited whenever he could. We greeted each other with the broadest of smiles, a handshake, a hug and the sense that we'd known one another for years. As we boarded the Airtrain to Jamaica Station and disappeared underground on the subway into Manhattan, I talked through my past few days on the road and together we exchanged tales of our adventures in New York. Mark dealt in Xerox installation by day, and website design and development by night, which provided him with the pocket money to fund this, his eleventh visit to the Big Apple.

'Where are we going to go tonight?' asked my excited host. 'There are plenty of delightful bars in TriBeCa, and one or two favourites there we can try?'

'I know Hell's Kitchen fairly well,' I offered. 'It's your birthday we're celebrating, up to you.'

'No, no, no – we're celebrating the Twitchhiker too!' announced Mark. 'I can see two very late and drunken nights ahead for us!'

'Absolutely,' I said. 'We'll drop my bags off at your hotel, and head straight back out.'

'Wonderful!' my host cheered. Mark was clearly delighted to have company in New York, for a short time at least.

Compared to the London Underground, travelling on the New York Subway is a treat. Trains run twenty-four hours a day with express services surging between major stops. The fares are obscenely cheap by comparison and there are no price bands or zoning; travel one stop down the line or 30 kilometres from the northern tip of the Bronx to Coney Island in Brooklyn, and it'll barely cost a couple of bucks. Subway carriages are broad, uncluttered and – and this is the deal-breaker – air-conditioned. Bliss. It's a little-known fact that a New York engineer called Willis Haviland invented electrical air conditioning in 1902; why over a century later Haviland's invention still eludes the management of the London Underground remains a mystery.

Beyond the decadent splendour of Grand Central, Midtown East is a largely unremarkable neighbourhood of Manhattan, dominated by skyscrapers and gentrified to the hilt, although towards the East River and Turtle Bay are occasional outcrops of older low-rise brownstones and businesses. Mark had checked into the Affinia 50, a three-star hotel at 50th Street and Third Avenue in Midtown East, and my bed for the next two nights was the spare queen-sized bed in Mark's room. We remained in the hotel room only long enough for me to shower and reward my feet with a fresh pair of socks, before heading out into the night. Mark had arrived only a few hours before me, and we were both bursting to see the city and celebrate. My body clock hadn't checked the time since Germany and was uneasy with the suggestion, but it was duly ignored in favour of adventure and beer. There was a bar on the West Side calling to me, a bar with a giant hollow pig stood outside. Mark concurred with my suggestion and wasted no time hailing a cab in the cool Manhattan air – we were soon heading cross-town to Hell's Kitchen, and to Rudy's.

The first to settle the stretch of Manhattan's western shoreline, called Hell's Kitchen, were Irish and German immigrants in the nineteenth century, working on the Hudson River docks in local slaughterhouses and factories. These streets were the brawn of Manhattan; gangs swaggered through the slums and brawling was commonplace. When alcohol was barred by Prohibition in the 1920s, the street gangs evolved into organised crime rackets with interests in everything from gambling and extortion to prostitution, and an influx of Puerto Rican immigrants in the 1950s brought about the return of the gang violence as romanticised in *West Side Story*.

There's little left to hint at this neighbourhood's tawdry and violent past. The eastern boundary of Hell's Kitchen at Eighth Avenue remains a seedy and occasionally intimidating stretch, littered with sex shops and strip bars – once a halfway house between the working class tenements to the west and the porn-peddling theatres of Times Square to the east. The residential streets connecting Ninth and Tenth Avenues are still spacious and airy; several blocks were protected by preservation orders in the 1970s that limited building height, although relaxed regulations in recent years have seen modern condominiums encroach on the low-rise skyline, and the streets awash with cranes and concrete and hods of fluorescent labourers drinking Schnapple. While some residents lament the further loss of New York's heritage, others are relieved that after years of neglect the area is finally receiving attention from developers.

When we arrived at Rudy's at 44th Street and Ninth Avenue, there wasn't even room for amateur cat-swinging inside. The booths were stuffed full with chatter and pitchers, so we squeezed in at the bar and bought our $3 pints of Budweiser and hit the bartender for a couple of free hot dogs. The barman was a bespectacled and bearded Glaswegian called Gary, a former boxer with a keen interest in the history of whaling; he recognised me immediately and shook me firmly by the hand, pouring complimentary shots for the two of us. I hadn't talked to Gary since a previous visit the year before and we'd only met once before that, but he treated Mark and me as if we propped up his bar every night of the week. Locals and laughter, loud music, free hot dogs and a barman who treated me like a regular whenever I dropped by. Perfect. Let's hear it for New York.

We stopped by Chelsea Grill further up Ninth Avenue, then turned right at 47th Street and crossed Eighth Avenue to arrive at a bar forgotten by time and fashion – the Rum House at the Edison Hotel. It was a dimly lit affair, a musty throwback to another century with its teak bar and nightly lounge singer. Its proximity to Times Square meant there were plenty of tourists taking up the stools, but like Rudy's it was a neighbourhood bar smack in the centre of

Manhattan, with regulars heckling the bar staff in good humour and taking their turn on the microphone. As dear as Rudy's was to me, the Rum House was equally close to Mark's heart. He first visited the city in November 2001 with his family, and befriended the staff at the bar. Mark's father died in 2004 and Mark made a point of calling by the bar on every visit; the same staff, Jose the barman and Karen the lounge singer, would always ask after his mother and sister and rarely accept anything close to the price of his bar tab. It was yet another reason I adored the city so much – people accuse New Yorkers of being rude; they're not, not really. If you take the time to give something to the city, even in a small way, it'll always remember you and welcome you back.

Our night of debauchery was nothing of the sort in the end. Mark and I rolled into our beds at the modest time of one o'clock – there were three hours of drinking still available in Manhattan's bars, but we'd both endured eight-hour flights and lacked resolve to drink New York dry. It was a blessing since I needed to be up early; bouncing around cities and continents like Doctor Sam Beckett had robbed me of a day's work and I'd need to knuckle down the next morning. When the lights went out and my head finally hit the pillow, I couldn't have been happier; it was twenty-four hours since I'd woken up in Eppelborn and my body was shouting at me to sleep; and I'd crossed a whole ocean without resorting to swimming.

Chapter 12

Day Six – Friday 6 March

Jetlag gently nudged me awake several hours before my eight o'clock alarm intended to. In the queen-sized bed to my right, Mark Milaszkiewicz from Wakefield slept soundly and silently – only the occasional smoker's hack and breaking of wind spoilt the calm. New York City was peaceful, no horns or sirens to shatter the calm, only the occasional glare of a headlight peeked through the sliver of view between the curtains. Gotham is famously the city that never sleeps – the bars won't turf you out till past four and countless other haunts will take your money later than that – but there's an hour or two when it might enjoy forty winks.

It was barely five o'clock, at least an hour before Manhattan would rise and shine. My limbs were gently aching and dark, puffy bags already propped up my eyes. It was the cumulative effect of not staying still for very long and would be easily cured by a full night's sleep, a luxury I'd last enjoyed in Paris. I flicked on the bedside lamp and wrestled my laptop from its cover – at least I could take advantage of my body's refusal to rest and set to work, and catch up on several hours of tweets.

As it was Friday morning, my three-day window for accepting offers meant I could look as far ahead as Monday. My itinerary for the following day was already set; Katy (@katyhaltertop) had emailed me an e-ticket to ride a 'Bolt Bus' from New York to Washington DC – no doubt the inference of speed would prove to be a cruel joke played on gullible tourists. Once in Washington, Allison (@ateedub) had arranged my accommodation – initially I was to sleep on Allison's sofa, but her recent tweets to Katy suggested she'd since booked a hotel room for me. I'd been expecting a change of heart at some point – by searching Twitter I could see the conversations people were having about Twitchhiker, and plenty baulked at the thought of allowing a stranger 'from the Internet' into their home. They were right, of course – I was strange. I drank wine out of mugs. I refused to eat a meal if I could readily identify any part of its anatomy. I'd flush the toilet halfway through urinating so I could race the flush to the finish. At least Allison was still prepared to help, whatever the reason for her decision.

Twitter had also determined a possible itinerary for Sunday. Somebody called Ken from somewhere called Frederick was insistent that I accept a road trip across three states to Pittsburgh, taking in sights along the way such as the Appalachian Trail and the National Road. His Twitter handle, @yenra, was already familiar to me – it had cropped up amongst tweets mentioning Twitchhiker before I'd left the UK. He'd struck me as being far too excitable about my journey for a grown man and I'd already pegged him as a mentalist with a fondness for duct tape and hacksaws. Having said that, his history of tweets prior to his obsession with me revealed him to be thoughtful and intelligent, a keen blogger and somebody with immediate family – a wife, a daughter, a son. That was encouraging – he was less likely to store body parts in the freezer if the missus kept the Sunday roast in there. Unless she was the Sunday roast.

I had no idea where Frederick was or how to reach it, but it wouldn't prove a problem. Ken had already conspired with @wordtravelsfast, a Washington-based tweep called Lauree who would drive me from Washington to Frederick on Sunday morning. So there was a plan; from Washington to Frederick and on to Pittsburgh. It was certainly a step in the right direction; several hundred kilometres inland from the East Coast and plenty of options in terms of a next step, plus a population of over two million in the Greater Pittsburgh area meant attracting attention wouldn't prove a problem.

> **twitchhiker** Ok. Time to take a risk. Going to accept @ yenra's offer to drive me from Frederick to Pittsburgh on Sunday.
>
> *9:38 AM Mar 6th*

Mark took himself out to Brooklyn for the day while I struggled to complete a day's work, the view from the fourth-floor window continually summoning my attention. I jealously eyed up the ever-increasing hubbub of Third Avenue, yearned to walk the cross streets of the East Village or lose myself amongst the sounds and stenches of Chinatown's fish markets. By lunchtime the beautiful chaos of the city proved too much and I fled my three-star prison. I strayed only as far as the breathlessly cosy Brooklyn Diner on 43rd and Broadway for lunch with a pair of tweeps who worked across the road at Condé Nast; Susan and her friend Zoe wanted to hear tales of my adventure and lack of clean underwear. Perhaps they didn't ask to hear about the latter topic, but I told them anyway. Instead of ordering a burger or some other hearty fare, I opted for hummus and pitta bread. I'd never ordered hummus for a main course in my life and I was so bone-gnawingly ravenous that it barely touched the sides, but I didn't wish to fulfil the stereotype of a loutish Brit abroad dribbling cow fat down his shirt and picking out gristle from between his crooked teeth.

Before heading back to Third Avenue, I peeked around the corner of Broadway and took a moment to soak up the neon of Times Square. It was a tourist trap for sure, bombastic and shallow, but that sense of the sensational, the colours, the sounds; it was quintessentially New York – like a walk through Greenwich in the warm autumn sun or a night lost amongst the dive bars of the Lower East Side, Times Square was an intoxicating experience unique to the city.

Back to the hotel, back to the desk where I poured my brain through my fingers into my keyboard once more. Twitter provided plenty more reasons to be cheerful, this time courtesy of Internet travel company Orbitz:

Orbitz @twitchhiker What you're doing is awesome! We want to offer you a flight plus 2 nights hotel to Chicago from Pittsburgh.

3:08 PM Mar 6th

The rules allowed me to accept offers from companies as well as individuals, and although it was a flight it was only a short hop between two cities. Nobody had made an alternative offer, and I sensed a need to keep up momentum, so I gladly accepted. It meant committing to spending Sunday night in Pittsburgh after Ken and I arrived there, and I still didn't have an offer of help from anyone in the city. There were still two days, however; no need for concern.

Tap tap tap. My fingers rattled away as the sun sank over the Hudson. Tap tap tap. My one day in New York slowly slipped away. There had been a handful of snide remarks from followers about how I'd wangled a free holiday – they were so far wide of the mark it wasn't funny. Then again, whenever I'd heard the moans of travel writers that it was a relentless, tiring profession that often sucked the joy out of travel, I'd thought much the same thing – but you're on holiday and it's *free*, you lucky, lucky bastard!

I was meeting the team from *charity: water* later that evening but there was also Mark's thirtieth birthday to celebrate, so I had planned to finish my work and join him at the Pig 'n' Whistle on Third Avenue for five o'clock. It was past seven when I eventually squeezed through the door of the bar and pushed my way through the slack-tied office workers. I manoeuvred onto a stool next to Mark at the far end of the bar, who introduced me to the barman he'd befriended over the past four pints I'd missed out on. I didn't catch the barman's name or a single syllable of the conversation over the din of the crowd.

I sat for a few minutes more, buying Mark a pint for his birthday while supping meekly at mine. Mark and I were bellowing in one another's ear, one asking the other to repeat himself while the other shook his head and complained he couldn't hear a word. Within moments I was struggling to stay awake, my eyes were barely open and my speech began to slur. The first opportunity to relax in the day, and my body had decided to turn in for the night.

It wasn't stated overtly, but I sensed Mark was irritated that I'd failed to live up to expectations; all my talk of painting the town red with reckless abandon had been just that. He had every right; I'd been abysmal company. All I could do was apologise before picking my way through the crowds to the sidewalk and stumbling five blocks back to the hotel room. I had an hour before I needed to make my way to Chelsea and meet the *charity: water* team, so I set the alarm on my mobile phone, placed it on the bedside cabinet, pulled the duvet tight around my chin and passed out a moment later.

The mobile vibrated and whined, but it wasn't the alarm. It was ringing. It was Jane. The time on the face of the handset snapped into focus as my eyes woke up. Nine o'clock in New York. It was two o'clock in the morning at home.

Something was wrong.

The call connected but before I could speak, uncontrollable sobs flooded down the phone. The boys. Not them, please.

It wasn't. It was our seven-month-old kitten Elly, a black and white rascally runt of fur and mischief with crooked whiskers. She'd begun having epileptic fits at Christmas time, one every three or four days. She'd been neutered just a month ago and since then the fits had stopped. But earlier that night, she'd had a seizure, followed by another, then another; they continued for a full hour, and in the end her fragile frame wore itself out.

I wasn't so upset about the cat – it wasn't pleasant news but it wasn't unexpected – but listening to my wife break her heart ripped mine clean out of my chest. I should have been there at home to smother her with hugs and hold her hand. It should have been me having to figure out the answers to those questions we rarely need to ask, like what to do with the body of a dead kitten at two o'clock on a Saturday morning. There was nothing I could do, except tell her I was sorry and I loved her. It didn't feel like nearly enough. I cried myself dry on the phone, apologising over and over again for being too far away to help explain to the boys what had happened. I'd been running on empty for the past couple of days and I hated myself for being so far away from my family. I wasn't even a week into this trip and I was in pieces. I had to pull myself together, not least because I still had a meeting with my chosen charity to attend before I could finally collapse for the night.

By the sixth day of travelling I'd raised nearly £2,300 for *charity: water*, but I'd begun to believe I could do far more good by banging the charity's promotional drum during interviews. Journalists called on a frequent basis for updates on my journey and there was a relentless rain of emails asking questions, so I took every opportunity to talk through the facts – that one in eight people in the world had no access to safe drinking water, that the simple lack of basic sanitation killed more people every year than all forms of violence, including war.

Charity: water is a New York-based organisation and founder Scott Harrison had become aware of my support after reading a magazine feature. He'd tweeted earlier in the week to wish me safe travels and again when I arrived in the city, inviting me to meet up with his team that night. My head was 5,000 kilometres away but I wasn't prepared to mope about the hotel room. Mark had bought me a subway pass, so I picked up the E train at Lexington Avenue down to 14th Street, then walked across to Ninth Avenue and 15th Street.

I met Scott and the team at Chelsea Market, an indoor arcade housing stalls and restaurants, bakeries and bars that sat on the border of Chelsea and the Meatpacking District. The market utilises the husk of the former Nabisco factory where the Oreo cookie was invented over a century ago, and you never stray far from that history as you follow the factory floor through the post-industrial mall, past beams and ducts and girders.

The team was preparing an art installation inside the market, due to open with a VIP event on Tuesday. Staff and volunteers were gearing up to work long into the night, fuelled by soda and long, oily slices of pepperoni pizza. I mustered up the bare bones of a conversation with them as I half-heartedly man-handled yellow jerrycans and balanced precariously on stools, and after two hours had neither the strength nor will to continue.

Scott and I hadn't met by the time I decided to leave – he was critiquing the work of his team and directing the efforts of others. I'd slip out and head back to the hotel, I thought – there was no point in introducing myself and promptly buggering off. That was plain rude.

'It's Paul, isn't it?' Curses. Scott had spotted me picking through the stack of coats. I apologised for my lacklustre effort, but he seemed positively thrilled I'd made it at all.

'You're doing a great thing, Paul,' commented Scott. 'You've brought people together, your journey is an inspiration. It's a sign there's good out there.'

I thanked the charitable entrepreneur with the insufferable good looks for his kind words and apologised again for my apathy.

'Don't worry about how tiring it is, just enjoy the adventure. You're not walking the road alone.'

He was right, of course. It was an adventure and a half, if not three-quarters.

As I sloped off towards the subway in Greenwich, delighted with my endorsement from Scott, my mobile rang again. It was a little past midnight – five o'clock in the morning at home – but it wasn't Jane calling. It was a New Yorker called Jesse, a friend I'd made several years ago by virtue of stumbling across his ex-girlfriend's music blog, arranging to meet up and subsequently sneaking into a Supergrass gig at the Bowery with her. Another sickeningly handsome man, poured from the mould of Pacino's Michael Corleone, Jesse was the very definition of a New York hipster – working at MySpace by day, directing short films in his spare time, living in Williamsburg in Brooklyn and spending plenty of time at parties in Los Angeles where the likes of Natalie Portman would drop by. Yet he was far removed from the shallow, self-centred stereotype – he was sincere, likeable and carefree, no pretensions or pomposity. While we didn't see one another more than once or twice a year, I considered him a good friend, and he'd been the witness at my wedding. So did I have time, he enquired, for a drink or three with him and his fiancée across town? The question didn't require a first thought, let alone a second.

There are a handful of establishments in New York that wrangle over the title of the city's oldest bar; in all cases it depends entirely on a handful of definitions. For example, the Bridge Cafe in the shadow of the Brooklyn Bridge has served continuously as a 'drinking establishment' since 1847, albeit under different names, while McSorley's in the East Village opened its doors in 1854 and boasts of being New York City's oldest continuously operated saloon. Then there's Pete's Tavern on 18th Street which opened a decade after McSorly's yet claims to be the 'longest continuously operating bar and restaurant' in the city.

The Old Town Bar further west along 18th Street doesn't indulge in the spats, founded as it was in 1892. Nevertheless, it is one of Gotham's great neighbourhood bars, blessed with the original fixtures and fittings that have welcomed New Yorkers for over a century. The worn mahogany and marble bar, the tin ceiling high above, the warped staircase leading to the tables and stalls of the upstairs restaurant; as with both McSorley's and Pete's, to visit the grand Old Town is to drink from Manhattan's history.

I found Jesse and his fiancée Melanie tucked away in one of the Old Town's downstairs booths, each pulling on a local brew. I was becoming delirious and numb with tiredness, but as I sank a pint of beer, then another, I finally unwound in the close company of my friends. Not that I knew Melanie very well – we'd only met once, the evening after my wedding – but as the night wore on we warmed to one another. The bar's other patrons told fantastical tales and drank and cheered and the evening had all the makings of one of those dear, treasured occasions you recall with affection in years to come.

At least the first hour was.

In my barely lucid state and three pints the worse for wear, I became a little too familiar with Melanie and felt at ease to make the most grotesquely offensive statement about her mother you might care to dream up.

Whatever you're imagining right now, let me assure you it was far worse.

'I can't believe you said that, Paul. That... Paul, that was really offensive.'

Melanie's eyes were wide and her jaw hung loose; her disbelief at what I'd said was obvious, but I was trapped in the moment of not knowing whether she was bluffing, so I kept on going, waiting for a wry smile to give the game away. It never did. I glanced at Jesse, who wasn't laughing either and far from considering it. What had I done? The evening immediately imploded, there was nothing to salvage, despite my mewling apologies. We had discussed moving on to another bar but the notion was never entertained again. Within minutes of my monstrous faux pas, Jesse and Melanie were leaving and with a warm handshake from Jesse and a cold stare from Melanie, the pair turned and continued into the night without me.

I turned in the opposite direction, walked for a little way towards Broadway, then stopped. My eyes were so full of tears I couldn't see the path ahead, and for the second time that night I fell to pieces and cried my heart out. Slumped against the wall, my chest heaved so hard I thought my sternum would snap in two and my thoughts turned dark and terrible. I knew what was happening, knew why I was crumbling away in the darkness. My exhaustion had forced me to submit to the chemical imbalance in my brain, allowing it to seize power and overthrow rational thought. It was a truth I'd deliberately withheld from Twitter, and if I didn't find a way to manage my condition I was going to be in spectacular trouble.

Throughout my time on planet Earth, I'd garnered a reputation for impatience and kerosene moods, so when I was diagnosed with bipolar disorder three years earlier, it didn't faze me in the slightest. In fact, it helped me to reconcile so many chapters of my life where I'd been profoundly reckless or hopelessly lost; in hindsight, I realised that I'd lived with the consequences of my mental disability since I was sixteen, perhaps younger, given my fondness for maintaining a dual identity at school as the superhero Green Lantern. The knowledge didn't excuse my past conduct but it did allow me to understand my behaviour and make peace with myself.

Before my diagnosis, one moment I'd be punch-drunk on thin air, my mood soaring into the stratosphere, blazing brighter and brighter before exploding in screams of colour and then, as if a switch had been flicked, I'd plunge deep into a lightless pit of loneliness and despair. I managed to keep this extreme mania hidden away from most, but the likes of Jane and Jon saw enough to know.

The diagnosis of my condition led to understanding and that understanding led to control. I learned what my triggers were, what made me prone to the influences of bipolar disorder. The key factor was sleep, or lack thereof; there was an obvious correlation between the instability of my moods and the number of consecutive school nights I crawled to bed late. With the help of medication I soon became capable of controlling my behaviour and when I did stumble, I had a small circle of friends who'd pick me up and dust me down.

I shared the facts concerning my condition whenever I could, to help dispel the ignorance surrounding mental disability. Bipolar disorder isn't necessarily some hellish purgatory that damns the afflicted to eternal suffering, but their treatment by others who blindly accept such stereotypes certainly can be. I felt I was a better person for my condition, as if it freed my head to burst and fizzle with ideas and energy. I still enjoyed the manic highs but the medication and a good night's sleep stabilised my see-saw moods and minimised the lows. I became a more rounded, less destructive version of my previous self.

Before setting out on my journey, I'd discussed with both Jane and Jon what complications my disorder might bring about. I didn't want to risk knowledge of my condition affecting the neutrality of Twitter, one way or another – ignorance might have made people think twice about becoming involved, or cause others to treat me as if I had special needs. Both my wife and my best friend questioned whether I could cope with the relentless nature of my trip; no routine, little rest, the fear of failure and the consequences of success. All we could do was accept I would be vulnerable and manage that however we could – through phone calls and texts, words of love and reassurance.

At one o'clock in the morning it was still too early to call home, so I sat there in the street, tucked away out of sight from Broadway, and forced myself to breathe out my despair. After an hour in the biting cold, the chaos subsided and there was rational, ordered thought once more.

Twitchhiker was becoming a persona in its own right, a more courageous version of my own personality. And twitchhikers didn't sit about darkened corners of Manhattan blubbing like drunk Oscar winners. Scott was right, mine truly was an adventure like no other; random and relentless and draining it may have been, but I wasn't alone in living it. Others had seen to it that I had the opportunity and it was time I manned up. Besides which, I couldn't feel my backside anymore and it was beginning to rain.

Chapter 13

Day Seven – Saturday 7 March

Saturday morning saw me wake up in a substantially more positive mood than the one I'd taken to bed with me. I managed six hours of sleep before the alarm licked its finger and wriggled it in my ear, vanquishing the demons of the night before.

Mark was a little prickly when he eventually came round from his evening of excess – I'd failed to make good on my promises of wild birthday celebrations. All remained civil as we exchanged gifts, although there was a moment of uncertainty as I handed Mark a bottle of shower gel, the present I'd received from Andrea in Eppelborn. Bemused by the overly practical nature of my gift, Mark pottered over to his case and tunnelled through his clothes, tearing out shirts and socks.

'Well, I have something altogether very proper and terribly British as my gift,' he announced triumphantly as he turned to reveal a blue, sealed cuboid package in his hands – eighty pristine two-cup tea bags from Ringtons, a Newcastle-based company founded over a century ago that still hand-delivers orders of tea door to door. I was tempted to slip a finger under the seal and pilfer a bag for a morning brew; while it is undeniably true that a proper cup of tea solves all problems – from day-to-day worries to world wars – such properties are lost on our US brethren. Throwing tea into a harbour was a protest by your ancestors, America; it's not how you actually make it.

There really wasn't room for eighty of Newcastle's finest amongst my packing, one bag of which was brimming with dirty laundry. Aside from a single clean pair of boxer shorts, everything was aching with sweat to a greater or lesser extent. Somebody had suggested I take washing powder with me, another sage piece of advice I'd duly ignored. I was certain I'd packed a fifth pair of fresh socks, and I was missing an adaptor, too – I dimly recalled intending to unplug it from a German wall socket.

Gifts exchanged and packing complete, Mark hailed a cab from Third Avenue and we headed off to the bus stop at 33rd and Seventh, from where I would catch the curiously named Bolt Bus. The day was fresh and warm, spring had blown into New York, and Washington was promising temperatures of 22°C. All this, and I was wearing clean underwear. Happy days. The journey was back on track.

Across from the sky-high glass facade of Madison Square Garden, one or two fellow passengers were already waiting outside the Sbarro pizza joint on the corner of 33rd Street. I had the e-ticket for my journey printed out and clenched in my fist; it cost just $15 for the four-hour bus ride to Washington. While Mark and I discussed whether this bargain price would see me having to get out and push, a slick, black coach glided slowly up 33rd Street and hissed gently to a stop at the kerb beside us, the paintwork buffed and lustrous in the Manhattan sunshine. This, ladies and gentlemen, was a Bolt Bus, and it was perhaps the greatest bus ever to please the weary traveller's eye. Not since Centraal Station in Amsterdam was I so excited by the prospect of my transportation – the livery promised free Wi-Fi on board. My road trip through the states of New Jersey, Pennsylvania, Maryland and into the District of Columbia wouldn't be four hours of dead time; I could work my way down the USA. Wi-Fi. On a bus. While it was moving! It was black magic, voodoo no less, but with less need for dolls or resurrecting the dead. All that remained was for a robust handshake and an unexpected hug from Mark – his unbridled fervour for both New York and Twitchhiker further heightened my new good mood.

twitchhiker Update: Halfway to DC. Stay tonight, Pittsburgh tomorrow. Nowhere to stay, can't reach airport on Monday for flight to Chicago.

12:29 PM Mar 7th

The four hours of dreary Interstate to DC gave me a chance to take stock of my itinerary. I was a human baton for the next twenty-four hours; Katy (@katyhaltertop) would meet me at the coach stop in DC. She would then pass me to Allison (@ateedub) who had arranged my accommodation in the city, – I still didn't know where exactly. Lauree (@wordtravelsfast) would collect me the next morning and drive me to Frederick where I'd hook up with Ken (@yenra), and together we'd follow the road to Pittsburgh. And breathe.

My road trip buddy still made my palms sweat; in my nervous state I felt this stranger's enthusiasm was suffocating, his half-hourly tweets seemed to me bordering on sycophantic. He was also breathlessly blogging about the drive to Pittsburgh:

> 'Later today, I'm going to the grocery store to buy some snacks and beverages. While I hope we stop for meals, I don't want us to be lacking. So I'll have a cooler full of ice and drinks and a box full of crunchy snacks and cookies. Please tweet @yenra if you have any snack suggestions.

> 'The same goes for music – let me know what songs you would like me to add to the playlist. This is a chance to shape the trip: tell me snacks to offer and songs to play.'

The blog also included photographs of magnetic car decals his daughter had painted; our names would be plastered either side of Ken's Mustang convertible. Why all the unnecessary fanfare?

twitchhiker Obama seems to be having every road in DC dug up simultaneously. When he referred to change, he meant the tarmac.

2:25 PM Mar 7th

Despite its unrivalled technological achievements, the Bolt Bus was capable of neither teleportation nor flight, so after picking through several kilometres of roadworks and diversions, it pulled into the coach park at the junction of 10th Street and H Street over half an hour late. The person who'd brought me to Washington was also my host for the afternoon, and that was Katy, a bubbly, buxom, brunette twenty-something-year-old working at an advertising agency in York, Pennsylvania.

'So I was thinking you might want to go on a tour or two,' said Katy with a cute Southern drawl. 'But we can do something else if you want?'

I knew exactly how I wanted to spend my time. I wanted to ooh and ahh at all the pretty buildings I'd seen on television.

'Can we just walk around and look at... well... stuff? The White House, Capitol Hill? Is that OK?'

'Sure we can,' Katy beamed back.

Saturday afternoon, blazing sunshine and I had an afternoon off from twitchhiking. It was the first time in my week of travelling I was going to play at being a tourist.

We drove a short distance to Third Avenue and mounted the kerb somewhere near the US Department of Health & Human Services building; it looked the double of the FBI headquarters I knew from nine seasons of *The X-Files*, as did most of the other buildings I spied on street corners. Nearby was the United States Capitol and the ample thoroughfare of the National Mall, the three-kilometre-long National Park that rolls out west from Capitol Hill to the Lincoln Memorial, dominated by the beacon-tipped obelisk of the Washington Monument. It punctures the skyline, a needle of stone that took forty years to complete and was the tallest structure on the planet for five years until the Eiffel Tower pushed beyond it in 1889. It lends to the epic scale of the setting – an endless lawn flanked by majestic buildings of government and countless ornamented museums. This is a setting favoured by history, where millions have gathered in both celebration and protest, while the country was at peace and at war. Like Central Park, however, the National Mall is also a recreational centre for the city's residents and visitors, and the day's good weather saw thousands of people drawn onto the lawn to enjoy picnics and long strolls amongst the joggers and gangs of marauding Frisbee throwers.

Before making further progress along the Mall, Katy and I visited the cafeteria at the National Museum of the American Indian for lunch. Again, my insistence to sample the more obscure delicacies on the menu saw me square up to a bowl of buffalo chilli. It appeared that an uncommonly sick buffalo had evacuated its bowels into my dish, more a rich brown soup of beans and knuckles of meat. The taste was little better – every mouthful reinforced the notion that buffalos are creatures fashioned entirely from cartilage.

The dish of beany gristle sat awkwardly in my gut as we walked forth up the National Mall, from Capitol Hill to the Washington Monument. We swung by a rather modest mansion-sized residence that would have been entirely unworthy of mention if it hadn't happened to be the White House. It's tiny.

'My Great Aunty Ann had a farmhouse in Kirkby Lonsdale that was larger,' I pointed out to Katy.

'Did she really?' said Katy.

'No, not really. She did own a lot of cows, though,' I said. 'She'd send me to the milking shed to take a bucket of fresh milk every morning. Now that shed was definitely bigger than the White House.'

'You milk your cows?' asked Katy.

'Yes, obviously. Why, what do you do with yours?'

'We barbecue them,' replied Katy, laughing.

We asked other tourists to take our photo in front of world-famous monuments, chatted and larked about in no particular rush to go anywhere. Katy enthused about studying at university in Denver and the joys of a Texan upbringing, describing the family barbecues where everything within a ten-kilometre radius was chargrilled and devoured.

As the embers of the early evening quietly died away, we met with Allison who had arranged my accommodation for the evening. Her photo on Twitter was of an eye, nothing else, so it was impossible to determine anything about her appearance other than her possession of at least one blue eye. She turned out to be blonde and slim, and in possession of both eyes, but also aloof and a little wary of me.

We drove a short way to the Banana Café on 8th Street, and Washington became a different city – no imperious pillars of marble or cold concrete office blocks, but dainty low-rise buildings, none taller than three storeys, all different styles and colours, squeezed and slumped against one another. This was the historic neighbourhood of Capitol Hill; a stone's throw from the home of the most powerful man in the world, it felt like we'd stepped out into small-town America.

The Banana Café was a bright yellow, two-floor Cuban joint, and the mellow evening had attracted the crowds. The three of us headed for the bar upstairs while we waited for a table to become available, and there met the red-headed Lauree (@wordtravelsfast), the tweep who would drive me from Washington to meet Ken in Frederick, and Kate (@wonderchook), a Washington-based Twitter user who'd noticed our messages flying back and forth and turned up out of curiosity. And so there were five of us, none of whom had met one another until that day. A jug or two of margarita later ('the best margaritas in town!' hollered the sign at the bar) and the awkward pauses melted away into tall tales and laughter. Eventually the tequila loosened Allison's tongue and the reason for my change in accommodation came to light.

'It's my boyfriend. I was all really excited about having the Twitchhiker coming to stay at our apartment, and he was like "what's a Twitchhiker?" so I explained I'd invited this guy I'd heard about on the Internet to come and stay on our sofa, and that's when he…'

'He… what?' I asked.

'*We* decided it would be better if you didn't stay on the sofa.'

'Ah,' I said, immediately feeling awkward.

Another round of margaritas and a double gift exchange ensued; Katy handed over a scented blue candle, and in return received the Ringtons teabags I'd been given by Mark in New York. The candle was then presented to Allison, the next tweep to assist me, who exchanged it for a hand-knitted scarf. I was quite taken by the long, turquoise snake of a thing and made a point of wearing it for the remainder of the evening.

We moved to an outside table and enjoyed the warm Washington evening – quesadillas were ordered all round (mine with extra jalapeños), except for Allison who ordered a dish called mofongo – a firm moulded heap of cooked banana-like plant. Allison had been timid and shy when we first met, but revealed herself to be a well-travelled, gorgeously goofy nerd who worked 'on the Hill' in communications. Lauree enthused about her work in community media and Katy was quite possibly the hardest woman I'd ever met. Short and toned with cropped black hair, she was a former roller-derby player, an American sport that involves strapping on roller skates and knocking seven bells out of other women. Like rugby, but on wheels.

My road trip to Pittsburgh began early the next day, so I arranged a time for Lauree to pick me up at the hotel and we said our goodbyes before midnight. Allison accompanied me in a cab north-east of Capitol Hill to The Henley Park Hotel and checked me in at reception, where we hugged one another like the oldest of friends and went our separate ways.

As I reached the charming décor and crisp linen of my room, a nagging sense of panic began prodding through the haze of tequila. I still hadn't resolved the increasingly urgent dilemma of where I was going to spend the following night. Two million people in Pittsburgh were so far ignoring me, which might have meant that I was less than eighteen hours away from my first night sleeping rough.

Chapter 14

Day Eight – Sunday 8 March

If you were staring an eight-hour road trip square in the eye, then you'd be a first-class fool to prepare by dining on authentic buffalo chilli and quesadillas with extra jalapeños. You just wouldn't do it, would you? Yet the consequences of my decidedly rich diet hadn't crossed my mind, at least not until my attempt to enjoy a seven-hour stretch between the sheets was rudely interrupted by insufferable stomach cramps and a full hour warming the toilet seat during the twilight hours. Housekeeping at The Henley Park Hotel wouldn't be best pleased with their international visitor later that morning.

My day promised to be long but exciting; while it was hardly a full-blown Route 66 coast-to-coast affair, my host Ken had gone to a great deal of trouble to ensure it was an unforgettable experience. The night before, the other Twitter users and I had discussed Ken's rampant enthusiasm for our journey. Was it only a matter of time before a deputy sheriff bagged my cannibalised limbs from an oversized cooking pot? Of course we joked about the mania that had gripped my host, but the prospect of being trapped in close quarters with a stranger was causing anxiety. At least the Mustang was a convertible – I could always throw myself over the door if it all became too unbearable.

Before I encountered Ken and my inevitable decapitation in the city of Frederick an hour's drive away, it was up to Lauree to drive me there from Washington DC. Her dishevelled Toyota Corolla rolled up outside the hotel ten minutes late and it was clear the previous night's Cuban excess had not been kind to her either – if her eyes had been any redder they'd have bled down her cheeks. Despite living locally in Arlington, on the opposite bank of the Potomac River to Washington, Lauree didn't appear too familiar with the roads of the capital. She also had serious relationship issues with her female-voiced GPS system, which stubbornly refused to show the correct route between DC and Frederick. When it eventually did, Lauree ignored it anyway and went the way she thought best, which meant I was treated to a tour of Washington's less-travelled roads through forested nooks and crannies by two women who weren't on speaking terms. Several wrong turns later and we were coasting north along Maryland's grey straight Interstates amongst the other Sunday morning traffic. The sun-kissed blue skies of the previous day had conceded to featureless stretches of cloud and we passed signs for Rockville, Germantown and Clarksburg.

As we zigged and then zagged across Frederick and took a final left into a street of modest one and two-storey homes, there was no doubting which was Ken's house; it was the one with Ken waiting outside for us. Before we'd even parked up, Ken's whole family was assembled outside, too.

'Lauree, can you do me a favour?' I whispered as I picked my bags from the boot of the silver Corolla.

'Sure.'

'Ken's address, the one you plugged into the sat-nav? Can you send that to my wife please?'

I tore a sheet of paper from a notebook stashed in a satchel and scribbled an email address across it.

'Just to be safe, you know.' I tried not to allow the mild terror I felt show on my face.

'You're scared, aren't you?' grinned Lauree. Rumbled.

There were perhaps a dozen steps between myself and Ken – from Lauree's car parked on the opposite side of the road to the driveway where the Mustang and Ken's family awaited – and in that brief distance I had to reconcile my fears with the celebration concerning my arrival.

The truth was I'd so far felt stomach-churningly nervous every time I'd met a new host. There were dozens of people on Twitter enquiring how I managed to roll up somewhere new every day and immediately place my trust in these strangers without question – I didn't have much of an answer for them; it was a very real leap of faith. Ken's focus on me over the past few days had felt intense, which only served to accentuate my anxiety.

'Paul! You made great time! We're just about ready!' Ken's grin was as broad as his shoulders; he was a stocky guy and tall, too. The firmness of his handshake fused the bones in my fingers together and then Ken went supernova.

'So this is my wife Laura, Timmy my son and my daughter Katherine, these are our two dogs Tod and Rosie, we've got this icebox sitting up front here,' Ken showed no sign of pausing for breath as he gestured to the massive black bin wedged between the seats of the Mustang. 'We've got these snacks too, I've made a CD, by the way, from all the suggestions sent on Twitter, there are some fantastic songs on there, you'll love it.'

I was right, he was maniacal, but not blood-lusting, serial-killing maniacal – he was Tom Hanks in *Big*, an over-excited thirteen-year-old child trapped in a grown man's body and dizzy at the prospect of an adventure. The rest of the family appeared startled by the fuss but unfazed that it was Ken responsible. Laura and Timmy edged their way back into the house while Ken gestured me closer to the Mustang to inspect his daughter's magnetic decals. Katherine had created intricate, swirling artwork showcasing our Twitter names and *charity: water*, too, which Ken had attached to both passenger doors and the rear of the car. And then we ran through an itinerary of the dozen different sodas in the icebox, through all the candy and snacks options. It was terrifying. And overwhelming. And it was infectious. Ken's boundless energy had me jealous of his grand expedition, until I remembered I was in the passenger seat alongside him.

I'd worn Allison's gift to me, the hand-knitted turquoise scarf, from Washington to Frederick, and despite Lauree's insistence I could keep it, I wanted my exchange to continue around the world. I uncoiled it from my neck and passed it to Lauree. In return, my bleary-eyed driver had for me a sealed deck of Atlantic City playing cards and a bumper sticker that read 'Virginia is for Lovers'. It smacked of a last-minute gift spotted on a bookshelf before bedtime while wasted on margaritas, but Ken was made up at receiving them. He exchanged them for a framed photo, the subject of which was Twitchhiker. Me. Ken had scanned the photos I'd posted online of my trip to date and created a montage. His face was bursting with pride, so much so I was concerned he might try and kiss me. It would make a wonderful gift to exchange with... Ah.

There were plenty of Twitter users repeating my online plea for accommodation that evening, but I may as well have been attempting to contact the dead. The population of Greater Pittsburgh was over 2.4 million but there wasn't a stray tweet, chirp, warble or peep to be heard. I was eight hours away from a night on the streets.

The city of Frederick was likely named after English nobleman Frederick Calvert, who became Proprietor Governor of the Province of Maryland in the mid-eighteenth century. He was also one of the greatest absentee landlords in history – when he inherited the title from his father, he also inherited all the revenue derived from the colony through taxes and rent. A monthly income of £10,000 in today's money would certainly lead to the occasional indulgence, so imagine what a twenty-year-old nobleman did when he found himself earning ten grand a month in 1751. Exactly. Calvert never once stepped foot in Maryland because he was far too busy enjoying coital relationships with the female population of Europe, while at various

145

times being accused and subsequently acquitted of rape and murder, as well as demonstrating appalling taste in interior decoration – his decadent renovations at Woodcote Park in Surrey were described as 'ridiculous' and 'tawdry', proving that even in the eighteenth century, money couldn't buy you taste. Frederick Calvert was a Georgian jet-setter – or as his Eton tutors preferred to label him, 'a disreputable and dissolute degenerate' – and he had little interest in spending eight weeks vomiting every meal overboard into the ocean to meet his tenants.

Instead of following freeways from Frederick to Pittsburgh, Ken had opted for a more picturesque route that took in much of the Historic National Road, one of the first roads surveyed and built by the US government two hundred years ago. First, however, there was the small matter of brunch that required us to head north, to the Mountain Gate Family Restaurant in Thurmont, a favourite of Ken's and famous amongst locals for the all-you-can-eat buffet at weekends. And they really did try to eat everything, piling plates as high as they were wide. A large, low-level dining room led through to rows of heated and chilled trays, brimming with salads and breads, beef and beets, puddings and pies, chicken and cheeses and a carvery staffed by a pensioner with faded tattoos that told a story or two. I started with macaroni and cheese, before helping myself to a plate of meat and finishing with ice cream – I didn't want to overdo it, obviously, what with my poor stomach and all – and noted every third person through the door modelled a mullet, women and children included.

Suitably stuffed, we rolled back to the Mustang and set our course for Pittsburgh. Anywhere that was a point of interest or a photo opportunity, so long as it wasn't too far out the way, we pulled up and stretched our legs.

'I think we'll make a quick stop at Catoctin,' decided Ken. 'We can take some great photos of you posing in the old furnaces!'

The centuries-old Catoctin Iron Furnace was where cannonballs were forged during the American Revolution. I ducked inside the filthy brickwork and worked the camera for Ken, a keen amateur photographer.

'What about Camp David?' said Ken. 'We can get pretty close before the Secret Service turn you away.'

'We don't want to upset the Secret Service, do we?'

'Don't worry, they wouldn't shoot you,' said Ken. 'The snipers in the woods probably would, though.'

Fortunately, our ambitious attempt to drive up from the gate of Catoctin Mountain Park past the President's country retreat was thwarted by barriers. The snipers stood down and I settled back to explore the endless depths of the icebox. I opted to try my first root beer, and instantly vowed never to try my second. I may as well have squeezed a tube of Deep Heat down my throat; I was guaranteed not to suffer any muscle strain on the journey, but I'd have to wash my mouth out with shampoo.

We headed west on Route 77, stopping where the road intersected the mighty Appalachian Trail, a public pathway stretching over 3,500 kilometres across fourteen states, from Georgia in the South to Hundred-Mile Wilderness in Maine.

'I really want to get some shots of you hiking through the woods!' announced Ken. 'The Twitchhiker conquers the Appalachian Trail!'

I didn't really conquer it, stopping some 3,500 kilometres short of doing so – we hiked no further than a hundred metres into the dense woodland, partly because our trainers weren't standard hiking equipment, but mostly because Ken's talk of snakes and bears on the trail caused a mild tightening of the rectum.

Further down the road I spied a nick in the distant skyline where the hillside had been neatly sliced through; it was Sideling Hill, a man-made mountain pass that plunges through hundreds of metres of rock strata. Ken pulled over once more, and as we clambered up the steps to the viewing platform high above the pass, it occurred to me how long I'd been travelling for:

> **twitchhiker** Twitchhiking is one week old! Currently at Sideling Hill in Maryland. Could somebody tell me how far I am from Newcastle?
>
> *1:02 PM Mar 8th*

Dozens of tweeps around the world plugged the two locations into a plethora of online distance calculators and came up with a collective answer: 5,720 kilometres. There was satisfaction to be gleaned from those numbers, regardless of how distant Campbell Island still remained; all those fleeting doubts of travelling no further than Newcastle city centre, and there I was heading towards the American Midwest. And Twitter had even better news for me moments later:

> **aikaterine71** @twitchhiker will def sponsor you tonight and get you to Pittsburgh airport Mon. Will coord meet spot & time with @yenra.
>
> *1:13 PM Mar 8th*

If the driver of the white articulated lorry driving west through Sideling Hill had happened to glance up at that moment, he would have seen some idiot tourist dancing a comical jig of delight. I wouldn't be sleeping rough that evening – the relief bled from every pore. Twitter hadn't let me down, it had found a way. Almost. The tweep making the offer, Katherine wasn't in Pittsburgh. We would have to head to Wheeling, West Virginia instead – a slight deviation from our route that meant heading further west. I was beyond made up at the prospect of a place to stay but bemused there hadn't been a whisper from anyone in Pittsburgh. Despite a news story running on MSNBC's website, I was dead to the Steel City; nobody wanted to know and if they did, they'd decided they were washing their hair or out to lunch. I'd argued that I stood the best chance of reaching New Zealand by crossing the US, yet there I was being staunchly ignored by over two million people. Hopefully it would be the first and last time.

We continued through the stranded towns and along the lonely roads of Maryland, Pennsylvania and West Virginia; dense dark woodland shrouded the landscape. We talked most of the way – except when I nodded off for a minute or thirty – discussing Twitter and iPhones, Ken's passion for England and my passion for chocolate-covered raisins. We discussed his work, or rather, I needled Ken into telling me about it.

'So you work for the Government?'

'I work for the Government, sure.'

'That must be interesting. What department?'

'Hmm. Can't really say.'

'Oh really? Why not?'

'Can't really tell you that either!'

'OK. Is there anything you can tell me?'

'Sure, it's a government job I can't tell you anything about.'

It was the only time on the trip I sensed a serious, no-nonsense tone in Ken's voice. Instead he explained how his enthusiasm for my adventure was born out of nothing more than the desire to be part of something unique. He'd missed out when Microsoft revolutionised computing, and the fear of future loss transformed him into an early adopter of technology – he was first to road-test any new gadget or online service to ensure he was never late to the party again. When the Internet began creeping into the mainstream, Ken became one of the US Government's first webmasters. He was helping me because Twitter was something new and exciting, and he didn't want to live with the regrets of inaction – a mindset I entirely identified with.

As promised in his blog posts and tweets of the past several days, Ken had compiled a playlist for the journey, based on requests and suggestions from other Twitter users:

'Take Me Home, Country Roads' – John Denver
'The Long and Winding Road' – The Beatles
'On the Road Again' – Willie Nelson

'Littlest Hobo Theme (Maybe Tomorrow)' – Terry Bush
'Ramblin' Man' – Allman Brothers Band
'Born to Run' – Bruce Springsteen & The E Street Band
'Road to Nowhere' – Talking Heads
'Born to Be Wild' – Steppenwolf
'Radar Love' – Golden Earring
'Rocky Mountain High' – John Denver
'It's a New Day' – Will.i.am
'Already Gone' – Eagles
'Sweet Home Alabama' – Lynyrd Skynyrd
'Don't Stop' – Fleetwood Mac
'Down Under' – Men at Work

I felt not unlike the Littlest Hobo, turning up somewhere new every day, in search of a good meal and a bed for the evening before leaving town for adventure and the open road. Or perhaps it was more Bill Bixby's Doctor David Banner, but without the disturbing piano solo. No, I was in a flying mood – while his boundless zeal had initially petrified me, Ken's fanaticism for my journey had proved as encouraging as it had unexpected. I needed more people like Ken on my side.

We arrived in Wheeling, West Virginia, a little after six in the evening, nearly eight hours after setting off from Frederick. Standing on the banks of the Ohio River, Wheeling is a typically tiny American city, boasting barely 30,000 residents. In England, cathedral cities with tiny populations are something of an anomaly, but in the US there are 'cities' everywhere. State law can determine whether a one-horse town becomes a one-horse city, hence the likes of Woodland Mills, Tennessee – a city three hours to the north of Memphis with a population under 300. And that's including the livestock.

Katherine was waiting for us on the sidewalk on a desolate North Main Street. There wasn't another car or pedestrian in sight – no doubt everyone had gone to Pittsburgh for the fancy special party I wasn't invited to. After parking up in the yard next to the apartment, Ken orchestrated a photo shoot to mark the end of our journey and then tucked in close to me while I pulled my bags from the boot of the Mustang.

'Here,' uttered Ken in a hushed tone, pressing a roll of bills into my palm. 'In case you get stuck, consider it another donation from Twitter.'

I looked down at the money. There was a lot of it, at least a couple of hundred dollars. Clearly Ken was whispering so his wife back in Frederick couldn't hear. I opened Ken's palm and pushed the bills back into it.

'Ken, that's a wonderful gesture and it's very much appreciated, but you've gone above and beyond for me today.' But Ken was adamant that he could do more. 'If it's burning a hole in your pocket, Ken, donate it to the charity,' I said. 'I'll get by without it, I promise.'

And he did. As well as taking a day out of his life to drive me cross-country for eight hours and after spending a small fortune on meals, snacks, soda and gas, the following day Ken donated £150 to *charity: water*. The man was a Good Samaritan of boundless spirit and giving.

And so to my new hosts, thirty-somethings Katherine and Alston. Both worked in the shadowy world of 'legal document services', processing court documents for rival international law firms. They were childhood sweethearts, peas in a pod, and if there were two more selfless individuals in Wheeling, you'd struggle to find them in broad daylight with a torch. The previous year, the couple had lost their possessions, their pets and in fact their entire home in a fire, and so were living in temporary accommodation while their house was rebuilt. Their apartment was tiny – a living room overlooked North Main Street with a kitchen-sink-sized kitchen at the rear, and doors leading off to a single bedroom and a wardrobe mistakenly fitted with a bathroom suite. They were squeezed into a one-bedroom apartment with rented furniture, yet were willing to offer a stranger their sofa for the night. Admittedly it wasn't their sofa, and perhaps that had been the deal-breaker.

Alston and I spent most of the evening putting the world of science fiction to rights; he relived the summer of '77 and his memories of watching *Star Wars* at a cinema just a few blocks away, while I ranted about the horse manure that was *Indiana Jones and the Kingdom of the Crystal Skull*. We did, however, show plenty of loving for *Firefly* – the greatest ever television show that barely was.

The evening's entertainment consisted of *Celebrity Apprentice* in HD and a pizza like no other I'd tasted, and I say that as someone who makes it their business to eat a lot of pizza. The base was crusty, like cracker bread, and only half the cheese was cooked; the rest was delivered in a paper bag and crumbled on before eating. This hot crust and cold topping approach was a sixty-year-old tradition of Di Carlo's, specifically their Elm Grove pizzeria on the National Road – Katherine assured me that the popular consensus of Wheeling folk was that the same order from Di Carlo's other outlets was patently inferior to Elm Grove. I wasn't convinced myself, but enjoyed both the pizza and the company nevertheless; Katherine and Alston had taken me into their makeshift home while a city of two million continued to pretend I wasn't there, so I forgave Wheeling its culinary folly and chomped away.

That day, I met three souls kinder than most. I didn't quite understand the machinations that had seen Twitter obscure my presence from Pittsburgh and redirect my journey an hour further west, but then it didn't matter. Like Dirk Gently and the little-understood art of Zen navigation, I didn't reach where I intended to go, but I did end up somewhere I needed to be.

Chapter 15

Day Nine – Monday 9 March

Perhaps the greatest unsolved mystery of *The X-Files* was that throughout the first five years of the show, Mulder spent his evenings sleeping on his couch. While fans were happy to entertain the notion of alien colonisation, television presenters who controlled the weather, and time-travelling serial killers, they considered it unrealistic that a grown man might sleep on his sofa night after night. Quite right, too – sofas are too uncomfortable for anything more than a long doze after a large Chinese meal. Many have thinly cushioned arms at right angles to the seat cushions that bring little relief to the vertebrae in the neck. Few three-seaters accommodate anyone of average height or taller without limbs protruding at awkward angles, causing numbness in the extremities. And while leather upholstery may suggest a night of regal rest, invariably it means peeling your sweaty limbs away with a sickening suck in the morning.

Yet there in Wheeling, the city where nothing was too much trouble for a stranger far from home, I'd spent a night on Katherine and Alston's sofa that was, in a word, perfect. Firm and even, a wool-mix upholstery with low padded arms and a good length on it – and it wasn't even their sofa. Who knew how many stranger's backsides had broken wind into the cushions before I pushed my face into them and slept like a baby. I didn't care, it was so damned comfortable.

It was a bright Monday morning, one week on from my arrival in Amsterdam, with my itinerary for the next two days set in stone. Later that day I would fly to Chicago courtesy of @orbitzgal, the customer service team for US travel website Orbitz. They were also taking care of my accommodation for two nights somewhere in the city. After that was a mystery. As had been the case throughout the past week, there were dozens of offers of help I couldn't take advantage of, because they were isolated by geography – there were train tickets and bus rides waiting to take me from point B to point C, but I was at point A, several thousand kilometres away, usually on a different continent. Something was sure to turn up – Wheeling had proved I could make my plans on the fly.

A week since Amsterdam meant there were more pressing matters to be dealt with. Katherine and Alston were aware that my four changes of underwear after nine days' travelling required the attention of a washing machine – hopefully they made the deduction through elementary mathematics rather than their sense of smell. It was uncomfortable watching another man handle my underwear but, ever the considerate host, Alston did insist.

While I eagerly awaited the tender brush of fresh cotton against skin once more, Katherine talked me through the packed lunch she'd prepared for me. Yes, I had a packed lunch. Yes, I was having my laundry done for me. Katherine and Alston were a joy. The highlight of my lunch was yet another pizza-based delicacy I hadn't encountered before – pepperoni rolls. It's thought they were invented in 1927 by Giuseppe Argiro, a resident of Fairmont, another miniature city some 100 kilometres to the south of Wheeling. The dinner roll-sized snacks were popular with coal miners across the state because they were a small and delicious meal-in-a-bun, and while you can occasionally pick them up from convenience stores elsewhere in the country, you'll find them everywhere in West Virginia. Indeed, Fairmont has declared itself the 'Pepperoni Roll Capital of the World' – not that there's a long queue of contenders knocking the door down.

My highly moreish pack of pepperoni mini-rolls was half-devoured by the time the big tub finished washing and spin-drying my clothes. I jumped in the shower first, though – I wanted to savour every moment of my first full clean set of clothes since Paris. Clean jeans. Sweat-free sweatshirt. Bliss.

Before repacking I handed over Ken's gift of the Twitchhiker montage to Katherine – there'd be no better reminder of her last-minute favour to me than my mug beaming back at her across the room. If Katherine and Alston ever considered having children, at least they already had a fireguard. To take on and give to my hosts in Chicago, Katherine presented me with a pack of locally produced chocolate-covered pretzels. If they were as exquisite as the pepperoni rolls, there wasn't much chance they'd make it to the Windy City.

Before heading for the Interstate and Pittsburgh, we forked right onto the National Road and across the Wheeling Suspension Bridge. It's a tiddler compared to modern-day structures, but was the longest suspension bridge in the world for two years up until 1851. Judging by Katherine's insistence that I experience the crossing, that fact still instils pride in the city's residents. Uncooked cheese toppings, pepperoni rolls, former world-record-holding suspension bridges – Wheeling packed a lot in.

The drive from Wheeling to Pittsburgh Airport was only an hour, but it took all my energy to stay awake for it. Except I ran out of energy after the first twenty minutes and snored loudly into Katherine's right ear. Nine days in, my body was a little sore at me for recklessly throwing it around the world. I came round shortly before we arrived at Departures and was eventually lucid enough to thank Katherine for her hospitality. Online, offline, in real time, she'd saved my skin. Katherine and Alston had embodied the spirit of Twitchhiker – they had little to offer, but they didn't hesitate in offering it regardless. There was a short delay at security after the passenger ahead was found to be carrying a knife, ornamental but still the long and stabby sort – he didn't understand what all the ensuing fuss was about, as if he was catching a flight to a point in time before September 2001 – and eventually I arrived at gate D88 for my American Airlines flight to Chicago's O'Hare airport. There must have been some mistake, I thought, staring down at the aircraft on the tarmac. It looked for all the world like a model jet from the outside. The interior confirmed it was a plane chartered from Lilliputian Airways. I counted the seats as I stooped to make progress along the aisle. Fifty-two in total, with a single row running along the left-hand side of the aircraft, and a pair across the aisle. Passengers had to be vacuum-packed in and if their hand luggage was too large, it became checked luggage because there was only one set of overhead bins. Even they were too tiny to fit much more than a multi-pack of crisps in.

The flight to O'Hare was sticky and claustrophobic but mercifully short; my attempt to find the shuttle bus, considerably less so. Gaggles of signs and directions to the information desk conspired to misdirect me and continuously contradicted one another – no sooner had they sent me up three levels of stairs than I was instructed to descend two. I was a rat in a maze – if Richard O'Brien had appeared playing a harmonica and bellowing 'Will you start the fans please!' I wouldn't have been the least bit fazed.

The airport shuttle bus eventually reached downtown Chicago and pulled over on the Magnificent Mile, where the driver motioned for me to step out. I'd visited the city once before, a 48-hour trip to produce a radio show from Navy Pier, and while there had been little time for sightseeing, I'd learned enough about that particular street to know I wouldn't be sharing dorms with a snoring Dutchman again. The Magnificent Mile has been the heart of upmarket retail shopping in Chicago since World War Two, a section of Michigan Avenue that stretches north of the Chicago River, packed with luxury boutiques, world-class restaurants, mainstream malls and sumptuous hotels. I'd paid little attention to my booking confirmation and so hadn't expected my hotel, the InterContinental, to be all that. It transpired it was all that and a big scoop of extra that on top – a lavish Art Deco skyscraper a stone's throw from both the equally decadent Chicago Tribune Tower and Wrigley Building, at the north end of Michigan Avenue Bridge.

A four-star hotel with a first-class zip code, with a sweaty foreigner loitering in reception. My host @orbitzgal arrived soon after to check me in, which was just as well because the concierge was eyeing up the firehose. It turned out my Twitter associate had two heads – not on the same body, that'd be hideous – because Orbitz used the Twitter account for customer services; more than one person at the company had access to it for dealing with questions and queries. So I was met by Laura and Kate – one tall, slim and blonde, the other shorter, slim and brunette – beautiful, the pair of them, and both appeared delighted to meet me. Nothing, but nothing massages the ego quite like the attentions of two stunning girls with dreamy American accents.

'Paul, we're so glad you've come to visit us in Chicago,' said Laura.

'It's really amazing to see you,' agreed Kate. 'It's been such a crappy day in the office, and having to come meet you meant we could leave early, so we're really grateful.'

Oh. I was an excuse for bunking off work. Never mind, then.

We didn't go overboard with the Chicago nightlife; Kate had other plans so Laura and I hunted down a cheap and cheerful restaurant and settled on Sol y Nieve, a tapas restaurant on East Ohio Street. We picked over meatballs and croquettes and olives and calamari, all perfectly pleasant enough, though the decor reminded me of my Nana's living room in that twee, is-it-really-still-the-1970s sort of way, but with more terra cotta and fewer horse brasses.

Tummy full and my host thanked, I retired to my eighteenth-floor room at the InterContinental. It was vast, quite too big for one person, and replete with rich mahogany furniture and antique lamps, with southerly views to the Wrigley Building and Chicago River, and east across the melee of the Magnificent Mile. I hung up a couple of tops and one of my three pairs of trousers in the wardrobe and made myself a coffee I had no particular thirst for, tested the taps in the bathrooms, flicked through the channels on the television without watching any one programme. Pointless-but-mandatory checklist of my accommodation complete, I pulled off my shoes, made a mental note to buy Odor-Eaters, popped open the laptop and rattled in my credit card number for Internet access.

Orbitz were looking after me for two nights in Chicago, but as of Wednesday I had no plans. It didn't feel right. I had over 6,000 followers, and every tweet I sent was repeated by dozens of others, meaning tens of thousands of people were aware of my situation. Dozens of people were asking questions and passing comment – Where was I? Where would I go next? Shouldn't I have reached Campbell Island already? – but scant few options had been put forward. Plenty of noise, very little signal. The rise in the number of followers hadn't translated into a proportional increase in support; my audience were becoming voyeurs, preferring to lurk in the shadows and remain passive to proceedings. Since leaving Wheeling earlier in the day there had been only one offer of any value, from a Twitter user called Peter West Carey from Washington State:

> **pwcarey** @twitchhiker would you consider a train ticket from Chicago to the west coast (Seattle)?
>
> *3:42 PM Mar 9th*

Now that certainly would have been an adventure and a half; over 3,000 kilometres through the Rockies to the Pacific. How many people took the time to cross North America by train? It was the very definition of epic and it would put me on the West Coast, exactly where I needed to be if I was to reach New Zealand.

Wait, Paul. Slow down. There was a problem. There was a reason why people preferred air travel to the trains in the US: time. It would take days to traverse the continent, hardly the Kessel Run in less than twelve parsecs. I'd panicked when I crossed the North Sea and lost touch with Twitter for a single night. Suddenly the epic adventure lost its sheen. Did US trains have Wi-Fi? Perhaps Peter would consider a ticket with breaks in service so I could hop off and on along the route? Three thousand kilometres non-stop could mean a couple of days without the Internet, and no Internet potentially meant no working, and no Twitter.

> **twitchhiker** @pwcarey A train from Chicago to Seattle might be interesting. Could I stop along on the way? Could I get WiFi on the train?
>
> *8:06 PM Mar 9th*

For the first time during my journey, a dilemma of my own making loomed, one that lurked in the rules I had set myself: unless another offer was forthcoming, I'd have to accept Peter's train ticket, regardless of the consequences. There was nothing else for it. I'd have to run a very deep, very hot bath and give the matter further thought before bedtime.

Chapter 16

Day Ten – Tuesday 10 March

'... yes?'

'Hello, is that Paul Smith?' enquired the man who'd rung my mobile at half past four in the morning.

'... yes. Yes it is.'

'Sorry, were you asleep?'

'Yes, it's half past four in the morning,' I explained.

'Is it?'

There was a brief pause during which time the caller, who I assumed to be a journalist, no doubt glanced at his watch, recalled that North America is several hours behind the UK, not ahead of it, and realised his error in ever picking up the phone and dialling my number.

'Oh right, of course, so it is. I'll call back later. Sorry to have disturbed you.'

Click.

It was barely a ten-second interruption to my sleep but enough for the synapses to fire up and whirr into life. I was wide-eyed after scarcely five hours' sleep. I was too tired to curse the idiot out loud, but too awake to nod back off so I pulled on my T-shirt and boxer shorts – not that I was expecting any peeping toms on the eighteenth floor – and shuffled over to the writing desk.

The view to the south across the Magnificent Mile was haunting, but spectacular. In the distance, the sodium street lighting across North Michigan Bridge illuminated the heavy brooding fog that cocooned the skyline. The terracotta tiled clocktower of the Wrigley Building, the headquarters built for chewing gum's William Wrigley Junior, was barely visible, its outline silhouetted by the washed-out orange smoulder of turrets and towers beyond it. Immediately outside my window, two colossal stone busts balanced on the lip of the building ledge, neo-gothic gladiators peering into the deserted street below. The Chicago night was a brooding beast, such a rich juxtaposition of architecture, modern skyscrapers alongside elaborate, classical forms. Chicago is famed around the world for its skyline, established through a sequence of events that began nearly 140 years ago. In October 1871, the Great Chicago Fire tore the heart out of the city, reducing several square kilometres of buildings and land to ash and rubble, and displacing a third of the population. The Chicago River provided little resistance to its fury as winds fanned the flames through the timber frames of homes, stores, ships and churches. Extraordinarily, fewer than 300 are thought to have died, even though over 17,000 buildings were destroyed.

The determination of the Chicagoans to rebuild their city ushered in a new era in architectural innovation that eventually led to the first modern skyscraper, the ten-storey Home Insurance Building, completed in 1885. The greatest architectural pioneers of the late nineteenth century used this blank, if somewhat charred, canvas to create a city that rose into the sky. The World's Columbian Exposition in 1893 celebrated the 400th anniversary of Columbus's arrival in the New World. Huge swathes of the city were transformed, and neo-classical and gothic influences appeared. And then Chicago reinvented the skyscraper again, this time in the 1960s, with a new structural process that led to the first super-skyscrapers – the John Hancock Center then the Sears Tower in Chicago, the World Trade Center in New York and every attempt to touch the heavens since.

In Chicago, you're witness to a fierce fusion of innovation and regeneration, ornate towers jostling with dizzying columns of glass and steel, and this passion, this architectural proficiency evident throughout the city, was born out of a brutal eruption of flame and fury.

The Tuesday morning I found myself staring into showed no such ferocity, as the sky lightened and features of the washed-out cityscape found definition. It was a day off from travelling, my first since the previous Friday, so I attempted to catch up on the writing I'd failed to fit in elsewhere. It was a brave effort, but my brain was having none of it. It was fuzzy and miserable, grouchy as hell and it all but refused to entertain the notion of hard work. The lack of sleep and consistency in my day meant I couldn't find any focus or clarity in my thinking. Being unable to concentrate was causing stress, which in turn was causing a lack of concentration. So for most of the day, I slumped over the desk in my hotel room and stared out across Chicago's magnificent Magnificent Mile, trying to will the words from my head onto the screen.

It wasn't helping my concentration that I needed to keep an eye on Twitter, watching out for an offer to move me on from Chicago the next day. By mid-morning I'd established from several Twitter users that to take the train from Chicago to Seattle would take a day and a half, with no opportunities for stopping off along the way. Then my Parisian host Chris delivered the deal-breaker – he tweeted to say the chances of on-board Wi-Fi on that route were non-existent, and that even a reliable mobile signal would be a struggle.

I couldn't take it. There was no way I could afford to go offline for so long, to then turn up in a city with no guarantee of a next step. Of course, if nobody trumped it with a better offer, my own rules stated I'd have to accept it regardless. Stupid rules. A second offer did appear, however, one that should have seen me breathe a long, slow sigh of relief:

chrisukstevens @twitchhiker – I'll fly you from Chicago to Dallas on Wednesday. And will put you up in a motel for a night when you get here.

08:13 AM Mar 10th, 2009

Saved from going off the rails by a tweet that took to the air. The trouble with the offer was that a friend had made it; Chris and I had known one another for years, we'd even lived together while both working at the BBC in London. More importantly, I'd argued the case for avoiding flights across the US wherever possible – I'd accepted the trip to Chicago in lieu of any other offers at the time.

The lack of support was disheartening and there was a nagging sense that perhaps Twitter was losing interest. Chatter about the challenge had barely risen above a whisper in the past couple of days, and charitable donations had slowed to a trickle. And so the devil climbed onto my shoulder, cackled menacingly and whispered mischief into my ear. I decided to make things interesting to re-energise Twitter and cajole followers into action.

> **twitchhiker** If I get no other offers by midday, I'll have to fly to Dallas. If I do get another offer, I'll put it to a public vote.
>
> *10:16 AM Mar 10th*

I'd learned from the very first time I'd asked Twitter to determine my fate that nothing whips up a crowd like the opportunity for control, to assume the role of the character Christof in *The Truman Show*. And Twitter didn't disappoint. Oh no.

> **ajmullin** @twitchhiker can get you a Megabus ticket from Chicago to Memphis, Kansas City or Minneapolis or more www.megabus.com.
>
> *11:19 AM Mar 10th*

Talk about kicking a man when he was down. The Megabus in the UK is the transportation of the desperate, the bankrupt, the student. It's an unappealing option for travelling any distance, ranking somewhere between being strapped to the wing of a plane, and skipping naked with your penis stuck in a live chicken. I looked up the timetables and swore very loudly; Kansas City – the destination that allowed me to make the most progress west – was ten hours away by Megabus. I was looking at a full day sat on an increasingly numb arse, offline and going broke. Because I already knew what was coming. Twitter's reaction was inevitable – there was no competition between a cushy flight and a half-day slog by bus. People would never let me take the easy route and fly, and if I hadn't found myself so miserable and tired again, I probably would have agreed. But I was. So I didn't. They were going to make me suffer, which is exactly what I would have done if some poor bastard had provided me with the opportunity to play puppet master.

I reluctantly set up the poll on Twitter and left people to have their wicked way in voting for my next step, and turned that frown upside down to meet up with Laura and Kate for lunch. We met at a restaurant a few blocks west of the hotel and ordered a Chicago-style pizza pie as wide as the moon and as deep as Sartre.

'Oh my God,' was Kate's reaction to my decision to call a vote. 'Why would you want to make it even harder for yourself?'

'I thought it'd spice things up. I'm a little like a modern Anneka Rice, but without the helicopter.'

'Who?' asked Laura.

The pizza pie was stodgy and dribbling with calories. It was magnificent, although as soon as I'd waved the pair off I breathed out and adjusted my belt. Nine days of sitting on my backside a great deal had seen my body turn to dough from navel to nipple. But my belly was full and so my mood improved as I walked back up North Michigan Avenue and returned to the hotel. The sidewalks were congested with quick-paced Chicagoans in suits and blouses, with their mobile phones glued to one ear while the other hand clasped a take-out tray of salad for lunch. Their faces were contorted in irritation as they encountered yet another brace of brash and trashy tourists dawdling along with their bunches of shopping bags from extravagant boutiques.

Then I remembered the poll. I glanced at some of the tweets on my phone, saw the discussion that had flared up while I'd demolished that pizza pie. Some were choosing the bus on environmental grounds, others because it would make for a 'better' travel experience, but most because they liked the idea of me suffering for ten hours. Bastards.

The Megabus to Kansas City won by a landslide. No, an avalanche. No, a landslide that obliterates everything in its path, swiftly followed by an avalanche which takes out the emergency services attempting to rescue those trapped by the landslide. Three-quarters of the vote put me on that bus. Of course I only had myself to blame. I'd cajoled Twitter into it, so I could hardly piss and moan because I didn't like the outcome. It was all about the journey, I reassured myself, not the destination.

The burst of activity breathed life back into Twitter, and into Twitchhiker. The mention of Kansas prompted a flurry of tweets from followers in Wichita, all eager that I pay them a visit, and the nearby Chicagoans realised I was amongst them too.

wibjess CHICAGO!!! Tweet-up tonight – 7pm at Kerryman for @Twitchhiker.

2:25 PM Mar 10th

Jess worked in the city at a travel website called Where I've Been, and had messaged me asking if I'd come out and play. I'd said yes, because I always said yes, because 'yes' was the default response to everyone when you wanted people to support you wherever you went. I needed to rest first, though – my belly-busting lunch had induced a food coma, my gut was distended and aching, it throbbed and threatened to explode. Oh pizza pie, how can you be so mouth-wateringly delicious yet so agonisingly painful? In my twenties, when I had a metabolism that could burn through coal, I'd promised myself I'd never sink to such a sorry state that my belly drooped over my belt. Burgers and pizza and curry and pie were seeing me skirt awfully close to breaking that promise. There was nothing else for it but to crawl back into bed and hope my gut didn't burst and make a mess of the sheets.

Two hours of unconscious digestion and a long, lukewarm shower later, I headed out of the hotel and into a torrential downpour. Tourists and locals alike scattered for cover and the street emptied of all but traffic. The bar I was going to, The Kerryman, was just five blocks away, but walking there was unthinkable. I'd just hail a ca–

Oh. No, I wouldn't just hail a cab, would I? I wasn't allowed. I zipped up my hoodless jacket neck and sprinted off down North Michigan Avenue, keeping tight to the base of the skyscrapers. There was no respite from the downpour, no dry shadows cast by the buildings as I zigged and zagged across the city blocks. At The Kerryman, the similarly soaked team from Where I've Been were already waiting upstairs to greet me. We were all in need of some warmth after being chilled to the bone, so a round of shots was ordered to break the ice.

About a dozen people passed through the bar, some lingered longer than others. Most worked with Jess at Where I've Been, the others were local bloggers, developers and designers, tour guides and the like – some knew one another well, for others it was the first time they'd met. Twitter united them all – well that, and the never-ending onslaught of shots that appeared at the table. As we all sunk another tequila, dispensed with another Jägermeister, slowly I became of the opinion that if I was going to spend ten hours on a bus, I might as well be hungover. I thought it made some sort of sense at the time, and of course in reality it made no sense whatsoever because I'd have the most wretched, brain-pounding, gut-clenching time imaginable on that bus, and of course I knew it and chose to ignore it. Guinness, Jägermeister, something pink with an umbrella – anything that could be poured down my throat was done so with a decreasing degree of accuracy. It was the sort of destructive, heavy-duty binge drinking that inevitably leads to trouble, although in this instance it led me into the Blue Frog.

As dive bars went, the Blue Frog would give the Mariana Trench a run for its money. It was a single windowless room, dirty, with furniture upholstered by a man with ten thumbs, fairy lights everywhere and a carpet you could wring out into your glass. And it got worse. Jess and the others had brought me to the Blue Frog for the singular purpose of karaoke. To the best of my knowledge I hadn't sung karaoke since Gran Canaria in 1996, and as a rule of thumb I ignored all social events that threatened to descend into yet another pissed-up recital of 'Angels' by Robbie Williams. But they had me. I'd attempted to drink all the booze in the world and I was gagging for the microphone.

I'd always thought I could sing 'God Only Knows' reasonably well. At least that was my perception when I'd sung along with speakers turned up so loud I couldn't hear my own voice. Or with headphones in. It turned out I'd been lying to myself for years, although I wasn't convinced the microphone was working correctly. Even then in my inebriated, tuneless state, I wasn't nearly as bad as the pin-striped suit who'd wandered in off the set of *Wall Street* and wouldn't know a melody if it kicked his face clean off his head. It was 'Love Shack', for crying out loud. How can you get that wrong?

Shortly after midnight I called time on my reckless shenanigans. Drunk as an inebriated skunk and having made a spectacular arse of myself in a bar full of strangers, I staggered back along Erie Street to my bed. The dread of what was to come at dawn had vanished, replaced by the quiet, light-headed contentment afforded by five hours of drinking Guinness and Jägermeister.

Chapter 17

Day Eleven – Wednesday 11 March

Whatever fool decided a ten-hour bus ride would be more entertaining with a hangover, if not from Hell itself, then certainly within the same postcode, is the same fool who left around a third of his clothes in the wardrobe of his room at the InterContinental in Chicago – a small bag of dirty washing flung in the far left corner, along with one of my three pairs of trousers, a shirt and a very nice jumper that was £32 from Burton. If it's still there, it's yours for a tenner. Room 1807. Cheers.

I didn't realise where my clothes were until two days after I left the hotel, but then I dare say my left arm could have been amputated during the night and I'd have been none the wiser until I wanted to wear a watch. My hangover was stinking out my skull, pounding harder and harder at my forehead. I could barely see, preferring to scrunch my eyes tight to avoid stray photons of light exploding on my retinas. What's that? I was so drunk last night that I married a horse? If you say so.

My vegetative state didn't last. The walk from the Magnificent Mile south to the bus stop in the sharp Chicago air cleared the clutter from behind my eyeballs. The sky was a brilliant fresh blue, the wind nipped at exposed ear lobes and nibs of noses, but it kept me suitably alert and took my mind off a stomach unhappy with me for attempting to dissolve it with copious amounts of booze. Along the way I picked up a litre of fresh orange juice and a pack of Advil, and slowly the sharp blows softened to dull thumps.

The pick-up for the Megabus was diagonally across from Union Station, yet another ornate, neo-classical building. I would never, ever normally consider crossing the road to visit a train station, but you have to when it's Union Station. Why? Two words – *The Untouchables* – and one of the most memorable scenes consigned to celluloid. The blonde-haired, blue-eyed babe in the pram tumbling down the steps of the station's Great Hall. Gangsters everywhere. Kevin Costner's no-nonsense federal agent Eliot Ness picks them off with his shotgun as he races to reach the pram. One villain left, Costner's out of ammo and he can't reach the pram, but into the scene enters Andy Garcia, tossing a loaded gun in slo-mo to Costner while sliding across the marble floor and underneath the pram. Baby safe. Bad guys dead. Bloody brilliant. And I was stood on those steps, in that Great Hall. And it truly was – Union Station is a cathedral, with its Corinthian columns and atrium ceiling. The likes of Union Station and New York's Grand Central Terminal are tourist attractions in their own right; in the UK, we have a pasty stall at London Kings Cross.

Outside I spotted the livery of a double-decker Megabus, identical to the brand's British colours. There were only six other people waiting at the stop, and the lack of passengers on board suggested Chicago was the first pick-up. I was eight years old again – I had to have the front seat on the top deck. Had to. As soon as the driver opened the doors, while the other passengers hauled their suitcases and backpacks to stow under the coach, I jumped on board and straight up to the front. Far from being the jalopy I was expecting, everything was new, no wear and no tear. And there was Wi-Fi. No power supply, but then not every bus can be a Bolt Bus, can it? Three or four hours' work was better than none at all. Most of the other passengers remained downstairs – perhaps there were a number of low-level bridges on the road to Kansas I wasn't aware of. There was only one other passenger upstairs, an obese lady four rows behind who kept clearing her sinuses and hocking into a handkerchief. I didn't want to talk to her.

The benefit of Wi-Fi was that I could react quickly to Twitter on my laptop, rather than struggle by on a mobile phone connection. Not that there had been much to react to following Twitter's decision to send me to Kansas City – as had happened in the case of Pittsburgh, there hadn't been a single tweet from the two million people in the city ahead. This time, however, I was far more relaxed about my fate. Having no plans was a strength, because it meant I could act on any offer at a moment's notice. Assuming, of course, somebody made me one.

I awoke from an unintended doze to find the view through the windscreen had transformed from the crowded white fascias of downtown Chicago to the cross-country wilderness of Illinois. The Interstate stretched on forever across the pancake-flat vista to a vanishing point on the horizon, straight and unwavering. There were no curves or peaks to be glimpsed, no gradients or angles to buckle the landscape. The endless stretch of road swept past lonely shacks and water towers, and battered billboards filled with bright and breezy 1950s-style advertising, faded by the silver sun.

After three hours, the coach pulled up at a truck-stop away from the Interstate. Colossal rigs lined the parking area, opposite a broken-down diner with wind-torn awnings. And it was bitter-cold. The cloudless sunshine, the swimming blue skies, the dust and desertion – from the warmth of my seat onboard the coach I'd expected a pleasing change in temperature from the chill of Chicago. No such luck.

twitchhiker Sweet muscular Jesus, it's cold out there. I think I just lost a nipple.

12:06 PM Mar 11th

The diner wasn't much warmer, and it was populated by every gum-chewing, flannel-shirted, rig-driving stereotype I'd ever seen on television. The dude who beat up Clark Kent in *Superman II*? There he was, shovelling down bacon and sausage swimming in syrup. The burger I ordered was burly and the accompanying fries were fat and greasy and hot, and together they dampened the roars of acid that licked at the back of my throat.

Back on the coach and once more on the road to nowhere, and Twitter detected signs of life in Lawrence, Kansas, some 50 kilometres to the west of Kansas City.

> **benasmith** @twitchhiker if you have no other offers, you can stay in Lawrence, KS tonight courtesy of @ljworld.
>
> *12:59PM Mar 11th*

Ben worked at Lawrence Journal-World, a newspaper and television operation keen to play a part in my journey. He also offered to pick me up from Kansas City. It was the best, and indeed only offer I'd had so the rules demanded I accept it – once more I was going to bypass a metropolis and find goodwill away from the bright lights. Quite how the far-flung folk of Lawrence had become aware of my itinerary at a day's notice was another happy mystery – Twitter was working its magic, six-degrees-of-separation style.

> **twitchhiker** @benasmith that's a great offer, I'd love to accept your help – thanks to @ljworld! I'm off to Lawrence via Kansas City!
>
> *1:26 PM Mar 11th*

And Lawrence couldn't get enough of me, because there was more to come.

> **JonEisen** @twitchhiker Leaving Lawrence, KS on Friday AM with my family for Denver, CO. Room for one more. Ride?
>
> *2:01 PM Mar 11th*

Denver. While in Washington, my host Katy had enthused about the mile-high city where she'd studied, but looking at the maps, Denver sat alone with nothing much in any direction. And not departing from Lawrence until Friday would mean sourcing accommodation for a second night. That said, Denver was over 800 kilometres due west, which pushed me ever closer to the West Coast where perhaps I'd find a way across the Pacific. It was a gamble and I was still drunk, and as I'd learned from past experience, such a concoction usually led to only one conclusion.

> **twitchhiker** @JonEisen has offered me a ride to Denver on Friday. I'd love to accept!
>
> *2:12 PM Mar 11th*

> **JonEisen** @twitchhiker Great! The family is excited, gonna be a tight squeeze, but a great experience. Will let you know final plans soon.
>
> *2:16 PM Mar 11th*

A nine-hour car journey, face pushed up against the window, arms folded into my ribs with a stranger's family poking at me the whole way. As long as it wasn't the Manson family, it didn't matter. He looked normal enough in his profile photo, but then didn't they all?

There was little variance in the landscape as the hours passed, but along the way I snapped photos of signs and scenery, posting them on Twitter so several thousand others could vicariously endure my trial by long-distance coach travel. The odd thing was that it wasn't a trial at all; I was thoroughly enjoying my day touring the forgotten freeways of the central states. When my laptop's battery coughed and spluttered and the screen faded to black, I had no option but to sit back and relax. For the first time since I'd left Newcastle, I had nothing much to do – no work, no Twitter, nobody to talk to, no expectations to live up to, no need to paint a smile across my face to hide how exhausted I felt – and slowly the realisation of what I had accomplished so far began to sink in. I'd lost sight of how wonderful and unique my journey was, how much support I'd had and how little I'd allowed myself to enjoy a sense of achievement. I was only a few hundred pounds short of the £3,000 target I'd set for *charity: water*, radio stations and journalists were still supporting me, even if the majority couldn't grasp the time difference when calling. More importantly, I was still travelling, still making the rules work for me. Phenomenal. And utterly ludicrous. Twitter continued to foster connections and establish trust between otherwise disparate individuals. I was having the adventure of a lifetime, and at long last I'd begun to realise it.

There was a second pick-up to be made in St Louis and, as the journey approached the halfway point, a stack of skyscrapers on the banks of the Mississippi River loomed into view, and another structure that caused a moment of disbelief and breathlessness – the futurama of the Gateway Arch. Completed in 1965, the single luminescent arch dwarfs the downtown buildings that stray too close to it. It reaches 192 metres into the sky, is the tallest monument in the United States and was quite easily the singular most striking sight I'd seen on my road trip. The lines and material can be compared to nothing else in the field of vision – it's as if the arch has been super-imposed on the city using Photoshop, an artist's impression of how St Louis may look in 2050.

'I've never been to St Louis before. The arch is an amazing sight, isn't it?' I commented to a chain-smoking passenger as we stretched our legs at the bus stop.

'It's not St *Luey*. It's St *Lewis*.' The squat, grey-haired woman in the ill-fitting tracksuit didn't bother turning to address me, but bellowed loudly in the direction she was already facing.

'Oh, really? The English would pronounce it "Luey".'

'The Americans would pronounce it "Lewis",' she spat back, my continued presence still unable to warrant eye contact. 'And they do.'

The western skies of Missouri shifted from blue to red as the twinkling Kansas City skyline began to fill up the view. The Interstate splintered and the coach peeled off towards the looming silhouettes of skyscrapers. I checked into Twitter on my mobile, and found a message from Ben, the tweep who had arranged my accommodation in Lawrence and would be waiting to collect me in Kansas City. Except he wasn't. Fortunately there was a Plan B – a friend of Ben's, @joey96, had offered to collect me from Kansas City and drive me to Lawrence. It didn't really matter, because I didn't have the first clue who Ben was either. The coach pulled up on an empty street in downtown Kansas City, and as I stepped onto the sidewalk a man called out my name from behind the door of a white jeep. I didn't even ask his, just threw my bags in the back and off we went. Blind trust.

From the lonely neighbourhood of Kansas City where the Megabus had deposited me, we drove west along Interstate 70 – the same Interstate Ken and I had weaved on and off while driving from Frederick to Wheeling – and Joey, as my chauffeur introduced himself to me, explained the history of Kansas and its role as a free state during the Civil War. Neighbouring state Missouri had been a slave state, and the road from Kansas City to Lawrence took us through the sites of the war's bloodiest battles. And despite the war ending over 140 years ago, there were still people and indeed whole families in both states that still refused to mix with one another; they were still fighting the Civil War to this day.

We reached Lawrence and pulled up at Johnny's Tavern on 2nd Street, just in time to miss quiz night. Lawrence is a big college town that loves its sports, and consequently there were frat boys everywhere, spilling pitchers of ale and doing their utmost to impress giggling cheerleader types. Joey put forward Johnny's pizzas as the best in town, but my stomach still craved meat, and a well-stacked burger was ordered.

'Joey isn't my real name, by the way,' Joey admitted as I doused another onion ring in ketchup.

'Really? What is it then?' This was an interesting twist.

'Well it definitely isn't Joey,' the man who wasn't called Joey grinned. 'I don't like sharing my personal information online, so I created an alternative identity.'

Uh huh.

'Yeah, I was going to call myself John Doe on Twitter, but that's a cliché.'

As long as it wasn't a criminal alias known to law enforcement officers, it was fine by me.

The Lawrence Journal-World had booked a room for me at the Marriott SpringHill Suites, and while I couldn't put my finger on it, there was something not entirely right about the building. The reception was far too open and bright, while the elevators were arthritically slow. And the corridors were… well, they were too wide. None of these features were of any great concern, but stood out enough to be noticeable.

The gift of free Wi-Fi proved to be a curse; I'd nearly fallen asleep in my burger at Johnny's, but felt compelled to sit up for an hour or two and work. On Twitter there was all sorts of chatter from tweeps in Wichita, eager to know if I would visit there next. It was unlikely since I was heading to Denver, but they did seem insistent. As the time ticked round to two in the morning, I dialled home on Skype for a video chat with Jane and the boys. I'd managed to call home whenever a reliable connection allowed it, and it was quickly becoming the highlight of my day. That was something new – seeing my wife and boys and every time appreciating how much I missed them, and how much I loved them. It was as if I had a crush on my own family, I didn't know how else to explain it. And on that morning, there were my boys, Jack and Sam, ready for school with their hair brushed and collars poking up through their jumpers at odd angles, sat on their mum's lap. Toothy grins, waves to the camera, giggling and laughing. And then Sam broke my heart with three little words:

'Come home, Daddy.'

I told Sam I wouldn't be long as my eyes filled with tears, promised him I'd be back soon for endless hugs and kisses. I'd had to travel around the world to realise that everything I needed to complete me was at home.

Twitchhiker had so far been about scratching a thoroughly selfish itch, raising money for a good cause and proving that goodwill was universal. But if you'd have told me the day before that after ten arse-numbing hours, three states and 900 kilometres that I'd be a happier person for it, I'd have asked if you were high on drugs. The journey to Campbell Island was proving as rich as chocolate-dipped doubloons, and while my spirit had wavered at times, I was more determined than ever.

Chapter 18

Day Twelve – Thursday 12 March

After throwing my tired bones around the globe for 259 hours and a smattering of minutes, I'd stumbled upon the middle of nowhere. I was pacing the forecourt of a lonely petrol station in Lawrence, Kansas, under a deep, crisp sky that betrayed the sub-zero temperatures flicking at my increasingly numb cheeks. The surrounding streets, bleached of their colour by the harsh white light of the day's sun, were quiet and lifeless. I was as far from the Pacific Ocean as I was from the Atlantic, and I was alone in a town where fish was rarely on the menu.

My morning had been chaotic, establishing the tone for a day that would be uncomfortable and surreal in equal measure. It began with a phone interview with a former radio colleague called Moose (or Hugh to his mother and bank manager) for a radio station in Manchester, followed swiftly by a television interview for Lawrence Journal-World, the newspaper company that was providing my accommodation, in the reception of the Bizarro Hotel.

'There's something odd about this hotel,' I confided in Christen, the news intern who was interviewing me. 'I'm not sure what it is, but it doesn't even look like a hotel.'

Christen smiled and tried not to encourage the paranoid foreigner, concluding her interview without comment on the setting, before driving me to the Lawrence Journal-World office so I could thank them for providing my accommodation. The business is something of an anomaly in local media, owning both a newspaper and cable television operation in the same market. In 1995 it became one of the first newspapers in the country to begin publishing on the Internet and editor Dennis Anderson brimmed with pride about the tri-media operation, almost as much as when he talked about basketball. The university team, the Kansas Jayhawks, were on a roll and everyone in the building was a fan.

While in Chicago, I'd passed on my chocolate-covered pretzels from Wheeling to the Orbitz girls, who in return had presented me with a tourist's guide to Chicago. The gift exchange had skipped a couple of steps after that; I'd received my ticket for the Megabus remotely by email, and I hadn't felt comfortable asking Joey to contribute, considering his last-minute drafting into the proceedings. So I still had the Chicago guide, which I exchanged with Dennis Anderson for a Kansas Jayhawks annual.

'Yeah, I went to college in Chicago,' said Dennis, staring down at the tourist guide in his hands. 'I managed a couple of papers there, too.'

It's the thought that counts.

'Yep, know that city very well. But thanks.'

I arrived back at the Marriott with less than two hours to spare before I had to check out, and I needed to find somewhere else to stay in Lawrence – I wasn't due to be cosying up with a man called Joe and his family of five for a day-long road trip to Denver until the following day. In my absence, however, there had been a full-blown revolution amongst my followers on Twitter. Wichitans wanted me to pay their city a visit, and they weren't taking no for an answer.

Ever since I'd arrived in Chicago, I'd noticed a steady rise in Twitter chatter about the possibility of diverting the Twitchhiker through southern Kansas. At first it was a stray comment or two, mostly wishful thinking and speculation, but since I had reached the same state there had been a mania of activity. Dozens of twitter users had synchronised their efforts and though they didn't have a way for me to reach them, they did have a plan to take me further on my journey – a road trip to Austin, Texas, which would see me arrive slap-bang in the middle of South By Southwest, the world-famous film, music and technology festival where Twitter was launched several years before. It would surely mean mingling amongst a swell of influential Twitter users; if ever there was an opportunity looking me straight in the face, SXSW was the gift horse with a gaze I shouldn't ignore.

Wichita had an exit strategy for me, but not one to ensure my arrival. Some six hours further around the globe, however, a Twitter user in Dublin called @chiarraigrrl saw the offer the Wichitans had put on the table and provided a solution:

chiarraigrrl @twitchhiker I can send you to Wichita by Greyhound if that's any good...

Sent 11:13 AM Mar 12th

I was more or less in the exact geographical centre of a different continent, and a nameless woman over 6,000 kilometres to the east in Dublin was buying me a bus ticket. Who was she? Why was she helping me? Was she attractive? I didn't care. Well, not much. I daydreamed for the merest of moments before accepting the offer from the exotic flame-haired, green-eyed Irish gal, and quickly bundled what few belongings I had left into my two messenger bags, this time managing not to leave a third of my clothing in the hotel wardrobe.

Wichita was a city I knew only from the lyrics of Glen Campbell's song that, let me tell you, is one of the greatest songs ever recorded. Don't argue, it absolutely is and I won't hear a word against it. Campbell sounds as if his breaking heart has been ripped whole from his chest as he sings those words to a distant love too far away to embrace. Don't tell me you couldn't cry all the moisture out your body when you listen to it.

There was nothing in my rules that prevented me changing my mind, so rather than walk myself into a moral maze, I wasted no time in accepting the Greyhound ticket from my new Twitter friend in Dublin, who in turn emailed me the ticket reference. The Wichitans went wild as I accepted a night's accommodation from a tweep called Carrie, and the road trip to Austin from two others called Shea and Tyler.

Finally, I tweeted @JonEisen to thank him for his offer of a lift to Denver and explain that I felt confident about the road to Wichita proving more fruitful.

Good. Except the new itinerary left me with less than an hour to reach the Greyhound pick-up point across the far side of Lawrence.

Once again it was Ben Smith (@benasmith) who came to my rescue.

Ben had meant to collect me in Kansas City, but he'd been seriously ill with a kidney infection in recent days. He arrived to collect me from the hotel several minutes later, and looked bloody terrible; sallow-faced, rakish of frame, ashen of skin and sunken of eye. He'd already done so much for me, and now I'd dragged him from his bed to save my skin once more. He was an expat hailing from Oxford, who'd arrived in Lawrence after falling for a sassy American girl with a sassy American accent, followed ten years later by a sassy separation.

I didn't know until we chatted in the car his motivation for helping me. It turned out Ben's involvement epitomised everything that was brilliant and bizarre about my journey, embodying the unspoken interconnectedness between strangers on Twitter.

Long before I'd boarded the ferry to Amsterdam, before I'd even conceived the idea in that supermarket bread aisle, Stephen Fry had tweeted something impossibly witty, as he does several times a day. In dozens of different countries around the globe, dozens of other Twitter users responded by tweeting a message back, and all their replies and remarks appeared on the Internet for anybody to search through and read. Ben was one such individual who searched Twitter to read those replies. He was struck by one comment in particular, and became friends with the woman who had sent it.

When I found myself heading towards Kansas City with not a soul to help me once I arrived, it was this woman who suggested Ben help me as a favour to her. Her name was Leanne, and she was a cute thirty-year-old designer with snow-white blonde hair, blue eyes and more piercings than most. Twitter knew her better as @minxlj – the very same person who had donated my ferry ticket to Amsterdam on day one.

So two strangers with not the slightest jot in common had fallen into one another's orbit through crazy random happenstance and come through for me, while the two million residents of Kansas City were busy washing their hair. Leanne just happened to know the right person in the right place to help me, at just the right time. Thank you, Leanne. And Stephen Fry too.

Ben swung the car onto a petrol forecourt and gently eased himself out of the driver's seat to open the boot.

'By the way, was everything OK at the hotel?' asked Ben.

'Everything was fine,' I replied. 'But now you mention it, there was something not quite right about it.'

'How so?'

'I'm not sure. The dimensions of the place were wrong, somehow. The corridors were too wide, and the lift was too slow for a passenger lift. It didn't feel like any hotel I've ever checked into.'

'That's probably because you've never checked into a shopping mall before.'

Well that would explain it, then. A decade before, the Marriott SpringHill Suites had been the less-than-successful Riverfront Mall. I'd probably spent the night in a former food court. Mystery solved.

The petrol forecourt was the pick-up point for the Greyhound coach to Wichita. A brace of homeless bums, their faces wearing well-worn creases, slouched on a broken old bench and squinted in the icy sunshine while I paced back and forth to keep warm. Then I realised the homeless bums had suitcases. They weren't vagrants, they were passengers. On my bus. The Greyhound. The backbone of American travel. The stuff of legends. The precursor of nightmares.

A coach pulled up alongside the forecourt, and I twice checked the livery to ensure I belonged on it. The paint was brilliant and new, no dents or chips, polished and buffed to perfection. The windows were tinted and clean, the bumpers attached to both the front and rear of the vehicle. It was a Greyhound to be sure, inviting and trustworthy. 'Aha!' exclaimed the coach in my direction. 'That will teach you to be so judgmental about America's iconic public transport!' It was right, to be fair.

The door hissed open, and a squat, sour-faced driver grumbled her way down the steps, peering over the rim of her glasses at the dishevelled trio assembled before her, before grudgingly opening the luggage hold for the other two passengers. Then she did something entirely unexpected, by me at least.

She asked to see our tickets.

While they appeared to be ramshackle jobless layabouts, the two vagrants ahead of me whipped tickets out from amongst their various layers. I pulled from my pocket the folded piece of hotel stationery with my ticket reference scribbled on. My flame-haired Irish filly hadn't mentioned a ticket. Balls.

'Ticket please,' came the expected and draining challenge.

'I don't have a ticket,' was my pathetic retort, 'but I do have my ticket reference number.'

'Then you can't get on this bus.'

'OK, I booked online two hours ago so I'm not sure how I'm meant to have a ticket?'

Her stare singed the spot in between my eyes, like a magnifying glass held over a wasp.

'You were meant to print your ticket out in there,' she spat, flinging her arm to the forecourt store.

'Well how the fuck was I meant to know that, you silly witch?' I said, but only in my head.

'Can I go and print it now?' were the actual words that passed between my frozen lips.

'No. This bus ain't waiting around.'

'Right. So there's nothing whatsoever I can do to get on that bus?'

There was more staring followed by an unnaturally long exhale of air.

'Give me your ID.'

I pulled out my wallet and handed over my driver's licence. She perused the details, the curious photo of the bearded chap that in no way resembled the bearer, and then, in an unexpected turn of events, put it in her pocket. At that moment I regretted ignoring the advice of everyone who had taken the time to give me it, by failing to make copies of my documents before leaving the UK.

'We'll have to print your ticket when we reach Wichita. I'll keep your ID until then.'

What was she going to do with it? I had no other choice, I had to board the bus. I waved Ben off as I stepped up to board.

My first impression of the Greyhound's interior was that it in no way reflected the blindingly clean exterior. My second, third and fourth impressions followed in rapid succession:

- this coach smells like a sow's armpit
- this coach looks like a sow's armpit
- the windows are obviously tinted to stop people seeing in

The coach wasn't full; in fact it was almost exactly half full – I knew this because everyone on board was taking up two seats. As I weaved in and out of the limbs spilt into the aisle, some passengers were folded up asleep, others sat slumped with their legs splayed open, inviting my gaze to their unsavoury crotches. Those that were awake simply watched as I sought a space, refusing to move the bin liners of possessions that enjoyed their own seat. They weren't the friendliest bunch of day-trippers, between them possessing fewer teeth than the Osmond family. A couple of old-timers in baseball caps and gingham shirts nodded their heads while holding my gaze just enough to acknowledge my existence, but nothing more.

I stumbled along until I finally found the last pair of free seats, the pair immediately before the back row, directly opposite the toilet. The stench of fifty strains of piss and shit was unbearable before I'd even had a chance to sit down.

The world record for the longest breath-hold currently rests with thirty-two-year-old Tom Sietas. In 2008, the German free diver held his breath underwater for seventeen minutes and nineteen seconds. I needed to find a way to not only equal his record, but beat it by a further 150 minutes, without the use of pure oxygen, losing weight to improve efficiency or any sort of training. And I'm reasonably convinced I would have smashed Sietas' effort, if the gap-toothed lady in the sleeping bag behind me hadn't started whispering to herself and the young offender in front hadn't reclined his seat into my chin.

I opened my bag but thought twice about firing up the laptop and working. Instead I pulled out the dog-eared card from Jane that she'd stowed away amongst my clothes eleven days ago, and glowed as I read the words once more. I was at peace with my journey now but I couldn't wait to see my family again, assuming the smell, the prisoners or the driver didn't gut me like a kipper first. What doesn't kill you only makes you stronger, I thought.

The average lifespan of a star such as our sun is ten billion years, give or take a few million. During my time endured on the Greyhound, it's likely several thousand celestial bodies ignited and faded, one after the other. Those three hours were a lifetime. I'd never wanted to reach Wichita so quickly in all my born days, and I'd never wanted to reach Wichita at all until six hours beforehand. Except it wasn't called 'Wichita', at least not according to the handful of jokers sat ahead of me.

'Wicha-where?'

'Wicha-there!'

'Yup, we're Wicha-here!'

And in case they hadn't laughed enough the first time, and they did laugh, they ran through their Wichita routine twice more before we arrived. Hilarious. Perhaps I wasn't feeling so jovial because I was still hemmed in in my seat next to the toilet, which had been frequented by half the passengers over the course of the journey. But even a bus ride with a stinking potty for company failed to dampen my spirits. The view through my window was of blue skies and golden plains of arid land; if I hadn't lost the feeling in my face before boarding, I'd have sworn it was T-shirt and shorts weather. The experience was ultimately calming, much like my journey from Chicago to Kansas City the previous day.

As the coach picked its way through the streets of Wichita, the blue skies were lost to sad grey clouds. The city's bus station was no cheerier, a dark and exhaust-soaked garage and a grim setting in which to meet my hastily arranged host for the evening. Her Twitter name was Carrie (@CarrieFollis) and, having accepted her offer of accommodation earlier, her name was all I knew of her. She was a petite lady, in her thirties perhaps, smartly dressed and sporting a head full of loose, blonde curls down to her shoulders. Accompanying her was Josh (@joshdutcher), a far looser, more relaxed character, wearing casual jeans and a daft, cheeky grin. Together they were easy to spot, since they were the only people accompanied by a cameraman called Corey from local television station KSN.

'Paul, hi, I'm Corey. Hi. Can you do that again?' he asked as I stepped off the bus and greeted Carrie and Josh.

'Hi. Yes. What?'

'Step off the bus and greet Carrie and Josh – can you do that again for me?'

I was keen to talk to my new host, but the local news network wanted the Twitchhiker project on the ten o'clock news, so I re-boarded the bus, much to the irritation of the driver who still held my ID. It was returned intact once I'd jumped through hoops at the customer service desk and soon we were on our way to Carrie's house, with Corey the cameraman in pursuit.

Carrie and Josh were the brains and brawn behind Naked City, a lifestyle and entertainment magazine for Wichita. I quickly figured out that they worked together, but as we chatted in the car it wasn't clear whether they were a couple or just good friends.

As we pulled up to Carrie's house, a detached cottage on a corner plot, the grey skies filled with snow. Not huge fluffy chunks of the stuff, but those fine and pointless spits that are neither use nor ornament.

'Snow? I thought Kansas had sunshine all year round?' I asked.

'Did you even hear what you just said?' laughed Josh.

'I know, I just thought it'd be warmer in March.'

'You're thinking of California,' replied Josh. 'Or Mexico. Or pretty much any place other than Kansas.'

Carrie's home was neat and snug, and unnaturally tidy. There were no piles of ironing stacked on chairs and tables, no breakfast pots left lurking in the sink since morning. Corey the cameraman set up in the spotless dining area and recorded a half-hour interview across Carrie's dinner table, before packing up and promising to see me later that night – more footage was required for the Twitchhiker special on the ten o'clock news on KSN, and there was talk of a tweet-up.

Carrie showed me to my bed for the night. It was that of a teenage boy, although the teenage boy wasn't in it, thankfully. I subtly clarified the situation to avoid causing offence – Carrie had kids, Josh wasn't the father, her husband was working and Josh was Carrie's co-worker who was goofing off work.

I threw myself in the shower for barely a minute, before returning to my room and unpacking my clothes. Where had I put my jumper, the one Katherine had washed for me in Wheeling? And that's when I finally realised:

twitchhiker Crap. I think I've left a jumper and some other clothes in the InterContinental in Chicago. Damn.

17:22 PM Mar 12th

Think of Kansas and you tend to picture fields of golden corn reaching up to a burning circle of sun, a sweet blue sky arching overhead. At least that was my imagination's portrait of the state before I arrived there. Life failed to imitate art, however, and the snow continued to fall into the evening, whipped around by occasional gusts of freezing wind.

Carrie drove us into downtown Wichita, to the last-minute tweet-up that had been organised to celebrate my impromptu visit. The city was a modest affair, not so crowded by steel towers of power and instead content with broad avenues and low-slung properties.

We parked up on a snow-swept East Douglas Avenue and headed inside The Anchor, a long horseshoe of a building, with the bar area along the right-hand side and a dining room to the left, half of which had been set aside for our get-together. Immediately my chest tightened with anxiety, because embarrassment was sure to follow – even when events had been orchestrated in major cities like Washington and Chicago, there hadn't been more than a dozen attendees. And sure enough, we were the only three in a space that catered for thirty.

Then the cameraman appeared. Except it wasn't Corey, it was another cameraman. And he wasn't from KSN, he was from rival affiliate station KWCH. He looked around, slightly confused by the lack of bodies, asked if he was at the party for the Twitchhiker and whether he could interview him.

And while he was asking questions and filming me, a second cameraman walked into the room, alongside a TV reporter. They weren't from KSN either, or KWCH. They were a crew from Wichita's third affiliate station, KAKE.

And then Corey turned up.

There were three local television networks in Wichita, and I was to appear on the 10 p.m. news across them all. And within a few minutes of the first interview's end, thirty or so people appeared to quell my embarrassment. The majority had been strangers to one another just a few months beforehand. In many cases, Twitter had allowed them to discover one another, but the dynamics of the situation changed soon after; Twitter became the back-channel to physical relationships, allowing users to keep in touch when they weren't meeting up in the real world. For this group of people, Twitter stretched beyond a social media network; it represented a gathering of firm and trusting friends. It was a microcosm of the Twitchhiker project, proving the power of community spirit. And of all the places I'd visited so far, none were more welcoming, and nowhere was more engrossed in Twitter. There are plenty of towns and cities where users put faces to avatars at tweet-ups, but Wichita felt unique.

Amongst the attendees were Shea and Tyler, the two kids from Wichita (and by 'kids', I mean they were in their early twenties – I use the term partly out of affection but mostly out of raging jealousy) who had offered me a ride to South By Southwest in Austin, Texas. Unless you study North American geography for more than a few moments, you never appreciate the colossal scale of the continent. On a map, Kansas to Austin looks like a three- or four-hour drive, including a toilet break at the services. Nope. Driving through the night and across three states from Kansas, through Oklahoma (Oklahoma!) and into Texas was a route nearly 900 kilometres in length, at least nine hours on the road.

At the beginning of the week, the thought of yet another road trip after spending two days on coaches of various states of comfort and sanitation would have no doubt driven me to tears. The Megabus had changed all that. The prospect of ten hours getting to know my companions and cruising down through the central states was exhilarating.

The attention of the cameras was a little overwhelming, the turnout of individuals was incredibly touching, and having KSN anchor Anita Cochran drag me outside to pose for photos with her kids was just plain surreal. And when the crowds dispersed and Carrie, Josh and I left the dining area and walked through the bar, there was my moon face splashed across the late night news. Josh asked the bar staff to change channels, and there I was again, saying all the same words but not necessarily in the same order.

Welcome to Wichita. I certainly was.

Chapter 19

Day Thirteen – Friday 13 March

The following morning in Wichita, I decided to weigh myself on Carrie's bathroom scales. The lack of sleep and exercise multiplied by a diet of deep-fried fat meant my chin was threatening to bypass my neck and join at the chest. Carrie had washed an armful of clothes for me the previous evening but my fresh shirt was feeling a little too snug about the collar. I tried holding my breath, gently rocking back and forth in an attempt to fool the scales but to no avail – I'd piled on ten pounds in less than a fortnight.

To celebrate my record weight gain, we headed out to The Donut Whole on East Douglas Street where Josh joined us. It was the first time I'd eaten donuts for breakfast – fat, lip-smacking donuts with sprinkles, and a few big slurps of coffee from a mug. Josh went one better, and fatter. Where Paris had presented a cornflakes and Coco Pops combo, and Eppelborn had offered an epic spread, Wichita was to play its part in a growing tradition of memorable breakfasts, by serving up bacon and maple syrup. On top of the donuts.

I took a bite; it was sweet and salty, the tastes and textures almost married up on my tongue, but not quite. Donuts were for elevenses and tea-time treats, I decided, to be filled with raspberry jam that squirted down your front. Bacon's proper place was in a white bap smothered with ketchup, where it could continue to cure hunger and hangovers.

> **twitchhiker** Morning from Wichita! Plans so far: road trip to SXSW tonight, will arrive about 2am, nowhere to stay yet.
>
> *9:42 PM Mar 13th*

I spent the day working from the offices of Naked City with Carrie and Josh, loafing about on their sofa trying not to doze off or get any fatter. There wasn't a shred of panic about what might or might not occur when I reached Austin, whether a Good Samaritan would show me shelter or whether I'd be shut out in the cold. Instead, I concentrated on knuckling down to write. Outside, Wichita's weather grumbled with occasional and inconsequential showers of light snow throughout the morning, but eventually the watery sun broke through and brought Josh and me no end of delight.

> **joshdutcher** Me: 'What's that?' @twitchhiker: 'That bright yellow ball in the sky?' Me: 'Yeah!' @twitchhiker: 'I think it's Jesus shining on us.'
>
> *12:48 PM Mar 13th*

We took lunch at Heroes, a broad and manly sports bar with a menu packed out with beer and meat. As the three of us sank into a booth, my mobile rang. It was an excitable Jon calling from home:

'Mate, you've done it! £3,000!'

'Wow, really?' I hadn't checked in on the total donations for a couple of days.

'Just a few minutes ago, you've passed your target!'

Hearing the news was so much more satisfying than the double deep-fried chicken strips that were turning my arteries and backside to lard. Twitter users had already made a difference by providing enough funding for a freshwater well in a foreign land, and there was plenty more goodwill and generosity to come. Returning from Heroes to Carrie's car, we were approached by mum-of-two Cindy (@WichitaCindy). I'd met her the previous evening at The Anchor, and while chatting I'd mentioned about so much of my underwear still being in Chicago.

'I happened to be in the mall today,' said Cindy, stood with her son in the car park and gesturing to a carrier bag she was holding, 'and I thought these would come in helpful.'

I accepted the bag and peered inside. It was a three-pack of boxer shorts, exactly the sort of charity I was in need of – new underwear was never something I'd buy for myself. I'd wear my socks until a stray toe or two poked through, my shoes until the soles flapped loose like a spaniel's tongue and relied on mundane Christmas presents for basic comforts such as underpants. I was delighted to accept clean undercrackers from a housewife in Wichita, who promptly asked if she could take a photo of me and my new three-pack of pants standing alongside her son. He'll treasure that memory forever, I'm sure.

Fresh underwear was all well and good, but it didn't solve the problem of where I was going to stay in Austin. The spotlight turned to a man from Norway.

arcticmatt @twitchhiker do you still need a place to stay? How does the Austin Hilton sound? Big couch in my room.

4:55 PM Mar 13th

The Twitter handle was familiar: arcticmatt... it swilled around my head for a few seconds before it clicked. He was the Norwegian who'd begun supporting me within minutes of sending my very first tweet about Twitchhiker. In fact, he was one of my very first followers and now he was in Texas, attending the South By Southwest Festival.

twitchhiker @arcticmatt Hey Matt! That sounds great! As long as you're ok with me turning up at 2 in the morning?

5:01 PM Mar 13th

Hotel couches are usually of a size intended to pay lip service to the form – they sell you the idea of a couch so you pay a few dollars more for your room, whereas in reality it'll be no wider than a door and just as comfortable to sit on. Not to worry, I conceded, because the offer guaranteed shelter, warmth and a toilet in working order, and that was all any man could ask for.

arcticmatt @twitchhiker just spoke with general manager of the Hilton and they are sending up a spare bed for you!

5:21 PM Mar 13th

It was as if the stranger could read my mind. So I had a place to crash once I arrived in Austin in the twilight hours. That said, it was a shame I wouldn't be able to attend any of the events at the festival. Tickets had no doubt sold out months ago, and had cost in the order of several hundred dollars. I'd have to be content at fraternising with attendees in the hotel bar and at late night parties, which was fine by me since I liked bars and parties.

arcticmatt @twitchhiker just hooked you up with a free SxSW pass :)

5:45 PM Mar 13th

And he really had. The Norwegian had walked into the office of the festival co-ordinator, noticed that he and the official shared the same surname, and talked him into believing they were related. It seemed a free pass worth the best part of a thousand bucks was the least the co-ordinator could offer a member of his own family.

Tyler and Shea arrived at Carrie's office a little after seven on the Friday evening; Shea's black Nissan Versa was loaded with coffee and snacks for our nine-hour road trip south through Oklahoma and into Texas. Shea was blonde and buxom and astonishingly easy to make giggle until she snorted coffee out of her nose, while Tyler was undeniably a hipster, a very cool customer but still easy to raise a smile from. They were good friends, with similar careers and similar interests – both worked in new media in the city, and both were craving the non-stop geekery and drinking until dawn that South By Southwest would provide in spades. The Jägermeister-induced brain trauma I'd suffered at the Blue Frog in Chicago was four days in the past, so it seemed likely I'd be tempted to join them.

If we reached Austin alive, that was. As the dusky skies of Friday evening turned to night and we slipped across the state line into Oklahoma, Shea displayed exemplary driving skills for a short-sighted octogenarian with a head injury. She just wasn't very good at it; every so often Shea would either be too busy talking or perhaps resting her eyes, and the car would slowly veer to the right for three or four seconds, before she threw the steering wheel to the left, squealing in relief at preventing the three of us becoming organ-donor demographics.

twitchhiker Halfway to Austin, stopped for Starbucks. Playing DJ in the car while blogging. Awesome, apparently.

10:59 PM Mar 13th

Shea's occasional swerves across several lanes of Interstate kept everyone alert, as did our frequent exits to take on supplies. Besides caffeine, we also pulled into a burger joint called Arby's, except it wasn't a burger joint at all. You already have McDonald's, Burger King, Wendy's and a multitude of other patty-flipping drive-thrus. No, Arby's made its name selling roast beef sandwiches. Not thick, hand-carved beef with lashings of horseradish sauce and gravy, but wafer-thin processed meatish flaps. Tyler and

Shea were ravenous for the '5 for $5.95' offer, as was I until my first bite of an Arby's Beef 'n' Cheddar.

'You two really like this?' I asked, making the face of a toddler sucking a lemon.

'Yeah, it cost $5.95 for five sandwiches,' replied Tyler between chews of whatever it was in his sandwich. 'You're not enjoying it?'

'Not really. Have you ever had roast beef for Sunday dinner? With mashed potato and Yorkshire puddings?'

'A what type of pudding?' asked Tyler.

'Yorkshire,' I confirmed.

'I've heard of pudding before,' announced Shea, 'and I really like that. Is it similar?'

'Nothing of the sort,' I explained. 'It's a sort of pancake mix, but cooked in an oven.'

'Awesome,' declared Tyler. My God, I thought it was a cliché that Americans referred to everything from healing evangelists to efficient bowel movements as awesome, but apparently not.

It was a long nine hours to Austin. Not because of the company, but because nine hours is a long time to drive anywhere, in spite of Shea's best efforts to spice up proceedings by threatening to take the scenic route cross-country. Through Oklahoma there had been little to see through the passenger window except darkness, but the moment we crossed the state line into Texas the roadsides filled up with giant fizzy neon shouting about liquor stores, stetsons and adult entertainment. Having said that, every one of the neon signs had letters missing, leaving us to guess what type of business might advertise HOT OW LS to passing motorists. As on any road trip we relieved the monotony by sharing dark secrets and tall tales, and played a variety of party games that led to embarrassment, hysteria and the occasional awkward silence. What goes on tour, stays on tour. Except what Shea will do for $50. That has to come out at some point.

After what seemed an eternity of suburbia had flashed by the windows of our Nissan Versa, we eventually reached downtown Austin. It was a little before four on a cold and crisp morning, and the streets were devoid of parties, drunks or other signs of festivities. We reached the Hilton, no signs of life outside or in, and I shook hands with Tyler and hugged it out with Shea, and promised to see them the next day. Once inside the grand open space of the reception area, however, there were drunken roars of laughter and life from the guest bar to the right; they were mostly kids in T-shirts packed in tight and awash with designer beer – festival attendees staying up late on a school night. I wanted my folding bed more than I wanted some legless hipster yapping at me.

Knuckling the button for the twelfth floor, I felt the adrenalin and anxiety burn in my chest once more. I'd never knocked on the door of a stranger at stupid o'clock in the morning before. And he was foreign. What if his English proved to be worse than my Norwegian?

Left out the elevator, and left again to room 1216, where I rapped on the door too quietly to be heard, and then louder, more assured. A thin, bald man opened the door, cocooned in a cotton-white dressing gown, his face decorated with glasses and a goatee beard. Definitely Norwegian.

'What fucking time of the morning do you call this?' he said with a grin.

Matt was from Cheshire and had emigrated to Tromsø several years before. Husband, father-of-two and a mad-keen football supporter, it came as no surprise that a fan of the beautiful game living in Norway followed Manchester United.

When we met we clicked immediately, as if we were old friends who'd stayed in touch with one another but not met in the flesh for an age. Thank God for that, I thought; awkward social relationships with a stranger when sober are rarely welcome. Especially in their bedroom.

Chapter 20

Day Fourteen – Saturday 14 March

Saturday began no more than three hours after I'd dropped into bed, with daylight prodding at my eyeballs a little after seven in the morning. Matt was already awake, sitting up in bed, smoking a cigarette. I hadn't paid much attention to his room earlier that morning, but it was certainly more than adequate for the purposes of dossing down in, with its pinstripe wallpaper and polished oak furniture.

'You staying tonight as well?' asked Matt.

'If you don't mind, that'd be great,' I replied. 'Be good to catch my breath and see a little of the festival.'

'No problem, pal,' said Matt, lighting up another cigarette. 'I'm here for the whole festival, stay as long as you like.'

My newly relaxed approach to securing assistance from Twitter meant I was making plans on the hoof, instead of the security of a three-day itinerary. And it was making for a far more enjoyable journey, even more of an adventure into the unknown.

I rubbed my eyes to life and rifled through my bags for my iPod Touch. After a couple of attempts it connected to the hotel's Wi-Fi. I had mail. Lots of it. One in particular caused my eyes to distend from their sockets:

Subject: Hi Paul – ABC's Good Morning America is calling...

Hi Paul,

We're trying to reach you – what's the best number to contact you at?

  Thank you

  Ted A Winner

I'd been to the US enough times to know that *Good Morning America* was a very big deal. It would no doubt mean giving up an hour or so to television cameras, but the possibility of promoting both the journey and *charity: water* on national breakfast television was too good to pass up. Was it the right thing to do, some Twitter users wondered aloud? Wasn't Twitchhiker about relying on Twitter for help, rather than the media? I could no longer make the distinction; since there'd been no effort by myself or anyone else to contact the media directly, all of the attention Twitchhiker was receiving was occurring as a result of Twitter. If journalists were aware of me, it was because Twitter had found a way to reach them. Every offer of help I'd received, every follower who watched from afar, every request for an interview – all of it could be traced back, directly or indirectly, to that very first tweet on 2 February.

If a *Good Morning America* camera crew happened to be in Austin, then it was a happy coincidence; I hadn't made the decision to abandon Denver in favour of Wichita and reach Austin for the sake of media exposure. I was there for a little Twitter-loving, figuring I'd never have a more receptive or savvy crowd than the thousands that had converged on the Texan capital for five days of unadulterated tech porn.

I called Ted to bottom out exactly what would be required of me. Could I do a live two-way with their presenter in New York at just after seven the next morning?

'That'll be no problem, Ted,' I replied, figuring a half past six alarm call wouldn't cause too much hardship – despite the fact that Matt and I were already making plans to misbehave with Captain Stella and first mate Jim Beam that evening.

'Great! So that's live on the East Coast just after seven, and for you that'll be a little after six.'

The time difference. I was an hour behind New York. A half past five alarm call it was, then.

'And we'll need to shoot some B-roll with you this afternoon,' continued Ted. 'I can have a camera crew meet you in Austin at, say, midday? You'll only be away an hour or so.'

B-roll is the footage that producers use to illustrate a live television interview before or during it. Taping it can see ice ages come and pass.

'That's great, Ted, look forward to it.'

I didn't.

I spent three hours with the camera team on Saturday afternoon. Up escalators, down escalators, up 6th Street, across it, down it. I stopped to take in the view of the colossal Texas State Capitol once, twice and perhaps a third time for luck. The whole process, like everything else in television production, moved at the pace of cold rice pudding.

At Auditorium Shores, a broad open park to the south of the city, the crew filmed me slowly running out of puff as I plodded up a hill and collapsed at the peak to take in the Austin skyline. Texas is fiercely Republican in its political leanings, yet Austin is buoyantly liberal and a fat melting pot of creativity and innovation, its reputation sealed by SXSW. It's through the combined interactive music and film festival that many visitors first learn about this liberal oasis in a desert of... well, desert; Texas is over five times the size of England with less than half the population. There's a whole lot of nothing in Texas, yet the whole world comes to Austin every March to play for ten days. When South By Southwest was launched in 1987 it was an event only for the music industry, a brave move considering it was far from the bright lights of other major cities. But Austin stayed firm in its belief that the world would go out of its way to attend. Through immigration the city enjoyed an eclectic music scene, and Austin had had a reputation as a full-on party town since the Civil War, when General Custer's command moved to the city and his troops drank in bars on 6th Street and 4th Street – a neighbourhood still renowned for its nightlife today, and one I'd familiarise myself with later that evening. If they ever let me off that bloody hill.

Three hours later, and the GMA team had all the footage of me walking, pointing, descending, ascending, sitting and staring vacantly into the middle distance that they needed. They returned me to the hotel, and at last it was time for my SXSW experience to begin. Except for the BBC, who wanted to record a quick interview inside the conference centre – at least I was edging closer to seeing something of the event. Fortunately, my interviewer Darren Waters was as eager as I was to explore the festival, so I filmed a piece to camera on the spot where we met, and was released from media captivity five minutes later.

Free! I hot-footed it up the escalators and into the trade hall, eager to see the future. Stalls and gizmos and graphics and mobiles and hyper-elevated levels of bullshit so self-indulgent you wouldn't believe. It was all here! I made small talk with the Google girls! Stole pens from Microsoft! And then further along the aisle, I spotted Jeff Jarvis. Wow! Jarvis was an associate professor at City University of New York's Graduate School of Journalism. He was the person responsible for creating *Entertainment Weekly*. His musings on publishing in the digital age were inspired. More importantly, we both wrote for *The Guardian* and he'd once replied to a message I sent him on Facebook. Practically best friends, then. So long as I didn't make a prize tit of myself in any obvious way, everything would be fine. And so I waited for Jarvis, or Jeff as his friends probably called him, to finish talking to some obsessive fanboy before I made my move.

'Hello Jeff, my name's Paul. Paul Smith? I don't know if you remember me, but you replied to a message of mine on Facebook a couple of years ago.'

There was a pause. Jeff's eyes narrowed. 'Hi Paul, great to meet you,' he replied, cautiously. Of course he didn't remember me. He was Jeff Jarvis, he received hundreds of emails and messages a day. What a stupid opening line that was.

'I write for *The Guardian* too!'

Common ground established. Good work, Smith.

'Great, how's that working out for you?' asked Jeff.

'Great. Really, really great.'

Exquisite wordplay from the writer. World class, bravo.

'That's... great.'

Panic. Followed by a silence you could roll a whale through.

'OK, well I just wanted to say hello, since we'd talked online before.'

Gah.

It's not unfair to say I made a complete dick of myself in front of Jeff Jarvis, a writer and thinker I deeply admire, and it was a level of gurning, speechless dickishness that was uncomfortable for all concerned.

Much more enjoyable was the hour spent catching up with Jemima Kiss, a journalist for *The Guardian*. We traipsed across downtown Austin to J. Kelly's Barbecue, a recommendation of other conference attendees. The menu offered just four main courses, all barbecued – sausage, ribs, brisket and chicken. Limited by the ferocious meatiness of the available options, vegetarian Jemima made do with picking at portions of the three side dishes, until we ascertained the smoky baked beans were almost certainly cut with a meat of undetermined origin.

215

There were dozens of seminars and panels at SXSW, of which I saw none. The scale of the event was overwhelming; world-changing product launches, the superstars of tech rubbing shoulders with college kids, uber-geeks and entrepreneurs.

Matt and I mooched about the conference centre for the remainder of the afternoon, before taking dinner with John Havens of BlogTalkRadio.

'If you ever want the freshest meal – in a restaurant, on a flight, whatever – always ask for the vegan option,' explained Matt as we perused the menus at Roy's, a 'Hawaiian-fusion' restaurant nearby.

'They always have to make it from scratch, and if you ask a place like this to prepare it, it shows how much effort they're willing to put into their dishes.'

Following the sales pitch from the waiter, a vegan dish didn't seem like such a bad option, even for a carnivore like myself. I've already mentioned Texas was a size that anyone living in the UK would find difficult to comprehend; despite being a coastal state, it's over 1,100 kilometres from the Gulf of Mexico to the northern border, and Austin is 300 kilometres short of the coast. That doesn't mean restaurants have to do without fresh fish, however.

'I'd also like to recommend the fish today, gentlemen,' concluded the waiter, 'we have some exceptional salmon available, FedExed to us just this morning.'

I'm sorry, what? People were not only expected to pay more for fish delivered by Federal Express, but were meant to be impressed by the fact? The only time I'd heard of such a thing was when my friend James sent an open bag of prawns by second-class post to an ex-girlfriend.

'I'll have the short ribs, please,' I offered in return.

By day, Austin was crawling with festival delegates, spilling out of the conference centre and into bars, out of hotels and into the conference centre. By night, the city was buzzing with bodies, thick shuffling packs of kids on the sidewalk, queuing up outside venues for parties thrown by the hottest tech brands, or hot-footing it from one block to another because a friend of a friend knew somebody who might be able to sneak them into the Facebook party. Fortunately for me, I had inside connections. Actually I had just one, but that wasn't bad going for the guy who just blew into town fifteen hours before. Shea was promoting an event for her client at Red Eyed Fly on Red River Street, and with a knowing look to security she secured my entry by the side door. The management were no doubt nervously eyeing up the county fire regulations that night. As in every other bar and venue I'd spotted while walking there, personal space was invaded by limbs clutching drinks in plastic cups. Shea suffered some sort of heart palpitation upon spotting actor B. J. Novak in the crowd. I had no idea who she was slurring about.

I made no real effort to drink the evening away – it's always difficult to relax when a five-thirty alarm call is heckling your efforts. A complimentary shot of tequila or two were thrown back with Shea and Tyler, and I did my best not to gag – tequila is a wicked liquor that had seen me green on many a blurry occasion. No matter how enticing a night the Texan hospitality was willing to provide, I couldn't muster the enthusiasm. Every hour spent mixing my drinks was an hour's less sleep and two additional hours of sore head.

I returned to Matt's room in the Hilton, past and through the gangs of geeks, and flipped open my MacBook before bed to see whether Twitter had plans for me the following day. And I'd nearly missed them.

> **marklad2020** @twitchhiker Just seen that you need to leave on Sunday, so can offer you a flight from Austin to San Francisco on Sunday?
>
> *2:08 PM Mar 14th*

The tweet had been sent nearly ten hours beforehand, and somehow I'd overlooked it while checking earlier in the day. It would mean once again abandoning my trip across North America by land, but with no other offers forthcoming, it was all I had. I rattled off a reply to accept the offering, hoping that the sender, Mark Seall, would be able to act on it despite my tardiness. The tweet had been sent from Zurich, some seven hours further around the world. Mark would be another mysterious stranger I'd never shake the hand of, another distant individual kind enough to help me on my way – if my reply reached him in time.

Chapter 21

Day Fifteen – Sunday 15 March

Bill Weir: 'Paul Smith has gone from the United Kingdom to Texas in fifteen days and has paid nothing for travel or lodging. How does he do it? He's using Twitter, the new social networking site that is all the rage, asking strangers for help, and he joins us this morning from Austin, Texas – a long way from home. Paul, good to see you, good morning.'

Me: 'Good morning... Bill.'

For a moment, I couldn't remember the presenter's name and paused for what seemed an eternity. I was live on national television and I couldn't recall a name whispered in my ear thirty seconds earlier. Damn the tequila.

Bill Weir: 'So how does this work? You send out a message on Twitter saying can I catch a ride, can I stay on your couch?'

Me: 'Essentially that, I put a message out and say "I'm here, I need help getting somewhere else and I need help with somewhere to stay" and I leave it to Twitter and the kindness of strangers to help me out and choose where I go next.'

Bill Weir: 'So it's twitchhiking, that's the term they've used.'

No Bill, that's my word, not theirs. I coined the phrase in a supermarket. You'll have to pop into Tesco Gateshead when you're passing through next. Quite an eye-opener.

Bill Weir: 'A lot of people might wonder about staying with strangers. Have you felt safe?'

Me: 'Absolutely, all the way through. Everyone's been very kind and very polite, there have been no problems at all, I've never once felt I've been in an unsafe situation. And I think that's the beauty of Twitter – any one of the people helping me isn't on there in isolation, there might be several hundred people watching them – anyone could be watching them in fact – and you get a good idea of what they're about by what they say.'

Bill Weir: 'What's been your favourite stop so far?'

Me: 'I think the favourite was Washington, because it's the only place I've managed to see any of the sights. I spent an afternoon there last weekend, and that was pretty neat.'

"Pretty neat"? Who talked like that? Of course – almost everyone I'd met in the past ten days. I was mimicking my hosts on national television. Damn the tequila.

Bill Weir: 'And you're also raising money for charity during this?'

Me: 'Yes, there's a charity called *charity: water*, it's got a very simple aim – there are over a billion people in the world who don't have access to clean drinking water and *charity: water* are trying to change that by sinking wells in developing countries and teaching people about water and its use, so we're raising money for that and have about $5,000 so far.'

Bill Weir: 'Well, you've got karma at your back, obviously. And I know you just got married, congratulations on that, and you told your newly-wed "hey honey, I'm gonna go round the world by myself and stay with strangers" five days after your wedding. You're a brave man.'

Me: 'That went well. In my mind I explained it thoroughly to her before deciding to go through with it, but in reality I did no such thing.'

Bill Weir: 'Well good luck to you, I know you're heading for the Antarctic Circle. Thanks Paul.'

All over. For two minutes and thirty-nine seconds, I was beamed into homes from the east coast to the west, from Florida to Seattle. Three hours of filming, two hours for producer Syd and his team to prepare the hotel bar for lighting and sound, all for less than three minutes of television. Madness. Still, I'd managed not to say fuck or bugger.

scottharrison @twitchhiker nice job on GMA!

10:33 AM Mar 15th, 2009

As of nine o'clock that morning, I'd been twitchhiking for exactly a fortnight. I'd spent over eighty hours travelling 11,575 kilometres by car, coach, train, plane and ferry. Point-to-point, the distance between Newcastle and Austin was only 7,660 kilometres – but who travels to be efficient? The occasional tweet attempted to catch me out for not being carbon-neutral or environmentally friendly, but that was a different challenge altogether. There were already plenty of individuals with fitter thighs riding their bicycles across continents or their horses pole-to-pole, or wherever. Two weeks and still moving! Two weeks and not dead! That was something to celebrate. I was still 13,000 kilometres shy of Campbell Island, but the bulk of that distance was the Pacific Ocean – short of a slow cruise to Hawaii, that journey would be all or nothing.

It was mid-afternoon in the UK, and the Hilton's woeful Wi-Fi held together long enough for a Skype video call home to my family. The past two or three calls had seen all of us crying intensely at one another for several minutes, unable to process whether we should be excited by my progress or heartbroken by my absence. Reaching the halfway point of my journey shifted our perspective – I was edging further away from home, but every day was a day closer to being together again. And life would be different when we were, I promised. I'd scoop them all up and squeeze them tight and perhaps for the first time appreciate how blessed I was to have them.

Twitter could have shown me the cold shoulder and sent me home at any time, but it wasn't ready to just yet. My man in Zurich had replied overnight, and I was all set to fly to San Francisco via San Diego later that afternoon. With one problem solved, two new dilemmas emerged – where would I stay in San Francisco, and how would I reach Austin-Bergstrom airport?

The latter was an aspect I hadn't considered before leaving the UK – cities were big places, and travelling across them is often a challenge in itself, even for the folks who live there. Marrying up two offers in the same city didn't always mean I'd solved the issue; JFK is 13 kilometres from downtown

Manhattan – if my host Mark hadn't met me at the airport and paid my fare, I would have had little option but to walk between the two. Assuming I could have walked, since airports are insulated by thick gussets of road and rarely built with pedestrian access in mind.

> **thumbble** @twitchhiker If you need a place to crash in SF, I've got an air mattress you're welcome to!
>
> *9:45 AM Mar 15th*

Christen (@thumbble) was happy to see me crash at her apartment in San Francisco for the night – it was my first offer of help from the West Coast and I accepted immediately. So arranging a place to crash over 2,000 kilometres away wasn't a problem, but reaching an airport less than half an hour's drive down the road? Not a peep from the tweeps was heard. It was frustrating and baffling. I'd taken up the offer of a road trip to Texas because I'd assumed the critical twittering mass attending SXSW would seal the deal and guarantee I'd never go without support for the rest of the trip, but it wasn't the case. Other Twitter users had established that it'd cost just a dollar for me to travel by bus from downtown Austin to the airport – they tweeted it, repeated it, repeated it some more, but not one single person at the festival offered to help.

I updated my blog, uploaded my photos to Flickr, cleared my inbox, glanced nervously at Twitter, rapped my fingers impatiently on the desk. Still nothing. My flight to San Francisco was with Southwest Airlines at 6.45 p.m. It was already past midday. A watched Twitter account never

tweets, as my Nana never said, on account of dying before
Twitter was invented.

> **twitchhiker** Gah! I've no way to get to Austin airport at
> 4pm. Gah again!
>
> *12:35 PM Mar 15th*

Another hour rolled by. Matt was threatening to force a
dollar for the airport bus into my hand, but I refused to
accept it. I didn't want more of his charity, not when I was
amongst the densest concentration of Twitter users in the
world, and not when I'd just explained my challenge on
live television to the third most populated country on the
planet. Somebody else must have heard my pleas, surely?
Short of carving my face onto the moon or revealing myself
to be the Second Coming, I couldn't do much more to draw
attention to my plight.

> **hallienoves** @twitchhiker I can take you to the airport!
> What time is your flight?
>
> *1:52 PM Mar 15th*

Yes! I had no idea who @hallienoves was but I was going
to hug her and kiss her, tongues if she requested. Exhale.
Relief. Relax! But not too much – my blasé attitude had
come close to sending me home. There was little more to
glean from Austin so I accepted the ride for half an hour
later and began to pack up my belongings – including the
promotional T-shirt Shea had asked me to wear on Good
Morning America. In return, I... Oh. My gift exchange had

broken down. In Wichita, Carrie had given me a copy of her magazine in exchange for my Kansas Jayhawks annual from the Lawrence Journal-World. Outside on the streets of Austin at four in the morning hadn't seemed like an ideal time to exchange gifts with Shea and Tyler, and there was too much interest in tequila and B. J. Novak for anybody to remember the previous evening. The exchange would have to skip a beat. I offered the magazine to Matt the non-Norwegian, who in return offered his beanie hat for my next host. He also had news for me.

'I've been tweeting Amber MacArthur and she's going to try and get you on net@night with Leo!'

Matt was beaming from ear to ear, at least until he recognised a face full of bewilderment staring back at him.

'Who? What's net@night when it's at home?'

Matt attempted to mask his faint disgust at my ignorance. He went on to explain that Leo Laporte was one of the most respected and influential technology authors and broadcasters in the world. Matt was convinced that appearing on the net@night webcast with Laporte and Amber MacArthur, a high profile web presenter, would provide bountiful support. But Laporte lived in Petaluma, a small city 60 kilometres north of San Francisco, and with no control over who would and wouldn't come to my aid, there was no guarantee I could reach a specific city on a given date, never mind an exact house number. But that was Matt all over – he had been beyond generous from the day that Twitchhiker had been announced, and he was doing everything he could to see me succeed.

One gruff manly hug between two Northerners later, and I left my host and hauled my bags out into the Texas sunshine. I'd been invisible to the thousands of conference attendees that milled about the streets, lost amongst the noise of SXSW, and my eventual saviour was a trainee librarian from north Austin. Helen (@hallienoves) had offered to help with accommodation several days earlier while I was still in Chicago but had now fulfilled the vital role of Texan taxi driver. We talked plenty, but I lost all track of our conversation after we stopped at a set of lights along 7th Street and spotted a figure on the sidewalk. He was a short chap, and young, perhaps in his early twenties, standing outside a car salesroom handing out leaflets. He was dressed in star-spangled paraphernalia that identified him as Uncle Sam – top hat, overcoat, white wig and matching stick-on goatee beard.

And he was blacked up.

Admittedly we were in the Deep South, and Texas was one of the original slave states that seceded from the Union before the American Civil War, so I was expecting to experience some ugly manifestation of racial intolerance. Yet Austin is liberal through and through, so a blacked-up Uncle Sam selling used cars really wasn't expected.

The remainder of the short journey to the airport passed without event and was perfectly comfortable, unlike the Southwest flight from Austin to San Diego, which was close to unbearable. Unrestricted seating on a full flight saw me wedged up against the bulkhead at the very back of the plane, in the middle seat. With my seat fixed upright, the snotty eight-year-old in front decided he would spend the flight continually reclining his seat to within a gnat's crotchet of my nose. For his trouble he received the occasional and sudden blow to the back of his headrest.

I was greeted at San Diego by a delayed flight, and joined in the waiting area by a full assembly of screaming children, and stared at throughout by a grizzled, wild-eyed cowboy, dressed in black from top to toe, including his ten-gallon hat. It allowed plenty of time to fix yet another critical oversight – my travel plans between San Francisco Airport and the city's Hayes Valley district, where my host Christen (@thumbble) would be waiting for me. The nature of all things interconnected rescued me once more; the offer of a ride came from a Wichitan called Eric, who had just moved to San Francisco and was aware of Twitchhiker through his friends and colleagues back in Kansas.

> **twitchhiker** If anybody has a number for @ericwestbrook, could they give him a call and let him know I'm suffering airline FAIL?
>
> *10:41 PM Mar 16th*

The flight delay slowly crept from fifty minutes to nearly three hours, pushing my expected arrival time to midnight, and I became increasingly nervous at stretching the goodwill of my hosts to a point that they might tell me to get stuffed. And it seemed I was right; when I eventually appeared in the luggage hall at San Francisco three hours late, there was nobody to greet me. Ten minutes turned into twenty, turned into thirty, and there was no sign of Eric.

Eventually, a car sped out of the darkness and shrieked to a halt at Arrivals. The driver asked if I was Paul, and that was all I needed to hear. I threw my bags on the back seat and jumped in without another thought on the matter. He could have been some mentalist who'd followed my real-time panic attack on Twitter, but fortunately he was Eric, a brown-haired, brown-eyed, good-looking web developer in a flannel shirt and ripped-up jeans.

The streets of San Francisco were quiet as we drove north along the Bayshore Freeway, forking onto the Central Freeway and then onto Market Street, before arriving in the Hayes Valley neighbourhood in the heart of the city. I was nearly four hours late, but Christen and her boyfriend Josh were kind enough to answer when I rang the bell of their apartment. It was a one-bedroom place, which is why I was sleeping on an air mattress in the living room. The late hour saw little more than brief pleasantries – Christen and Josh returned to bed and I crashed out on the floor. Fifteen days down, fifteen to go, and I'd made it to the West Coast of America. All that stood between me and Campbell Island was 11,000 kilometres of the largest ocean on earth.

Chapter 22

Day Sixteen – Monday 16 March

I'd visited San Francisco five years earlier during my honeymoon, or rather *non*-honeymoon, following my non-marriage to my non-wife in Las Vegas. It was a week of confused, conflicting emotions; Jane was distant and inconsolable, and I was mostly drunk and equally broken. We'd taken the city tour, kicked about the rubble of Alcatraz and slouched opposite one another in cafes and restaurants, unable to offer words that mattered. It rained most days, that cold damp rain that creeps inside your bones, which complemented the mood. My return was under far more positive circumstances, and so much had changed in the intervening years – our eventual marriage, and my diagnosis.

The airbed provided the best night's sleep of my trip to date. When I woke, my legs were horribly sore from the previous evening's flights, but otherwise my mood was buoyant that day, even though I saw very little of the city. I'd realised that would have to be the case before my trip began – trying to work while travelling invariably meant staying behind in class while the other kids played rounders outside. So when my hosts left for work, I sat about in my underwear from early morning until late afternoon, MacBook perched on my naked legs, super-heating my thighs and gently sterilising my sperm. I was spending two or three hours every couple of days replying to Twitter users, answering emails from journalists and writing posts for my Twitchhiker blog. That I was unable to write about my experiences until after I'd visited a location served to confuse myself and other fans of linear continuity. I would review events three days after the fact while planning the next three days ahead, effectively eradicating any notion of chronology I once possessed and adding to the already surreal nature of the journey.

The next leg of my journey presented itself early afternoon – two Twitter users had put their virtual heads together to invite me to Petaluma. A very insistent lady called Anastasia (@AccessInspirati) was adamant she would chauffeur me to and around Petaluma, a city to the north of San Francisco, while another called Kate (@kateHamptonInn) offered two nights at the Hampton Inn and Suites at the nearby Rohnert Park. I had to stay on in San Francisco for a second night before Anastasia could collect me; fortunately Christen and Josh were happy to see the airbed remain inflated for a second night.

I'd also been offered a flight to Portland in Oregon, further north towards the Canadian border, but time was becoming precious and I had to make the impossible leap across the ocean; I chose to stick close to San Francisco because if a flight appeared, it was likely to be from there or further south, in Los Angeles. My best option, and my only option, was to potter up and down the coast, bide my time and hope for something extraordinary to happen once more. After all, there's a very good reason why nobody holds the record for swimming the Pacific, and I wasn't about to smear myself in goose fat and attempt it.

> **twitchhiker** @AccessInspirati Hello, have decided to take the plunge – I'd love to take you up on your offer of a trip to Sonoma County!
>
> *2:41 PM Mar 16th*

'Why does every street around here smell of pot?' I asked Christen as we walked through the Mission District that evening. The answer, quite simply, was because we were walking through the Mission District, and it smelled of pot quite a lot of the time. Our destination was a bar called Zeitgeist, the venue for yet another meet-up with local Twitter users. I hadn't taken in much of the scenery on my arrival the previous evening, but as Christen and I walked south through the Mission, I was reacquainted with the crucial elements of the more colourful San Franciscan neighbourhoods. Hills? Check. BART? Check. Ranting drunks? Yep. The heady aroma of drugs in all directions? You betcha.

The Mission is the city's oldest neighbourhood; the building from which the name is derived, is the Mission San Francisco de Asís, founded by the Franciscan Order in 1776 to convert Native Americans to Christianity. The past fifty years have seen thousands of families from Mexico and Central America settle there, and so the neighbourhood is littered with independent businesses – cafes, markets, restaurants and taquerías. The relentless and universal force of gentrification has diluted the fiercely Latin vibe and raised real estate prices, but it's still a zesty, colourful place, more so when there's drinking to be done.

We passed underneath the Central Freeway on our way to Valencia Street and arrived at Zeitgeist, a busted-up shack of a dive bar populated by locals and drunks, and local drunks. We were joined at our picnic table in the backyard by other San Franciscan tweeps – including Jeff Scott, founder of the iPhone apps review site 148apps.com. He was a big guy, with a fine grey beard – like a giant, bearded badger – and together with Jeff's wife and @HeatherHAL, who arrived after a disappointing turnout at her book club, we drank many a real ale in Zeitgeist and watched our little corner of San Francisco get smashed out of its skull.

The evening was topped off with a mosey down Valencia Street, past a colourful jumble of both shopfronts and passers-by, to 16th Street and a Pakistani restaurant called Pakwan, which appeared to have arrived from 1979 entirely unscathed. Generic wooden furniture and kebab shop floor tiling, complemented by peach-toned walls and framed paintings produced by a colour-blind artist. None of us cared, because the food was outstanding and so cheap as to arouse suspicion. $6.99 for a chicken achar would usually include the feet, but we failed to identify any evidence of talons or scales to support our theory. Together with mushroom pilau, popadoms, naan bread and a glass of mango lassi, it was a majestic meal that left us all quietly aching with satisfaction. Except for the mango lassi – it tasted like a glass of flu. My belt was definitely going to have to loosen another notch, and my investment in sweatpants was looking ever more likely.

Day Seventeen – Monday 16 March

'Do I have to wear it? Now?' asked Christen, holding the multicoloured beanie hat as if she'd fished it out of a latrine.

'Don't worry, it's clean – and yes, right now,' I said. 'I'd like a photograph of how delighted you are to receive it.'

Christen had the air of a woman altogether un-delighted about her gift from Matt in Austin, but humoured me anyway and wore both the hat and a smile which said 'show anybody that photo and I will kill you'.

Christen disappeared into her bedroom and emerged with a book that could rightly be described as a tome.

'You've heard of *The Rule of Four*, right?' asked Christen.

'Nope.'

'Oh, well it was written by an alumnus from my high school. It was a pretty big deal in the States.'

'It's a big book,' I observed. Thankfully I'd be able pass it straight on to my next host when she arrived, rather than cram it in amongst my dirty washing.

Anastasia (@AccessInspirati) arrived shortly after lunchtime to pick me up. She was older than me, refined and very gracious, Mediterranean in appearance with dark eyes and olive skin. A wife, mother and businesswoman working in the travel industry, Anastasia bundled me into her SUV and away we headed north to Petaluma, an hour's drive from San Francisco. My host agreed to indulge me in a spot of sightseeing, so after traversing the Golden Gate Bridge, we pulled into the parking lot at the northern exit and delighted in the sight of San Francisco Bay, the distant skyscrapers of downtown sliced in half by a blade of silver mist. The bridge was completed in 1937 – before it was built, the Golden Gate Ferry Company operated across the bay, connecting the city and Marin County to the north. The day before it was officially opened to public vehicles, San Franciscans were invited to walk across the bridge. Over 200,000 residents did so, many keen to complete the distance in some unique and memorable way – on roller skates, stilts, tap-dancing from end to end. I'd wanted to take in the view because I'd recently met somebody who had been amongst the crowds on that day, 27 May 1937. The chaplain at my wedding in Brooklyn, Beth Lamont, was barely eight years old when she skipped across the bay – a kiss with history a lifetime ago.

We cruised north along Interstate 101 across fresh green hills that rolled and swayed across the landscape, and into Petaluma. Like San Francisco and other prominent communities on the West Coast, the region was pioneered by the Spanish in the eighteenth century. Unlike San Francisco, Petaluma survived the 1906 earthquake relatively unscathed (four-fifths of the buildings in San Francisco were destroyed by the quake and the fires that followed), and as a result the old-town homes and buildings of the city became a popular location for Hollywood, its streets forever consigned to celluloid in blockbusters such as *American Graffiti*, *Basic Instinct* and *Howard the Duck*.

Our first port of call was a single-storey house in an anonymous suburban street, unworthy of mention except for the fact that it was the headquarters of net@night. With little effort or need to orchestrate events, I'd managed to make my scheduled appearance with Leo Laporte and Amber MacArthur, as Matt had arranged three days previously. I'd since discovered that Leo's TWiT.tv shows were so popular that many people would have paid serious money and indulged in deviant behaviour to appear in my place. His audience figures are stratospheric – 600,000 pairs of ears listen to his podcasts every week, and over two million fans watch the live webcasts every month. And at the heart of this incredibly successful and influential media operation? A study no bigger than a modest-sized bathroom, which was crammed floor-to-ceiling with PCs, laptops, professional cameras and monitors everywhere, mics, lighting rigs and wires. I took a seat in the tech bazaar and could see myself simultaneously from three different angles on a screen opposite, immediately recalling many a man's dread of trying on a shirt in the dressing rooms of Next while sporting a receding hairline.

'If it gets to the point where you can't get outta here, we'll get you outta here,' said Leo. 'If you could choose anywhere, where would you go?'

'I'd have to say Australasia,' I said, bluntly. 'That's where I need to get to.'

'And if you can't get a ticket to Australasia from here?'

'Then I'd need to get to somewhere I could.'

'How about Hawaii?' asked Leo.

'That'd be horrible. Why on earth would anyone want to go to Hawaii? That'd be a terrible place to be stuck.'

'Oh wait, is that sarcasm?' asked Amber.

> **twitchhiker** At the HQ of TWiT.tv. Twittering live while streaming live. Awesome is the word, I believe.
>
> *3:10 PM Mar 17th*

There was one last stop before the Hampton Inn: it was St Patrick's Day, so we drove into the centre of Petaluma and headed to Maguires on Kentucky Street. Outside, crowds slopped Guinness over the sidewalk and each other as they watched teenage girls in embroidered dresses perform Irish stepdance, the older gents gently mimicking the movements while attempting not to spill their pints, and amusing themselves no end at their failure to do so.

We headed upstairs to join Anastasia's husband and her two children, and their friend and fellow Twitter user Thom (@QuickAmusements) for dinner – a rich Irish spread of ham and potatoes, kale and gravy.

At the bar, the Guinness was flowing like, well, Guinness on St Patrick's Day, but I refrained from over-indulging. I'd celebrated St Patrick's Day in New York the previous year, where the bars were adamant that no drink be enjoyed without the addition of green food dye, an evening which concluded with me prolifically vomiting into a gutter. So in Petaluma I chose to raise only a pint or two of tar to the man of the hour, and held the dye. While I was waiting for the second, the thick-fisted gent next to me brayed at the bar as he flung a fourth shot of bourbon down his increasingly raw throat. I baulked at the mere thought of it. I was aware I'd spent a few too many evenings on the sauce – not because of a crippling dependency on alcohol, but through the desire of both my hosts and myself to celebrate every milestone of my journey. A night of sobriety would do me no harm, and I asked Anastasia if she could drive me to the hotel to check in. The Petalumans would have to drink themselves blind without me.

Day Eighteen – Wednesday 18 March

'It's morning!' hollered the sunshine through a nick in the curtains of my room. It certainly was, I agreed, as I sat up in bed to welcome my third day in northern California. Since I had accepted her offer to travel north of San Francisco to Sonoma County, Anastasia had arranged a full itinerary of sightseeing and wine tasting, a day-long escapade through the spectacular landscape of Sonoma Valley. I didn't really have the time to be enjoying such a decadent jolly, but I didn't have anywhere else to be. I'd decided to stay close to San Francisco in the hope of the offer of a flight to New Zealand from Los Angeles; the majority of airlines flew trans-Pacific routes to Australasia from there. My reluctance to consider other offers in lieu of that hope was irritating the good people of Oregon:

TravelCoosBay @twitchhiker, maybe you missed my offer, we can bring you to Coos Bay Oregon! And help you get to Portland after that.

7:16 PM Mar 17th

Whether or not I accepted the offer was becoming increasingly academic – I had to depart Petaluma the next day otherwise I'd be booking a one-way flight to the UK.

twitchhiker I have one offer of a trip North to Oregon; if there's no second offer by 6pm tonight, I'll have to take it.

7:01 AM Mar 18th

There were plenty of other individuals being very vocal about Twitchhiker, but hardly in a manner that could be considered helpful. Since the beginning, a small group of Twitter users and commentators had made a concerted effort to make life unpleasant for me. On the same day I'd announced the project in February, one Twitter user actively demanded that people refuse to assist me, believing I wouldn't 'suffer' enough in the name of charity as I might if I attempted to run the length of Africa or have my face chewed off by crocodiles while swimming the course of the Amazon. New York journalist Jeff Koyen published a blog post offering $500 if somebody deliberately led me into a situation that resulted in my death. Delightful. That morning I found a number of comments on my blog denouncing my efforts as fraudulent, calling me to account over a journey that cost more to fund than it had so far raised for charity. Not only had the comments been posted on my blog, but on several other websites that had promoted Twitchhiker. Somebody was investing a substantial amount of time and effort into discrediting me.

Instead of rising above it, I took the bait. I totted up the costs of the trip so far, proved they were far less than the amount of money raised for the charity, and went on to play the troll at his own game, by monetising the global awareness that *charity: water* had received. How much would a thirty-second advertising spot on *Good Morning America* have cost? Tens of thousands of dollars, probably. The public doesn't spontaneously become aware of a charity and then donate to it; even charities have to pay to market themselves, and individuals have to spend money to raise money – if you're going to run a marathon, somebody has to buy your trainers. Go screw yourself, was my considered response.

An hour before I was due to leave the Hampton Inn and take the tour of Sonoma Valley, the tweet I'd wanted to see so badly arrived on my screen.

alienelvis @twitchhiker would you like to take Flight 712 from Oakland to Los Angeles leaving after lunch tomorrow?

8:23 AM Mar 18th

twitchhiker @alienelvis That's brilliant, thank you! Tomorrow would be perfect.

8:35 AM Mar 18th

Anastasia had already offered to take me wherever I needed to go the following day, and Oakland was only across the bay from San Francisco. I exchanged details with @alienelvis and we spoke on the phone; his name was Ben, an older-sounding gentleman with a gentle Californian accent. He was happy to arrange my flight, collect me from the airport and provide a bed for the night at his apartment to the north of Los Angeles, in the San Fernando Valley. So LA was in the bag – there was nothing more I could do, except wait and hope that Twitter would somehow provide the means to fling me clean across the Pacific towards my target.

It was a wait of approximately thirty-four minutes.

AIRNZUSA @twitchhiker Have you made it to New Zealand yet? We can help you from the West Coast.

9:09 AM Mar 18th

My eyes widened and I squealed through a grin as wide as the sky. Air New Zealand! My fingers dashed out a response, a tiny patter of adrenalin exploded in my chest. It was an offer to put me not only in the same hemisphere as Campbell Island, but the same territory! Tweets flew back and forth in a frenzy, and the deal was done. I'd fly from Los Angeles on Saturday afternoon, and arrive in Auckland on… Monday morning? That wasn't right, was it? Why did it take over a day to fly between the two cities?

Of course the answer was that it didn't; the flight was fourteen hours end-to-end, but en route it crossed the International Date Line. The US West Coast was eight hours behind GMT, but New Zealand was thirteen hours ahead (the extra hour was due to daylight saving time). The net effect of this chronological debacle was that, although my flight would land Sunday morning from LA's point of view, it'd be early Monday morning in Auckland. I was effectively losing a day's worth of travel and I'd have just a week remaining in which to complete the challenge.

I was still swimming in delirium from the speed at which my plans had progressed when Anastasia arrived at the hotel with our host Mimi from California Wine Tours (@ CalWineTours).

'I've got it!' I fizzed, rushing to embrace Anastasia as she entered the lobby. 'The flight to New Zealand, I've got it!'

'Oh my, how wonderful!' exclaimed the ever-gracious Anastasia, unfazed by the bear-hug from the stranger she'd first met barely eighteen hours earlier.

From the Hampton Inn, we wound through Sonoma Valley in a ridiculously well-endowed coach, packed with gadgets, champagne and wine. I sat on the leather-upholstered seating, champagne flute in one hand, iPod Touch lapping up the on-board Wi-Fi in the other. It felt preposterously indulgent but my plans for the next day were set, so I decided to enjoy my good fortune and not play the martyr. I'd scoffed snails in Paris and barbecue in Texas, so to visit Sonoma Valley and not indulge in a splash or two of vino and bubbles would have been rude, I told myself.

The sky was endlessly blue, accompanied by the sort of startling sunshine seen in the UK for a fortnight in August (and only then during the two weeks you're away with the family in Magaluf), and Sonoma Valley had splashed out on a view that caught the breath in my chest. Gentle hills of impossibly green hue swept either side of the road, with each turn a landscape more eye-widening and lush than the last. It was a mellow, easy-going day, both for me and the world outside.

Our first stop was the Imagery Estate Winery where Mimi introduced me to a pair of local oenophiles, Daedalus Howell and Chris Sawyer. Now you simply cannot meet a man christened Daedalus and let it pass without comment. Long slick black hair, dressed top-to-toe in black, a soul patch hanging beneath his bottom lip – Daedalus was a full-on, good-looking hipster who'd lived the media life in LA and relocated north to become the official cultural ambassador for Sonoma County. All things considered, a man with such an outlandish name, dressed in black on a beltingly hot day and with idiotic facial hair, should have been nothing short of a prize tit. He wasn't. He was a stupidly handsome guy who liked fine wine, made short films and was utterly charming to me from the word go. Bastard.

Chris Sawyer was something of a legend in wine tasting circles, a writer and sommelier to the stars that visited the region, so he was no doubt aghast to find himself educating a beer-swilling Northerner who could barely distinguish white wine from red, and who thought rosé was produced by mixing the two in the bottle. Together with Anastasia and Mimi, we stood at the regal bar area of the winery, where I swirled and smelled and swished and swallowed and detected next to none of the subtle textures Chris could.

'Hold it by the stem, don't cup the bowl in your palm,' instructed Chris. 'It can change the taste of the wine.'

'Got it,' I replied. 'Do I have to spit it out, by the way?'

'You don't have to,' said Daedalus.

'What happens if I don't? Does it impair the taste of the next wine we try?'

'Not really,' said Daedalus. 'You just get drunk quicker.'

'This one is packed with blackcurrants and berries,' continued Chris, 'notes of liquorice, and maybe a hint of tobacco leaf, too.'

Like many people, I'd long suspected the wine-tasting profession to be little more than a well-executed ruse to embarrass non-connoisseurs who splashed their palate with any old bottle of £3.99 pigswill. That's not what wine tasting is about, however, and Daedalus and Chris made the point very clearly; what matters is your opinion – do you like the taste, or don't you? Enthusing about the intricacies of wine is no different to how we critique music, or football, or politics. It's not a hard and fast science because every tongue is different, but you can train your palate to pick through the textures and tannins in that mouthful of liquid.

From the Imagery Estate, we travelled together to the Kunde Estate Winery; anybody who knows anything about wine will know that to meet Jeff Kunde in the flesh is something of an honour. As I knew nothing about wine whatsoever, he was just another guy running an award-winning century-old family-owned business in the Sonoma Valley. The estate was purchased by Louis Kunde in 1904, although the earliest vines that are still harvested were planted in 1882 by a gentleman called John Drummond, a winemaking pioneer in these parts. The estate's pedigree meant I wasn't going to pick up a £3.99 bottle of red there – the 2005 Reserve Zinfandel cost more than I'd spend on a steak dinner for two. We toured high into the hills of the estate with Jeff as our personal guide. I showed him the wonders of Twitter on my iPod Touch, he poured wine and explained the history of the knotted and gnarled century vines on his estate. I may have profited most from the arrangement.

'So on the screen I can see what people around the world are talking about,' I explained.

'Uh huh,' said Jeff.

'And if I tap *this*, I can see if they're talking to me.'

'Uh huh.'

'Then I can reply and talk to them.'

'Paul, that's great,' said Jeff. 'But I have no idea what you just showed me.'

While we drank and baked in the Sonoma sun, both Jeff and Chris performed a party trick involving a screw-top bottle; the end of the bottle is rolled along the arm at speed, from the inside of the elbow to the wrist, unscrewing the top and spinning it up into the air, where it is caught in an altogether impressive manner. Of course it was fun to have the clueless Englishman attempt their well-practised turn, and as might be expected I spent the rest of the day wearing a rather expensive bottle of the 2006 Chardonnay.

The day rolled on into the afternoon, and our coach rolled on into Sonoma, the tone never once dipping below thoroughly and indecently enjoyable. We indulged in an epic $10 beer and burger at the Big 3 diner, had an interview at the offices of the *Sonoma Index-Tribune*, and took up the suggestions from Twitter users that we take refreshment at the Swiss Hotel on the broad and peaceful Sonoma Square. Anastasia, Mimi, Daedalus and I took seats on the porch, ordered up beers and I slowly turned a gentle shade of pink in the late-afternoon sun. I had a silly, kid-ish grin slapped across my face – I'd stumbled upon the playground of northern California's rich and famous, where Daedalus introduced me to further big shots in winemaking, people like Jeff Bundschu and Chris Benziger. The evening was warm, the chatter was friendly and Sonoma was a wonderful, wonderful place to be. Throughout the trip I'd occasionally daydreamed about whether I'd pass through a place I'd like to live. There had been a couple, but Sonoma Valley probably edged them out. If it was good enough for

John Lasseter and George Lucas, it was rudely adequate for Paul Smith.

The beer was flowing a little too freely and easily when I received the call from New Zealand. Could I be available for a pre-recorded interview for Campbell Live, a national news programme in New Zealand? In an hour? Um. I'd slowly pickled myself over the previous eight hours and wasn't confident I could get through four minutes without saying something inappropriate, or without slurring. But it was pre-recorded, and if Twitter had indirectly created this opportunity to rustle up support in New Zealand, I had to take it. Steve the freelance cameraman from San Francisco was to meet me at my room in the Hampton Inn in an hour, so I said goodbye to my new millionaire winemaker friends, and to Daedalus. On reflection it was a fine name, and fitting of the unique individual it was bequeathed upon.

The interview wasn't a complete disaster. I appeared slightly sunburnt from my day romping around wineries and supping cold beer at the Swiss Hotel, and I did ramble on an awful lot, to the point where news anchor John Campbell was forced to interrupt me and conclude the interview. I'm glad he did – I'd been talking for so long I'd forgotten the point of his question.

Day Nineteen – Thursday 19 March

'Ouch,' said my head out loud, as my eyes blinked open and engaged with my brain. Not too sore, but dim and fuzzy, like a broken television with a screen full of static. A prescribed course of a long lukewarm shower, coffee and orange juice helped to alleviate the rhythmic pounding of my temples. I'd ignored the wisdom of many an old fishwife: 'Wine before beer makes you feel queer, beer before wine and you'll feel fine', although I'd probably polished off enough beer during my travels to make a nonsense of the second point too.

Thursday morning saw me take up the offer from Ben (@alienelvis) and fly from Oakland to Los Angeles. My exchanging of gifts between tweeps had fallen down in a few places, through forgetfulness or due to the speed at which some encounters had occurred. It had managed to reach Sonoma, at least; Anastasia already had the hardback book from Christen, and upon me Anastasia bestowed Clo the Cow, a fat-faced Friesian with a toothy grin and the mascot of the Clover Stornetta dairy farms in North California. The cow would have presented far less difficulty packing than the *New York Times* bestseller.

To the airport! We crossed the San Rafael Bridge from Marin County to Richmond and sauntered through the lunchtime traffic, down the east coast of San Francisco bay on a bright and clear spring day. We arrived at Oakland Airport, and Anastasia morphed from host and friend into my mother, maternal instincts kicking in as she hugged me and wished me farewell.

'Are you sure you have everything? You've not left anything in your room?'

'Yeah, think I got everything.'

'Your passport and ticket, you've got them too?'

'Yes,' I replied, patting the pocket of my messenger bag in a deliberately exaggerated manner to reassure her that, despite all behaviour to the contrary, I wasn't a total idiot.

'OK. And can you tweet once you land so I know you've arrived safely?'

'Of course I can!'

After delaying me in San Diego on Sunday evening, Southwest Airlines were spitting-keen to ruin my itinerary further, by overselling the flight to Los Angeles. It meant more delays, more shuffling of bodies, more busybodies in uniforms herding weary passengers here, there and every bloody where. When would the flight take off, I enquired? You'll have to wait and see, was the curt reply. When will I know if I'm even on the flight, I fired back? You'll have to wait and see. Two hours later and the plane was still on the ground due to sheer popularity. There was nothing I could do, except eat overpriced tacos in the departure area.

After Southwest came to their collective senses and realised that too many people wanting to board the same flight wasn't a watertight reason to stop most of them boarding, I took my seat and departed for the City of Angels. It was the briefest of hops down the California coast, barely an hour between the two cities, and waiting for me at the exit in LAX was Ben, a giant of a man in his fifties, a former software engineer and lecturer with a face full of stories; the crow's feet around his eyes told tales of laughter and fun. Although Ben lived in the San Fernando Valley, we took in a more scenic route along Malibu Beach. At least it would have been if the freeway hadn't been flanked by fog – we saw nothing that even hinted at the ocean beyond, except the rear entrance of beachside residences costing a million or five.

A few minutes inland, and we were driving along Mulholland Highway. The chewed-up gridlock of LA could have been on another world; no row upon row of crawling tail lights, in fact barely any traffic at all. Ben pulled over, and I stood and gawped at the valleys and green knuckles of mountain to rival the Lake District. Was this really Los Angeles? Or round the corner from Ullswater?

After the previous day of decadence, the evening was spent at Ben's apartment in the valley, typing away and watching appalling American television commercials interrupted by the occasional minute or two of programmes. Ben was a divorcee who lived frugally; the two-bedroom apartment was somewhat claustrophobic and cluttered; the threadbare scraps of carpet complemented the decrepit sofa. My heart sank further at the sight of the brutalised mattress in the spare room that was my bed. At least I wasn't curled up in a downtown doorway – and I certainly couldn't find fault with Ben's generous nature. Through his personal beliefs in the power of karma, and because it seemed like a fun thing to do, he had bankrolled my flight from Oakland to Los Angeles, fed me in Malibu, proved a jovial, intelligent, larger-than-life character throughout and welcomed me into his home.

It was a place to rest, nothing more. In less than forty-eight hours I'd be in the air once more and crossing the Pacific Ocean. I was closing in on Campbell Island.

At least, I thought I was. The events of the next morning would throw everything into doubt.

Chapter 23

Day Twenty – Friday 20 March

The San Fernando Valley is massive. Really quite huge. Home to two million people, more than half of Los Angeles' land lies within the valley – geography fanatics would note that Malta could comfortably fit twice over. It's less a sleepy suburban community to the real razzle-dazzle, more a city in its own right, and indeed has attempted to secede from the rest of Los Angeles in recent years. Many of LA's major film and television companies are based there, including Walt Disney, and nine out of ten legal US pornographic films are filmed in the valley. And I was in amongst this throbbing throng of innocence and sex, unaware of its proud twin traditions of world-famous animation and felching for the camera.

I lay on my tired mattress amongst the clutter in Ben's spare room, hemmed in by broken and unloved furniture, crates of trinkets and oddities buried in dust. The valley had woken early, bathed in orange-roast sunshine and the shudder of pneumatic drills – 7 a.m. was apparently an acceptable time to start reducing sidewalks and freeway to rubble. The bare windowpanes exposed my lair to the outside world, there were no curtains or blinds to stall the sunlight. Neither was there air-conditioning; every stretch of my skin was crawling with oozy, oily sweat. I hadn't appreciated how good I'd had it up until then, even though I'd expected to find myself in places far worse.

I'd taken advantage of Ben's washing machine the evening before, so after rising from my mattress I slipped into my first set of fresh underwear in three days. Sinking into Ben's knackered sofa, I prodded the laptop into life and quickly picked over the lengthy list of emails. Interview requests, editors enquiring as to when the articles I'd promised them would be filed, or even started, and an email from a PR company in the UK that worked with Tourism New Zealand. The PR people had received a message from the country's official tourist board, and in turn contacted me. It was far from good news; in fact, it was heartbreaking. The email from the Kiwis rated my chances of reaching Campbell Island – my final destination since the beginning of the journey – as roughly zero:

'Campbell Island is an uninhabited island nature reserve 700 kilometres off the coast of NZ. One of the sub-Antarctic islands, it is actually a UNESCO World Heritage Site administered by The Dept of Conservation.

'It has no airstrip, and can only be reached by ship. It is three days at sea from Invercargill (at the bottom of the South Island). The only boats that go there are occasional fishing boats, and tour operator Heritage Expeditions – their next trip to the island is in December.

'As the island is so ecologically important, (even if he found a way to get there) he would need a DOC permit to visit the island (which he wouldn't get in a week).

'There is no way he'd get there by helicopter either. The only time we've heard of a helicopter go there is on a 'daring' rescue in 1992 when a DOC ranger was attacked by a shark while snorkelling off the coast.'

So helicopters were ten a penny for idiots choosing to swim in shark-infested waters, but not for daring modern-day adventurers? I'd known it was a UNESCO World Heritage Site from day one; I hadn't appreciated that meant a lengthy application process if I wanted to visit. Yes, it was remote, even in relation to New Zealand, but I hadn't realised that no vessels passed by at all outside the summer months, and without the ability to bend time I couldn't wait until December. The facts weren't a surprise. I hadn't deliberately ignored the scope of the challenge, but hoped that the cosmos would continue finding order amongst the chaos and create opportunities for me. It was the first time somebody had told me that I should expect to fail.

'We suggest he sets his sights on another island – Stewart Island. It's on the way to Campbell Island, has about 400 inhabitants, and is also home to New Zealand's newest national park. There are also lots of little islands off the coast of Stewart Island, including the Muttonbird (Titi) Islands.'

What? They were attempting to fob me off with a different island, as if I wouldn't notice the difference. Of course I would. No, absolutely not. Stewart Island sounded all very nice and pleasant, but I couldn't give up on Campbell Island

yet. With nine days to go, I couldn't move the goalposts –
why would anybody continue to support me if I changed the
rules? Ben appeared in a dressing gown and towel, grunted
his salutations and shuffled into the bathroom. I chewed my
lip, eyeballed the email for several minutes more, reading it
over and over again, each time becoming a little more upset,
a little more angry. They would have me get so close to that
damned island, but not close enough for it to matter.

Ben was relaxed about me staying a second night, but I
wanted to see more of the city rather than mope about the
apartment like a scorned child. I took to Twitter to find me
a home for the evening, and Twitter duly obliged:

> **patricktoneill** @twitchhiker welcome to LA, twitchhiker.
> Photo shoots, house parties and Hollywood await. Oh, and
> a place to stay. With a view.
>
> *9:27 AM Mar 20th*

Sold to the man I'd never met before. I had no idea whether
it was LA bravado and bullshit or a genuine offer to sample
the Hollywood high life, but I accepted it without a second
thought and made arrangements with the tweep called
Patrick, before heading out into the city for lunch with Ben.

We parked up on Gardner Street, and walked the short
distance south onto Sunset Boulevard. There were lazy palm
trees every few metres, under a dusty blue sky that yellowed
towards the horizon. What was surprising about LA was
the skyline's lack of obvious razzmatazz – the buildings
along Sunset were low and cluttered, not a single building
in sight was taller than two storeys. Without the restrictions

of mountains or seas, the city has sprawled in all directions; there's no need to raise fifty-storey towers on every corner when land isn't so scarce. Of course there are skyscrapers in downtown Los Angeles, but they're corporate penis extensions that nobody visits outside office hours, and so don't count. Instead you drive down Hollywood and Sunset Boulevards, along the cross streets on Fairfax and La Brea, and you find street after street of lazy squat buildings, plenty of them ramshackle in appearance. Film studios for music videos and commercials are tucked away amongst the residential roads, while the main thoroughfares are chocked with stores and restaurants.

We took lunch at Cheebo, a favourite of Ben's, and I eyed up a menu that announced 'organic dishes, free of nitrates and hormones!' I hadn't realised I'd been stuffing my face with nitrates up until that point, and as far as a selling point for a restaurant was concerned, a lack of polyatomic ions hardly seemed to be a deal-breaker. Unlike, say:

'NO BODY PARTS. NO TIGERS. NO KILLER BEES.'

Now that was a more exciting food policy; easier to police in the kitchens. I certainly couldn't spot a rogue nitrate in my fusilli puttanesca, but I'd be delighted to know my meal was prepared by a chef willing to ward off killer bees. You're welcome, Cheebo.

It was a squeeze at the table, the restaurant already full of LA stereotypes doing lunch – the gossip girls and their Gucci accessories, the budding actor talking up his part, the British art director who thinks he has enough swagger

253

round town to carry off a well 'ard, mockney, Ray Winstone impression.

Pepperoni pizza and fusilli puttanesca devoured in the comfort of a nitrate-and-killer-bee-free environment, Ben chauffeured me onto my drop-off point. For his trouble I presented my host with Anastasia's stuffed cow called Clo, and in return received a blue Indian shawl. Ben was a deeply spiritual man, with an open mind and a kind heart. Life hadn't been too smooth for him, but his faith in the universe and cosmic karma was unwavering. I'd never seen quite so much happiness expressed in a man's eyes before.

Patrick arrived at our meeting point on Wilshire Boulevard in a black Porsche 911. He was a highly successful 30-something-year-old creative director with global advertising agency TBWA\Chiat\Day. Blonde hair, lantern jaw, sun-kissed and handsome – four qualities people use to describe me only upon offer of payment. I wasn't staying with Patrick that evening; he'd instead booked me into the well-to-do Chamberlain Hotel in West Hollywood. Of course I was grateful, but it didn't matter any more. I'd slept on airbeds, mattresses and sofas, and crawled between crisp linen in five-star hotels, and after three weeks, I'd stopped distinguishing between the humble and the excessive. The room was vast and ornately decorated, in a blue-ash palette that hasn't been favoured much since the mid 80s. And yes, it had a power shower and five too many pillows on a queen-sized bed that was no doubt stuffed with the shorn locks of

1,000 newborn lambs. I didn't care whether the next bed had a mini-bar within arm's reach or a view, because every time my routine was the same; I'd work, I'd sleep, I'd wash and I'd leave an unspecified amount of my clothing in the wardrobe for the cleaner to discover several hours after I'd left the state; I was missing a T-shirt and another pair of socks.

Patrick also made good on his tweeted promise of parties. After picking me up in West Hollywood, we cruised down Hollywood Boulevard, another main thoroughfare, wide and flanked by low-level buildings, and bathed in lurid neon.

'You good to go a little crazy tonight?' enquired Patrick. 'Have a few beers, meet a few people?'

When was I not?

'Absolutely, wherever you want to go.'

'Well, I did have this invite to a party that Eva Mendes is going to be at,' name-dropped Patrick, 'but I missed the RSVP date for the guest list; it was last week or something.'

'So we're not going there?' I asked, confused.

'No, we'll go, I'll phone a few people,' said Patrick, very nonchalantly. 'I'll know somebody who can get us in.'

And he did. Past the crowds at Grauman's Chinese Theatre with an unscheduled stop within sight of the Capitol Records building to check directions, we arrived at an LA Fashion Week event at the Confederacy Boutique. Outside, a throng of people sold one another on their latest projects, air-kissing and squealing in sycophantic tones that had me scouring the sidewalk for a half-brick. They were all impeccably dressed and presented, models and actors and executives with not a hair out of place and teeth white as a nun's conscience. And there was me, wearing that same jumper and pair of stinking brown trainers I'd worn every other day for the past three weeks.

We mingled amongst the masses inside and I drank away my lack of self-confidence, slowly relaxing into the mire of shallow bullshit that permeated the air. Then the squealy, yappy chatter reached fever pitch, causing permanent hearing loss to a colony of bats in the Hollywood Hills, and a huddle of well-groomed bodies stampeded to the entrance. We'd been joined at the party by Eva Mendes and Liv Tyler – Hollywood had truly arrived in my Los Angeles. Mendes looked like a well-made-up housewife in a white flour bag, but Liv – Liv was stunning. And tall. Wow, she was tall. A blue-eyed beauty, she was the girl for me. I made the schoolboy error of tweeting the details of our guests, and of course everyone on Twitter demanded proof. If they couldn't see it, they yelled, it didn't happen. Damn. I wasn't nearly drunk enough to ask A-list actresses for a snapshot and I'd have left it there, if Patrick hadn't convinced me that Liv Tyler would be sympathetic to my story, having once lived a hippie lifestyle and the like. Uh huh. I gulped down a bottle or three's worth of Dutch courage, fought back my bladder's insistence on popping to the toilet yet again and walked up to Liv Tyler. Liv bloody Tyler.

'Hello, excuse me, Liv?'

'Yes, hi!'

'Hello Liv. My name's Paul – you don't know me, but I'm hitchhiking around the world and–' 'Hitchhiking? That's so cool! Nobody hitchhikes anymore! Tell me all about it!'

Unreal. I was talking to Liv Tyler and she wanted me to talk to her.

'Really? Oh, OK, so I'm hitchhiking around the world using Twitter, and–'

'Twitter?'

'Yes, Twitter!'

'What's Twitter?'

'It's a social media network on the Internet that–'

'Oh. Right.' Instead of maintaining eye contact, her gaze began darting across the faces of friends for an exit. Our worlds had collided and smashed one another to teeny tiny pieces. To be fair to Liv, she humoured me for a good couple of minutes longer than necessary, and didn't call security when I asked for a photo to prove the naysayers wrong.

We waved goodbye to Eva, Liv and assorted stars from *24* and – as we walked out through the front door – Jessica Alba, and departed for a house party in Hollywood Hills. The occasion was the birthday of Patrick's friend, clearly the wealthy sort who had money to splash out on valet parking for her guests. It seems like a ridiculous extravagance, but in a city without a reliable or widespread public transport network, if you want to throw a party then you've got to cater for drivers.

More air-kissing, more bombastic drivel about music video projects that were going to be so explosive they'd blow brains clean out of noses (my interpretation, not theirs), but there on the patio at the rear of the house, sat talking to a friend, was a woman I recognised immediately. Holy Moly, it was Jorja Fox – Sara Sidle in *CSI* – right there in front of me! Buoyed by my earlier success plus several beers and shorts in the meantime, I loitered with intent, waiting for a break in the conversation, ready to introduce myself and refrain from dribbling as I gushed with praise.

It's possible that at this point I appeared to be a wild-eyed, leering madman, which may have come across as vaguely threatening. Apparently sensing that I was standing a little too close to be innocently passing by, *CSI*'s Sara Sidle stood up and... well... ran away from me. She wasn't so rude as to sprint, but Jorja Fox certainly didn't take her time to spare my feelings, and legged it into the house through the back door.

There wasn't really a positive to glean from the encounter, except that the police were never called. The actress who spent her days handling severed heads, dismembered torsos and mutilated organs had fled in terror at the sight of me. As claims to fame go, it was hardly up there with schmoozing with Liv Tyler.

Chapter 24

Day Twenty-one – Saturday 21 March

The flight from Los Angeles to Auckland would mean no Twitter contact for fourteen hours; fortunately there was no end to the support offered by the New Zealanders. Their newspapers had been following my progress since the day I announced Campbell Island as my intended destination; one of the first press features about Twitchhiker appeared in *The New Zealand Herald*. Together with other online coverage and my ruddy-faced appearance on national current affairs show *Campbell Live*, New Zealand appeared well prepared to receive the distant traveller.

Before Patrick had collected me from The Chamberlain on Saturday morning, I had a full itinerary stretching out to Tuesday, a full three days ahead for the first time in weeks. Air New Zealand was flying me across the Pacific later that day. A Twitter user called Mel (@proudkiwi) happened to be marketing manager of the SKYCITY Grand Hotel in Auckland city centre, and was adamant I rest my bones in comfort. Then there was Helen (@msbehaviour) who offered to collect me from the airport, even though my flight landed at the sleep-crippling time of 4 a.m. Alan at The Falls restaurant in Henderson (@THEFALLSNZ) wanted to shout me lunch, Jayson, the proprietor of The Wine Vault (@thewinevault), would throw a tweet-up on Monday evening, and Robert (@globtrav) bought a flight using his air miles to see me to Wellington on Tuesday evening.

Plenty of businesses, a few individuals – all of them ferociously keen. Despite the blunt refusal of Tourism New Zealand to entertain my folly, many others refused to give up on me.

It was by far the most colossal pastrami sandwich I had ever seen. Really quite huge. A dozen folded slices of pink peppered meat, book-ended by wedges of wholemeal bread. And then there was the side dish – thick, English-style fingers of hot fried potato, with gooey yellow cheddar oozed over them. Between the sandwich and cheese fries, I was lunching my way to a coronary. Patrick and I had stopped by Canter's Deli on Fairfax Avenue in West Hollywood. We'd made strenuous efforts to travel into the hills and marvel at the HOLLYWOOD sign that morning, but road closures, police incidents and an assortment of circular diversions made us retreat to the famous deli.

Everyone in Los Angeles knows Canter's, a family business founded in New Jersey. The Canter brothers arrived on the West Coast in 1931, and cold meats, lox and knishes have been served up in their name ever since. Monroe, Travolta, Cosby, Ali – all the stars have temporarily descended from the heavens to take a table amongst mere mortals and order a bowl of hot chicken soup in Canter's.

All very well for the celebrity crowd, but I hadn't travelled for three weeks and 15,000 kilometres to order soup. As I'd done throughout the trip, I sent followers photos of my beast of a meal, who proceeded to critique my lacklustre photography skills and predict my imminent death by gluttony, and to inform me they'd be joining us shortly. Wait, what?

saintblake @twitchhiker Please stay there... We're on our way!

12:23 PM Mar 21st

Somebody could tell where I was in central Los Angeles from a photograph of a sandwich? Unlikely, or so I thought. Barely halfway through the meal, our gum-chewing waitress returned to the table.

'Couple of guys at the front, they say they know you. OK if they come through?'

I looked at Patrick. Patrick looked back at me. He shrugged. I shrugged. The restaurant was busy, plenty of witnesses if trouble walked through the door.

'That's fine, they're friends, thanks.'

Through the archway, two men appeared. More boys, actually. Students, perhaps. One was tall, awkward in his stance, flat cap and glasses, the other was shorter with a strip of black beard hugging his chin. They were Jonathan (@clede) and Doug (@saintblake), and they were Twitchhiker groupies.

'So how did you find me?'

'We recognised the cover of the menu in one of your photos,' explained Doug.

'We weren't far away,' added Jonathan. 'We've been hanging out hoping to meet you since you arrived in the city.'

'Really?' I asked.

Really. The pair had been doggedly determined to track me down all morning, a relentless effort that had escaped my attention on Twitter:

clede @twitchhiker Where in LA are you? I'm in West Hollywood and would love to shake your hand before your flight!

10:14 AM Mar 21st

clede Anyone know where in LA the @twitchhiker is right now?

10:15 AM Mar 21st

clede @twitchhiker I'm at Fairfax and Santa Monica. You nearby?

10:18 AM Mar 21st

saintblake Trying to meet @twitchhiker before he leaves LA.

10:23 AM Mar 21st

Waiter, the champagne, for I have stalkers! I'm so Hollywood, darling! What do you mean, no bubbles? Very well, four flutes of your finest chicken soup!

They were breathless in their desire to meet the Twitchhiker in the flesh, and I hadn't the first clue what to say. We posed for a series of impromptu photos outside Canter's. The final shot was of Jonathan, Doug and myself arm-in-arm and performing high kicks for the camera. It was a thoroughly surreal but delightfully sweet experience.

Patrick and I waved off the two founding members (and indeed, the only members) of the Twitchhiker fan club, and bid farewell to Canter's Deli on our way to Los Angeles International Airport. With a couple of hours to kill, we cruised south through LA to the freeway, and east to Venice Beach. The boardwalk along the beachfront was thick with locals, gangs of kids, tourists and tricks and turns with tattoos, bustling stores and broken-down stalls screaming reggae music from knackered ghetto blasters and the occasional stray scent of marijuana, quite possibly emanating from those easy traders enjoying their reggae.

Since I was wearing my 'Don't Hassel The Hoff' T-shirt, it seemed only fitting I ignore the NO CLIMBING signs on the lifeguard towers and clamber up to adopt a steely pose befitting the bouffant knight-riding hero. The Pacific was subdued; its blue waters lapped the shore with little effort or intent. Lost amongst those waters, thousands of kilometres distant was a lonely slab of rock and shale, insignificant to nearly every other person on planet Earth. Would I ever reach its shores?

Finally, since it was only a short drive from the airport, Patrick suggested a tour of his office. I feigned excitement at the opportunity to inspect the kitchen facilities and vending machine selection, since it was clearly going to blow my mind clean through the top of my skull. Really? A tour of an office? And that was worth leaving the beach for?

It was no ordinary office, however; TBWA\Chiat\Day is one of the largest and most celebrated advertising agencies in the world. To prove the point, not only did they insist on inappropriate use of obliques, but their office wasn't an office. It was a warehouse, a maze of colour and shapes, with a sprawling indoor park, a full-size basketball court and, instead of cubicles, there were steel shipping containers, stacked one on top of the other, bright yellow, sliced in two to reveal workstations and meeting rooms. Certainly a far greater source of inspiration than a magnolia canteen and communal fridge stuffed full of out-of-date Müller Rice. Patrick and his colleagues produced advertising campaigns costing millions of dollars for the world's biggest brands – the likes of Apple, Pepsi and VISA. I was sickeningly jealous; I spent five years as a radio copywriter, and had the soul-sapping displeasure of working with jumped-up caravan salesmen and carpet remnant outlets, meaning I spent most meetings staring out the window and yearning for a career in Victorian coal mining.

'Mister Smith, can I ask you to wait over there please. Now, please.'

'Is there a problem with my ticket?'

'No, Mister Smith. No problem. Please wait over there. No, there. There.'

The e-ticket I'd printed earlier at the hotel had caused a degree of concern and flapping about at the Air New Zealand check-in desk, requiring the staff to make phone calls and rat-a-tat-tat at the keyboard, before I was eventually told to stand over there, somewhere, for some reason. Eventually a tanned gentleman in uniform arrived at the desk, and confirmed with the staff that I was the one causing all the trouble.

'Mister Smith? I am Thierry,' said Thierry in a stilted French accent. 'Can I take your bags?'

'I'm fine, thanks, there's just the two.'

'Allow me to take them, Mister Smith.'

It was more of an order than a request, so I handed over my possessions and followed the Frenchman as he brusquely cut a swathe through the queues waiting for passport inspections, and bundled me to the front of the queue at security. The other passengers glowered at me in a manner usually reserved for paedophiles and door-to-door salesmen. There was no small talk, no fleeting pleasantries, just sustained marching through the terminal building, up a flight of stairs, to a set of frosted doors. It was the Koru Club, Air New Zealand's first-class lounge, a taste of the high life arranged for me by Sarah, the staff member behind @AIRNZUSA. I'd never bought anything other than economy-class tickets before, so had never stepped foot in an airport lounge. Thierry was the lounge concierge, and allowed a gentle smile to break his staunch expression before leading me on a tour of my new-found wonderland, one of showers and Wi-Fi and cold meat platters.

Thierry showed me to a section of eight plush chairs reserved for VIPs, brought over a flute of chilled champagne, and left me to revel in my newly acquired status. I had no right to be there, my jowls unshaved and my clothes un-ironed – I wasn't a VIP by any measurement, certainly none found in Los Angeles. Not like, say, Rhys Ifans, who at that moment walked into the lounge and up to a reserved table four seats away, where he slouched into a chair and started thumbing through a newspaper. There was no doubt we would have got on famously, Rhys and I, if he hadn't chosen the seat in the VIP section farthest from me.

'I'm sorry sir, but I'll have to ask you to move please.'

Thierry had reappeared in the lounge. He wasn't addressing me, however.

'Is there a problem with sitting here?' asked Rhys Ifans.

'Yes sir, this area is reserved,' said Thierry. 'There are plenty of seats elsewhere in the lounge.'

'But there's nobody sitting here, apart from him.' Rhys Ifans was referring to me, the phony VIP sat opposite.

'Yes sir, but we are expecting other guests to arrive shortly,' explained Thierry.

'Can't I stay until they arrive?'

Thierry's eyes narrowed.

'We are expecting them *very* soon.'

The only hand that Ifans had left to play was to make a song and dance about being the star of several notable and distinguished productions for the stage and screen. If he'd tried pulling that caper, I was more than prepared to pipe up to Thierry about *Garfield 2*. To his credit he did no such thing, although he was clearly irked by the exchange, shrugging his shoulders as he stood up and wandered off someplace else. The grubby Northerner sat opposite with a bag full of dirty washing smiled and waved apologetically at the BAFTA-winning actor.

Curiously enough, no other VIPs turned up, at least not while I sat there. Thierry was still smiling, though.

twitchhiker Need to catch my flight. Thanks to everyone who's supported me this far and to those in NZ willing me on. Can't wait to see you, Auckland!

5:55 PM Mar 21st

Chapter 25

Day Twenty-two (ish)

There have been plenty of instances where, due to extreme buffoonery on my part, I've wished a single day could be deleted from the history of the world. There have been other days that have effectively been erased by illness, apathy or booze-riddled shenanigans. I'd certainly never been careless enough to lose a whole day while on board a plane, yet somewhere over the Pacific, the pilot proceeded from Saturday evening to Monday morning, leapfrogging Sunday in the process. Because I'd previously travelled east from Europe to the Pacific, I'd slowly gained time as I'd reset my watch earlier and earlier in each new time zone. And so day twenty-two of my journey was dismissed as naught but a chronological inconsistency as we crossed the International Date Line and plunged straight into day twenty-three.

While evading the passage of linear time, the Air New Zealand stewards buzzed about me, eager to hear tales of the exotic from my travels. The chief steward was keen to let me know that nothing was too much trouble, and that the airline's senior management had asked I be made a fuss of.

I had a seat in premium economy that provided plenty of legroom for unfurling my awkward frame, although sleep proved frustratingly elusive. It was the fault of my hands, as usual. The opportunity for forty winks on a plane (or a train, for that matter) is nearly always wasted because I'm never sure what to do with my hands. Wherever I put them – on my legs, folded across my chest, down by my sides – it feels so unnatural it prevents me nodding off. Just where are they meant to go? The dilemma was eventually solved by the chief steward, who waited for passengers in the business-class cabin to fall asleep before leading me through to the one remaining flat bed. I'd slipped into an alternate reality of comfortable air travel, a secret Masonic realm I'd never before encountered. So that's what passengers on long-haul flights paid thousands of pounds for – to sit behind that curtain of exclusivity, out of sight from prying commoners, and experience a superior quality of customer service by sleeping right through it. I couldn't decide whether that was a shrewd investment or a monumental waste of money.

Chapter 26

Day Twenty-three – Monday 23 March

Fourteen hours after departing Los Angeles on Saturday evening, it was early Monday morning in Auckland. I dozed for perhaps four or five hours, but it was hardly a peaceful spell of rest – every jar and jolt as the 747 buckarooed through clear-air turbulence snapped my eyes open. Turbulence is disconcerting while sat upright; it was pant-wettingly terrifying while lying down and half-asleep. During our time in Las Vegas, Jane and I had taken a sightseeing flight to the Grand Canyon on a propeller plane that seated barely a dozen tourists and the pilot. As the plane was tossed about and the passengers browned their trousers, a recorded message calmly suggested we think of air turbulence like taking a drive along a country lane full of potholes. It was nothing more sinister or dangerous than that – nothing to worry about, folks, reassured the Texan twang through our headsets, failing to acknowledge that if a car suffers a punctured tyre or broken fan belt, it doesn't explode, or plunge thousands of metres out of the sky to the ground at terminal velocity while passengers scream, pass out or recite the Hail Mary. Otherwise, the analogy was entirely reassuring.

Helen (@MsBehaviour) was waiting to meet me in the arrivals hall at Auckland airport, easily identified by her hand-scrawled sign that shouted 'KIA ORA TWITCHHIKER!' She was a tall, slim, blue-eyed Kiwi with a head of long purple hair, and she appeared unnaturally delighted to be awake before five o'clock on a Monday morning, in contrast to myself who was stiff and confused by the time of day. Even the drive through the deserted suburbs of Auckland was disorientating; New Zealand's road signs and rules are near identical to those in the UK, but weeks of left-hand drive cars on the right-hand carriage of European autobahns and US freeways meant the familiar had become foreign. Beyond the city centre and its thrusting profile (dominated by the Sky Tower, the tallest structure in the southern hemisphere), there were few high-rise buildings in Auckland, and instead we passed through a peaceful suburbia of modest housing that sprawled for several kilometres in all directions.

As I was largely ignorant to the culture or history of New Zealand, it was startling to see how dominant the Maori language was. Road signs led the way to the likes of Waitakere, Manukau, and Pakuranga, and Helen's greeting to me at the airport – kia ora – are two of the many Maori words that have entered the vocabulary of all New Zealanders (although still to this day, it remains too orangey for crows).

It was fascinating, and unexpected. We British are very much a mongrel breed derived from two thousand years of conquest by the Romans, the Vikings, the Germans, the

Danes, the French and anybody else who turned up on our doorstep and fancied a quick rape and pillage; any unique culture our island once possessed was assimilated long ago. And, of course, when early European settlers set sail across the Atlantic, life didn't turn out too well for the American Indians. I'd mistakenly assumed that's how history had played out elsewhere in the world, but not in New Zealand. That's not to say the Europeans that settled in the country en masse in the nineteenth century didn't cause all manner of trouble, because they did; the indigenous Maori population plummeted, to the point where it was feared they would become extinct. Yet the Maori were resilient and they prospered. Today, fourteen per cent of the country's population is Maori and their heritage is embraced and celebrated in New Zealand, a cultural symbiosis. I was a green, naive traveller for sure but it was uplifting to witness, and to realise my forefathers hadn't managed to trample everyone they met.

We stopped by Kiwi FM in Ponsonby, where we met breakfast host Wammo (as with most radio presenters, it wasn't his real name, which was Glenn) and I managed to sound reasonably coherent during an hour-long interview. From there it was a short drive to Titirangi, the home of Helen and husband Chelfyn, an expat who hailed from near Whitley Bay, the weekend summertime destination of myself and many a child growing up in the north-east of England. Chelfyn and Kiwi-born Helen married on the Pyramid Stage at Glastonbury Festival in 2000, before moving to New Zealand the following year to start their digital company Mohawk Media.

'Are you hungry?' asked Chelfyn.

'Starving,' I replied. I'd only picked through my meal on board the flight from Los Angeles.

'Great,' said Chelfyn, 'I was hoping you would be. I bought supplies especially.'

Chelfyn correctly deduced my diet for the past three weeks had been lacking in bacon and egg sandwiches, and quickly righted that wrong.

'I don't suppose you have a travel plug for New Zealand, have you?' asked Helen.

I hadn't, I admitted. I'd packed European and American adaptors, but I was ill-prepared for the southern hemisphere.

'Thought not,' said Helen. 'Think we've still got a spare you can have.'

Before returning to Auckland so that I could check in to the SKYCITY Grand Hotel, Helen and I headed out towards Piha on the Tasman Sea coast, to the west of the city. We navigated skinny roads that snaked and doubled back and veered high into the Waitakere Ranges, hemmed in by dense fauna, until we reached a viewing point near the summit of a hill.

My jaw slackened and my eyes opened up wide. From left to right, from my feet to the horizon, my field of vision was filled with New Zealand rainforest. Speckles of trees on the faraway ridge tumbled into the city-sized basin far below; the scale was breathtaking, almost incomprehensible.

We descended to the coast, past secluded homes tucked out of sight, behind creeps of trees, to the black sand beaches of Piha and the hulk of Lion Rock, a colossal fist of magma sitting on Piha Beach. Beyond the cove were further crags and crescents of beach, rainforest tumbling off the hills behind. It was early autumn in New Zealand but Helen and I had the beach to ourselves. For the people of Auckland, the Waitakere Ranges and the beaches along the Tasman Sea are their backyard, where they spend their weekends trekking through the bush, enjoying the surf or doing nothing whatsoever of consequence. It was New Zealand's equivalent of Whitley Bay; for me, it was paradise found.

Monday afternoon was all about rest, a few hours' sleep perhaps. At least, that was the plan before lunchtime, but reality had refused to even glance at the plan, and instead nipped down the pub while it thought I wasn't looking. I checked into the magnificent SKYCITY Grand Hotel in downtown Auckland, its reception area an orgy of excess and grandeur, extravagant stone and wood. The floor-to-ceiling windows in my room on the sixteenth floor allowed the view of the city to pour in; the bejewelled waters of Waitemata Harbour were straight ahead, and to my right the colossal Sky Tower that pierced the skyline.

My sense of balance deserted me. I slumped onto the bed and gently teased the shoes from my heels. Everything ached. I was light-headed, happy but exhausted. I needed to rest up, close my eyes for an hour or two, or risk a sudden plunge in my mood. Since leaving Chicago on the Megabus, since that day of peace and tranquillity travelling through the arid vacuum of Illinois and Missouri, I'd managed my bipolar disorder with surprisingly little effort. The occasional pang of loneliness and isolation was to be expected, otherwise I'd revelled in the journey; exhilaration and determination had kept my condition at bay. But I needed to rest, and not allow my head and hopes to drop.

Before I had the opportunity to draw the curtains and crawl into the acre of bed before me, the room's telephone shrieked for attention; it was my host Melinda (@proudkiwi) who had offered me the room at the hotel. Accompanied by others from the hotel's marketing team, she'd arrived in reception to welcome me. I considered trotting out some excuse about tiredness or jet lag or washing my hair, but I agreed to meet them in a few minutes instead. I made haste to the bathroom, dragging my weary bones into the shower to quickly hose myself down and wash away a day's worth of aches and pains and perspiration. Soothed, relaxed and smelling less like an unwashed adolescent rugby team, I sat down on the toilet to conclude my ablutions and promptly nodded off, at least until a concerned Melinda rang again twenty minutes later.

'Paul, it's Mel. Are you joining us in reception?'

The presence of a landline in a bathroom in itself is disconcerting, but for it to ring while I was asleep on the throne caused no end of panic.

'Yes, what? Yes, Mel! Hello. Yes.'

'So you're coming down to reception soon?'

'Sorry, yes. Very soon. As soon as my trousers are fastened.'

'What?'

> **twitchhiker** I've finally buckled and picked out a Red Bull from the mini-bar. Mmm, Taurine. Caffeine. Glucuronolactone.
>
> *5:31 PM Mar 23rd*

There had been a smattering of tweet-ups to celebrate my arrival at various cities around the globe – Washington, Chicago, Wichita, San Francisco – and Auckland was chomping at the bit to join in. They were going to put the rest of the world to shame, and they were going to start by hosting their knees-up in a wine shop, which was arguably game over for everyone else. I'd learned the stereotype of the UK as a nation of borderline alcoholics was universal, so it was no great surprise to discover that the proprietor of The Wine Vault in Grey Lynn was an expat from Basingstoke, Jayson. The shop itself was a small affair, a terraced property with one floor of wine, storage space and clutter on the floor above, and a patio area to the rear. Yet The Wine Vault's reputation far outstripped its physical presence – not only was Jayson ferociously active on Twitter, but on Facebook too, promoting wines and fielding queries from amateur connoisseurs. With a household video camera, Jayson filmed weekly wine tastings on a minimal set above the shop for his *Wine Vault TV* series, distributed through YouTube and Viddler. This modest store in a suburban street engaged and conversed with thousands of potential customers not only in Auckland but across the country. Jayson was proof that you didn't need grand designs or pertinacious advice from social media gurus (shudder) to be noticed; you only needed something interesting to say, and an engaging way to say it.

As daylight turned to a gentle dusk, the patio area slowly filled up with Auckland tweeps and conversation, becoming ever more boisterous as Jayson uncorked another bottle or four of rich thick red wine. There was Wammo, the breakfast show host from earlier in the day, Helen and Cheflyn too, Jo from Air New Zealand's headquarters in Auckland, Ande the radio programmer who had turned me down for a job in the UK four years before; half a world away from home, amongst the strangers, there were people I knew in the flesh, too.

Plenty of Twitter users already knew one another, while a handful stood on the fringes of the conversations, shy and quietly observing. One such person was Robert (@globtrav), the Kiwi who had used his air miles to provide my flight from Auckland to Wellington the following afternoon.

If it were possible to sprout wings, Robert would no doubt have already done so. He was able to work remotely through his laptop from anywhere, just as I was, no nine-to-five routine shackling him to an anonymous cubicle in a claustrophobic tower block. Unlike me, Robert chose not to sit hunched over a desk in his dining room or his local Starbucks. He adored flying to the point that he lived, and worked, in the clouds.

'So you spend your days flying? As a passenger?' I asked.

'Some days more than others,' explained Robert. 'Some days I'll take four or five flights, working on board the flights or while I'm waiting in the terminal. Then I'll take a break, get some rest, maybe arrange to meet friends for dinner in one of the airport lounges.'

'So where do you fly to?'

'All over. A lot of domestic flights, but I travel internationally all the time too.'

Robert's life truly was a flight of fancy, taxiing from one pre-flight safety demonstration to the next; all the delays, those intolerable waits for connecting flights – they were the perfect excuse for another coffee break or enjoying a long lunch with friends. I was a little envious of the nomadic lifestyle led by Robert – he was the very definition of a frequent flyer, although I wasn't sure I'd choose to spend so much time away from terra firma.

One by one the Twitter well-wishers called time on the night, leaving an ever-decreasing group of ever-increasing lushes, of which I was one. The clock struck ten, three hours on from the plucking of the evening's first cork, and in a prodigious example of a drunk man's logic, Jayson reasoned it would be the ideal time to record an episode of *Wine Vault TV*. This was a supremely idiotic suggestion, but when filtered through several litres of fermented grape juice, I could only concur with his reasoning.

We tripped up the stairs to the set of *Wine Vault TV*; a plain table ably assisted by a pair of functional chairs, with a white-washed wall as the backdrop. Fortunately, I felt I'd learned enough patter from Daedalus and Chris Sawyer in Sonoma to bluff my way through a wine-tasting session. Unfortunately, we weren't going to taste wine; to celebrate my arrival in New Zealand, Jayson had decided we would apply the science of wine tasting to beer. The attempt started poorly and quickly hurtled downhill; Jayson and I stretched our experience of sniffing, swirling, swilling and spitting booze to the very limit. Not that far, then. In our increasingly slurred opinion, the fragrance and tones of the beers ranged from 'old dirty couch' to 'nutty, right the way down to the crack'. Shameful. And immediately uploaded to YouTube for future generations to ignore in lieu of a cat playing a piano.

Having attempted to drink all of Jayson's hospitality, the half a dozen stalwarts that remained decamped next door to the seductive Gypsy Tea Room, where we attempted to drink all their wine instead, and everything else besides. Round after round of shots were slung back, a gallant attempt to exorcise all sobriety from the night. From there, the last three of us standing retreated to the casinos at SKYCITY. I immediately felt uncomfortable in the surroundings as another demon from my past reappeared; I once had a crippling gambling addiction that cleaned out the only savings account Jane and I had, unbeknownst to her at the time. I hadn't strayed near a blackjack table in four years, for fear of deluding myself into believing I could second-guess the chaos of the cards and play my way out of overdrafts and mortgage arrears.

I stuck close to the last two survivors of the evening, Mel and her hotel marketing friend Lucy (@kiwilucy), and chose to nurse a beer instead of risking what few New Zealand dollars I had on faded memories of probability. Eventually, in a rare demonstration of common sense, I wished my companions goodnight and swayed my way back to the hotel, desperately ready for my first full night's sleep in three days. It would be nothing short of glorious.

Chapter 27

Day Twenty-four – Tuesday 24 March

Morning! No it wasn't, it was still dark. In fact it was three o'clock and I'd slept for barely two hours. Fortunately I was still paralytic and so my rage at not being asleep was tempered. I scuffed my feet along the carpet to the bathroom and into the shower, and let the water run until I relaxed enough to slip back into sleep.

Morning! No, it was an hour after I'd eventually fallen asleep for the second time, so barely five o'clock. Jet lag had rendered my internal chronometer as much use as tits on a window. Worse, there was a hangover beginning to rap its knuckles impatiently against the crust of my skull. Pathetic. I winced and gulped down a couple of painkillers, and firmly cradled my forehead in my hand.

Morning! Yes, yes it was, at last. The alarm on my mobile heralded the arrival of half past seven, and a samurai-sharp blade of sunlight sliced through the curtains. The hangover was manageable but my left hand was cramping with pins and needles, my legs felt dull and numb. My body wasn't enjoying the constant travelling as much as I was. I stumbled once more into the shower cubicle, the unsullied bath looking on in disgust at my apparent defection. There was little time for such selfish luxuries; within the hour, I was due to appear on national radio with Mike Hosking, presenter of the breakfast show on Newstalk ZB, and host of New Zealand's version of *Who Wants To Be A Millionaire?*

Reaching across Cook Strait to New Zealand's South Island with news of my challenge was critical to the success of my journey; the South Island is as large as England and Wales combined, but barely a million people live there. Over a third of that population is clumped in Christchurch, nowhere near the southern tip of the island. It wouldn't matter if the rest of the world was willing me on – the person that'd see me achieve my goal had to be on the South Island, they had to be on Twitter, they had to know I was heading their way and they had to be willing to help me. Percentages of percentages of percentages.

twitchhiker Right, off to an interview with Mike Hoskings on Newstalk ZB in about 20 minutes. Will catch up on blog and tweets after that. On to Wellington tonight.

7:46 AM Mar 24th

As I've already mentioned, not everybody who learned of my journey was a paid-up member of the Twitchhiker fan club. New Zealanders had been overwhelmingly supportive throughout the month, but there had been a handful of exceptions. Overnight, a story about my adventure had appeared on CNN's website, and immediately invoked the wrath of a Kiwi called Linda in the comments section:

> 'Campbell Island is difficult to enter for a reason; it is a predator-free refuge for rare and protected species. A lot of time, money and effort by dedicated New Zealanders have gone into making and preserving this sanctuary. We as a people should not let one arrogant and ignorant Briton enter this reserve just because it is geographically opposite to his home-town.'

I certainly wasn't ignorant to Campbell Island's status as a World Heritage Site. Was I arrogant? I hadn't presumed I'd be whisked across the Pacific without question and allowed to strut about the island to my heart's content. It was faith; faith that, with a doff of the hat to Dirk Gently, the interconnectedness of all things would find a way to make it happen.

Or perhaps I was plain naive? I'd already been given my marching orders by Tourism New Zealand, who believed I had little chance of reaching Campbell Island. The latest press release from the tourist board, published upon my arrival in the country, was celebratory in tone and cited Twitchhiker as 'an opportunity to gain positive media coverage about New Zealand and our spirit of Manaakitanga (or hospitality)'. Unfortunately, it never once mentioned Campbell Island or my intention to reach it, and instead stated I was visiting the country for the purposes of sightseeing. I'd being privately told to expect failure and publicly supported in a manner that didn't encourage success.

Mel and the team at SKYCITY Grand Hotel had invited me to lunch, and in turn I'd invited my contact at Tourism New Zealand, Rebecca, to join us. Along with Jo Brothers from Air New Zealand (@jobrothers), who I'd met the previous evening, and Andy Blood (@thebloodster), we met in the Sky Tower's revolving restaurant, nearly 200 metres above Auckland. The skies were clear, and the views rolled down and across the cityscape, and off out into Waitemata Harbour, to North Shore, to Rangitoto and Waiheke Islands and farther across the Hauraki Gulf. It was as exotic a sight as it sounded, Mel and Jo describing the panorama in a seamless bouquet of English and Maori sounds. The view was interrupted by the occasional screams of tourists throwing themselves off the tower; the Sky Jump from the platform immediately above the restaurant allowed idiots of various nationalities to leap off and hurtle towards the ground, before a safety wire slowed their descent and prevented a mess on the pavement. No thank you.

'We're heading into New Zealand's winter,' Rebecca pointed out during lunch. 'Sailing beyond the South Island isn't particularly safe at this time of year.'

'...'

'And it's a six-day round-trip to Campbell Island by boat.'

What were the chances of finding a boat captain who'd risk his crew and vessel for a six-day voyage? Unpaid? My resolve crumbled a little, and for the first time I was willing to concede – to a point.

'What if I could fly there?' I suggested. 'Not to land on it or even over it, but maybe just close enough so I could see it in the distance?'

I didn't have to step foot on Campbell Island, I told myself; even if it was nothing more than a fleeting glimpse of a speckle on the horizon, that would be enough.

'Perhaps,' conceded Rebecca. 'There are airfields in the Southland region of the South Island, but then you'd have to find a private charter willing to fly out across the sea.'

'Can't you just stop bleating on about reaching that bloody island?!' seemed to be the underlying tone to our discussion. And then the subject came up about my leaving Jane so soon after our wedding. As I was sneaking another helping of carrots onto my plate, Rebecca looked me square in the eye and commented: 'I would never let my husband do something like this.'

No hint of humour, no playful narrowing of the eyes, no curling of a smile. I'd abandoned my wife, and the lady from the tourism board didn't appear too impressed about it. Another tourist screamed past the window and I considered joining them for a little light relief.

Before packing for Wellington, I checked in to Twitter to see whether New Zealand still believed in my cause:

ExploreMoreNZ @twitchhiker – @kiwiexperience driver @SmileyKiwi is happy to take you and @MauiRentals camper as far south as Stewart Island.

1:56 PM Mar 24th

Explore More New Zealand organised tourist excursions with partner companies, and offered to pull together everything I needed to reach the southern tip of the mainland and a little way beyond, to Stewart Island, the small inhabited island 30 kilometres further off the South Island. They'd also arrange my passage on the ferry between Wellington on the North Island and Picton on the South Island.

There was even better news. Potentially better news, at least. Waiting patiently for me in my inbox was an email from an anonymous follower, who had contacted New Zealand's Department of Conservation on my behalf and forwarded me their response:

Hi Twitchhiker Supporter

Your email has been forwarded to me as the DOC's Southern Islands Area manages the New Zealand sub-Antarctic Nature Reserves including Campbell Island. I appreciate that Twitchhiker is keen to get to Campbell, as are thousands of others, unfortunately it's not that simple when it comes to getting to the islands.

At present there are no visits to Campbell planned until November, and that is a commercial cruise company, so given his timeline of the end of this month I can't see anyway to facilitate his journey.

If you do think of a way to get him down (some rich benefactor comes up with a ship especially for the trip) then we will forward you/him the permit application, as all landings on the islands require a permit, and work through any issues that may arise.

The DOC had confirmed what I already knew, although they'd been a little more pleasant in their wording; the probability of me reaching Campbell was only a gnat's IQ higher than zero. But – and it took a galactic stretch of faith to reach that 'but' – if I did somehow find a way to reach the island, they'd assist in securing a permit for me to drop anchor and clamber onto land. All I needed was a boat and crew who were prepared to go out to sea unpaid for six days and fund all costs from their own pocket. And were on Twitter. Stranger things had happened along the way so far, but not many. It was so infinitesimal it could only perhaps be weighed using a mass spectrometer, but there was still hope.

The Air New Zealand flight to Wellington was quiet, barely an hour-long hop, skip and a jump of a commuter flight for the souls travelling between the North Island's two major cities. Lucy, who I'd met at the previous evening's wine orgy, had tweeted out the offer of a ride to the airport, and with that my itinerary for the following three days was set – one that would take me to Stewart Island.

My Wellington host Narelle (@narelle_NZ) was waiting for me on arrival, holding a printout of my hastily conceived Twitchhiker logo and wearing a lively smile. It was a little past eight o'clock in the evening and already dark, so the streets and form of New Zealand's capital city were shrouded by the veil of night, but it was apparent Wellington had a very different personality to Auckland. Narelle lived downtown in Te Aro, but there were very few high-rise buildings, and little consistency in the style and layout of the neighbourhood. Despite being the capital, Wellington appeared more relaxed and akin to a small town.

There were tweeps aplenty waiting for us at a bar named the Southern Cross for what was my second consecutive excuse for booze in as many nights. I was as tired as a put-upon field mouse but keen to spend time with people who wanted to spend time with me; they were all the family I had while on the road to Campbell Island. Over a dozen Twitter users crowded around a long table in the Southern Cross; some were known to Narelle, others had turned up out of curiosity, and one face was familiar to me – a girl called Alex (@alex_bettylou) who I'd last seen in Newcastle six months before. We'd worked together briefly before she'd emigrated to New Zealand with her boyfriend Kiwi (not his actual name, I suspected) – Twitter had connected me to familiar faces around the world, as well as new and unexpected ones.

It was never intended to be a late or drunken night, because I had little capacity spare for such raucousness. That said, it wasn't a terrible surprise when the evening turned late of hour and steaming drunk, after a small pack of us staggered on to a second venue, the Matterhorn, on Cuba Street. It was a classy affair, or at least the near-total absence of light suggested it was; I couldn't see much further than the end of my nose, although that may have been the drink. Dirty, dangerous Jägermeister was ordered and necked and ordered again, and tall tales were told concerning the cast of *The Lord of the Rings*. Everybody had a story to tell – it must be a tradition, an old charter or something.

The city is home to Weta Digital, the special effects company co-founded by director Peter Jackson, and many of the scenes in *The Lord of the Rings* trilogy were filmed on soundstages in Wellington. The Matterhorn had been a regular haunt for many of the actors, including a certain Ms Liv Tyler, who starred in all three films. It was surely written in the stars above that I was fated to be with the Hollywood actress. That, or I'd unwittingly become a stalker.

As last orders were called, the half-dozen of us that remained piled out onto Cuba Mall, past the city's famous Bucket Fountain – a water feature well known to Wellingtonians and briefly made world-famous by Elijah Wood relieving himself in it after a heavy night on the town. As the headlines no doubt chuckled at the time, urinating in public was a filthy Hobbit. And if they didn't take advantage of such a perfect pun, more fool them. I wouldn't be taking Wood's lead – I'd deliberately slowed my drinking pace down towards the end of the night. My time at Narelle's would be the last opportunity to work until the trip concluded and I arrived home in the UK, whenever that would be. So far I'd earned barely a third of my wage for the month.

Narelle's apartment in Te Aro was a grand three-bedroom duplex, high ceilings and contemporary finishes. We shared the dregs of a bottle of red and talked about Narelle's work as a web designer and developer for the government before drawing a line under the evening. My work would have to wait until the morning, before I left Wellington and began what would be the penultimate stage of my journey towards Campbell Island.

Chapter 28

Day Twenty-five – Wednesday 25 March

Since arriving in New Zealand my gift exchange had gone to hell in a handcart. At Los Angeles airport, I'd presented my second LA host Patrick with the silk shawl from Ben, my first LA host. Of course Patrick had no idea he would be asked for a gift; my trail of tweets throughout the trip had passed him by. He popped open the glovebox and rummaged through the sort of crapola we all stash away in there. Eventually he extracted a CD in a scratched jewel case; it was a home-made compilation of his current favourite disco anthems and mash-ups. A haphazard gift, but perfectly personal.

That CD had sat in my bags all the way across the Pacific, and through transience or ineptitude I'd failed to pass it on to any of the people who'd assisted me in Auckland. I had remembered to give it to Narelle earlier that morning, who ripped a copy onto her laptop and passed it back to me. She also had a gift for me – a glass globe the size of a golf ball, cradled in a glass stand. The countries and continents were etched on its surface; holding it to the light and looking at

New Zealand, I could see the UK waiting for me on the other side of the world.

Wellington's ferry terminal was the second I'd visited during the trip; unlike the terminal at North Shields which had reminded me of a parochial airport, Wellington was more like a city centre bus interchange, bustling with locals, elderly tourists and backpackers. As well as the passengers, the stern loading doors had a trickle of vehicles boarding it, including cars, camper vans, lorries and freight-bearing rail carriages; the Interislander ferries allow the North and South islands to operate a single rail system.

Smaller than the ferry that had chugged me across the North Sea to Amsterdam all those days ago, this vessel possessed a curiously sharp aroma of farmyard that singed the nostrils. Parked near the stern were several cattle wagons, now empty of their cargo of sheep but retaining a journey's worth of dung; just what the captain ordered for a three-hour ferry crossing. Fortunately the seas remained calm and the stench of my bile didn't add to the odour.

I'd already witnessed the wild beauty of Piha to the west of Auckland, but the voyage across the Cook Strait into Picton was breathtaking, and not because of the smell. Now, that may appear to be a lazy description and indeed, *breathtaking* is a word that is overused to describe everyday, mundane occurrences that do no such thing. Trust me when I say the sight of dolphins jumping across the path of the ferry while travelling through the forested magnificence of the Marlborough Sounds caused my jaw to loosen and my lungs to be gently squeezed empty of air. Underneath a peerless blue sky, I was experiencing the very real sensation of Mother Nature applying a firm hand to my sternum. To bear witness to the mountainous valleys we sailed through was to view the world in high-definition – an infinite wash of shapes and colours, a cascading stream of contours and textures that overwhelmed the senses, too much for the eye to comprehend or the brain to process. It was a rich and simple beauty.

> **twitchhiker** Dolphins are jumping across the bow of the ferry. This place is like nowhere else. It's so wondrous I could cry. I won't, obviously.
>
> *4:37 PM Mar 25th*

I did, obviously, but I wasn't going to admit it. It was quite the most magnificent, serene, perfect spectacle and it moved me to tears with little effort.

My ticket from @ExploreMoreNZ meant I had access to the VIP suite of the ferry. Always one for a perk or two, I used my swipe card to unlock the lounge door, to find myself in a room almost identical to everywhere else on the ship. Admittedly there was a free newspaper and a jug of orange juice, although both failed to make me feel as very important as I'd been led to believe they would. There was also a grizzled, sun-kissed driver from one of the cattle lorries; I needed no Holmesian powers of deduction to guess his career, merely a nose in reasonable working order – he stank of sheep shit. He grudgingly acknowledged my existence, and with nobody else in the lounge to strike up a conversation with, asked about my business on the ferry.

'Twitter? Never heard of it,' said he, as I attempted to explain myself.

'It's a way to talk to other people around the world using the Internet,' I offered hopefully.

'The Internet? Load of bollocks. Pointless, mate. Won't catch on.'

Donald, for that was his name, went on to explain that communities had been ruined by the Internet, with people preferring to 'bury their face in a bloody computer screen' rather than knock on a neighbour's door. He became aerated by the intolerability of mankind's digital enslavement, so I changed the topic and asked about family. Donald had two daughters, both living in the UK.

'You won't get to see them very often,' I offered by way of consolation.

'Nah, see them all the time,' said Donald. 'Had a chat with one of them on Skype at the weekend.'

The weather-ravaged face staring at me coughed up the words without a shred of irony. On my children's lives.

Despite the horror stories I'd been told about the ferry crossing across Cook Strait, it was tranquil and restful and passed without a hint of gagging or spewing in another passenger's lap. While in Auckland, Mel had recounted a tale of abject horror from her formative years, of a ferry crossing lasting twelve hours because the waters at both Wellington and Picton were so treacherous that the ferry captain didn't dare attempt to make port. Back and forth across the hellish strait the ferry sailed, attempting to dock at the South Island, then the North, back and forth once more, until eventually the waters calmed enough for the ferry to reach Wellington and allow hundreds of ashen-faced, empty-stomached passengers to disembark a vessel that was, in Mel's words, 'caked floor to ceiling in vom'.

I've talked an awful lot about throwing up so far, don't you think? Probably far more than either of us was expecting. Perhaps I should have instigated some sort of warning procedure IN BOLD LETTERING, in case you were enjoying a nice sandwich at the time of reading. If you were, and found your sandwich considerably less appealing after I recounted yet another tale of involuntary regurgitation, then I'll buy you another sandwich should we ever meet. I have to be honest with you, there are more tales of vomiting to come. No, I'm not happy about it either, but there we are.

Picton was a speckle at the head of Queen Charlotte Sound that slowly bloomed into a small town as we approached it. The port dominated the shore, while homes and buildings were scattered across the giant folds of forest to either side. Here and there were residential properties abandoned on the shoreline with no visible means of access except by boat. What a life they must have enjoyed – no traffic except the passing ferries and occasional yacht from the marina, no busloads of backpackers, no nosey tourists or double glazing salesmen, no surprise visits by family, or neighbours playing loud fusion jazz at Christ o'clock in the morning.

Silence. Serenity. And a view delivered from paradise. One to bear in mind for the retirement plans.

After disembarking I was met by Smiley – not his real name, obviously – a driver from Kiwi Experience who was to be my chauffeur on the South Island. He wasn't too difficult to spot; he was propped up against a camper van, wearing a sunhat, sunglasses and shorts, together with a grin that stretched from ear to ear and crammed full of teeth that made friends everywhere they went. Thick curls of blonde hair, built like a brick outhouse, Smiley was a rugged Kiwi who'd driven tourists up and down New Zealand for years.

'Mate, how are ya? Can I get those for yer? How was the ferry? Do you want to get goin'? You hungry? I bought plenty of food so just say if you're peckish.'

My host had been briefed to be my concierge, but that aside Smiley was damned pleased to see me, and with good reason.

'Full pay, mate, just got to drive you up and down the island, so you take as long as you like. Easy money, see the sights, nothing too taxing – not a bad way to earn a living, mate!'

Like half the population in New Zealand, Smiley had worked as a production assistant on *The Lord of the Rings* trilogy, with the likes of – yes, you already saw it coming – Liv Tyler, but after years of a career in film production he'd discovered bus driving proved far more satisfying.

A couple of hours on the road, and it was easy to understand why. We travelled the coastal road to Kaikoura that evening, and as the sun set over the rolling foothills of the Southern Alps, ash-blue mists swirled in over the charcoal-grey beaches. New Zealand kept peeling back further layers to reveal new sensations, and every time my heart pounded a little harder, my eyes widened a little further. As we arched around a wide cove, a surfer tried his luck in the twilight waves, but otherwise we were alone on our travels. In fact all the routes on the South Island were lonely; a land mass the size of England and Wales with only one million inhabitants meant we could drive for twenty or thirty minutes without spotting another soul.

By nightfall we arrived in Kaikoura on the East Coast, where the Top Spot hostel had offered Smiley and me beds for the evening. It was a small two-storey building, overrun by a coach-full of teen backpackers and winged beasties. It was difficult to figure out which were the more irritating of the two; the teenagers had clearly been travelling together a few weeks – awkward silences and yearning glances told a story of drunken casual sex followed by that morning-after regret and embarrassment that hung in the air for days and was no more avoidable than a cabbagey fart in a lift. So there was that. That and, as is always the case for a group of backpackers, one twat with a guitar. The floppy-haired youngster could play no more than three chords but he attempted to woo the girls and rile the alpha males regardless. Quite, quite agonising, but also fascinating to observe those teenagers struggle with self-awareness and emotions heightened by cheap vodka.

twitchhiker Parked up at the Top Spot hostel in Kaikoura, with a teenager strumming a guitar and wailing Oasis. We've all been there.

9:19 PM Mar 25th

Smiley and I tore into chunks of barbecued chicken and sausage that the group's coach driver had kept for us, before heading to our rooms. Mine was a single room with a private bathroom area through a doorless doorway. A bed was the only furniture in the room, but otherwise it was clean and devoid of exploding hormones. I'd struck hostel gold, it seemed. Of course, I hadn't. For one thing it was hotter than the loins of my backpacking associates; for another, the windows and sliding door were all shut tight, but the whirrs and cricks and zips of the insects I'd heard outside, I could also hear *inside*.

As I looked around at the faded yellow walls, I began noticing the dark spots on the paintwork were in motion. Some had shells. Some had wings. Some scuttled. Some hummed a sinewy, high-pitched hum. It was no doubt poor karma, but it was getting late and I couldn't be screwed with poor karma landing on my forehead and sucking blood out of my veins all night, so I took the one clean towel from the shower area and proceeded to flick the little bastards to death. While some had the good grace to fall silently to the floor, others flitted from wall to ceiling to avoid squishing.

twitchhiker Sick of killing things with wings. Slowly being eaten alive :(

11:28 PM Mar 25th

When I could beat and squash and swear no more, I crawled into bed, unable to pull the sheets tight around my neck because of the intolerable heat. I was tired enough to nod off despite the temperature, but terrified by the occasional sensation of something brushing past my face. The lack of a reliable 3G signal on my phone also caused irritation and fear – since arriving on the South Island, it had become near-impossible to access Twitter while on the move; the hostel didn't have Internet access and we weren't likely to find any the next day. Occasionally a stray bar of mobile signal would illuminate the handset's screen, granting a sliver of time in which to tweet and reach the world beyond. Nothing was a certainty anymore.

Chapter 29

Day Twenty-six – Thursday 26 March

twitchhiker Sweet muscular Jesus. Something the size of
a Triumph Dolomite just landed on my pillow.

2:30 AM Mar 26th

With any luck the rest of the guests at the hostel didn't hear
the bat-pitched shrieks of terror from my room. I hadn't
imagined it; I'd been woken up by a something or another
inches from my face. From lying down to standing up in a
fraction of a second, I'd leaped the few short steps to the light
switch on the wall opposite, felt the corpse of an earlier victim
crunch and ooze between my toes, and flicked the switch.

There on the pillow was a hard-shelled fist of a beetle, a
cockroach the size of a small horse. I whipped the towel
from the bottom of the bed and thrashed the beast, squealing
again when it scuttled off the sheets and threatened to stray
near my feet. Forget the previous day's endless gushing – I
hated New Zealand by night and every six-legged freak still
standing on it.

@

Against my better judgement, I'd nodded off after my encounter with the daddy-sized cockroach in my room and slept on until morning. After rustling up a delicious plateful of eggs Benedict in the camper van, Smiley dropped me off at an Internet cafe in Kaikoura so I could reach out to the digital world in the hope of further news. There was none. Aside from a stray comment or two from Twitter users in Invercargill, and a man in Christchurch keen to bundle me into the back of his van for purposes unknown, there were no options to take me further than Stewart Island. There were plenty of well-wishers and donations for *charity: water* continued to appear, but goodwill was no longer enough, no match for an endless ocean.

We were only a day away from Stewart Island, so Smiley and I were happy to ease off the gas and spend the morning whale watching. Because of the kilometre-deep Kaikoura Canyon that lies off the town's coast and the unique transition of ocean currents found there, Kaikoura is renowned for attracting whales. The canyon is also the home of the mythical giant squid; although proof of the submarine-sized beasts is scarce, remains are washed up along the beaches from time to time.

Before boarding the catamaran, Smiley wanted to show off the view from his favourite spot in Kaikoura; it was a dusty trail near Maui Street, high above sea level on the peninsula that separated the North and South bays of the town. Our vantage point was barely above a gentle sliver of mist that bisected the scene; below it, the smoke-black beach hooked to the right, flanked by Kaikoura to one side and the opal ocean to the other – above, a distant saw-blade of mountains tore at the clear blue sky.

The country was ridiculously eager to please; like a giddy young pup that barks and wags its tail until you throw the bloody ball for the twentieth time, New Zealand couldn't help itself but continually attempt to top its previous best spectacle. No matter how distant your home is, you must promise yourself to visit; shuffle about your mental Things To Do list and put it somewhere in the top ten – you may have to save for a year or two, but I guarantee you will not regret it. It's not like I've lived my life in a cellar, totally ignorant to pleasing sights in the world – be it the Lake District or the North Yorkshire Moors on a summer's day, sailing along the Nile or casting nets in a quiet fishing village in the Canary Islands. But New Zealand is beyond compare – I'd arrived barely three days beforehand and yet I'd seen a world's worth of beauty.

What I didn't see, however, were whales.

The pay-off for riding a buckaroo-ing catamaran that attempted to eject my eggs Benedict out through any hole available was a stray albatross and a heightened suspicion of water-faring vessels. It wasn't the fault of the ocean; more the fact that our boat bombed along like a boy racer was at the helm. There wasn't – the captain was a huge Maori chap who occasionally killed the engines to submerge a giant listening horn under the waves, hoping to catch a whisper of song. As it transpired, the sperm whales that were commonplace to the feeding grounds remained just as elusive as their squidular nemesis; there was plenty of horizon and the occasional bird for those who cared, but otherwise it was very much a whale fail.

From Kaikoura, we continued south to Christchurch along State Highway 1 – New Zealand's senior highway, connecting the tip of the North Island to the foot of its southern counterpart, with the obvious interruption of Cook Strait between the two. And for most of its length, it's single carriageway. Through the likes of Auckland and Christchurch the SH 1 expands to accommodate urban traffic, and there are numerous short sections where additional lanes are provided for overtaking. Otherwise, the major highway in the whole of the country is just two lanes wide. Incredible, but any more would have been excessive; March is off-peak as far as the tourist trade is concerned, and there was only Smiley and I to keep the silent glory of the countryside company.

Our intended route had been to head straight on to the Southland region and Invercargill, but a phone call saw us head west instead. Smiley's girlfriend called from their home in Queenstown; a close relative had been taken ill and she was on the phone in tears.

'I'd really appreciate it if we could head there for the night, mate,' said Smiley after explaining the situation. 'It's up to you though, you need to get wherever you're going.'

I did, it was true, but it made no odds whether I arrived in Invercargill later that night or early the next morning. I had a breakfast interview at a radio station in the city, otherwise the route and timings by which we arrived were irrelevant. Driving to Queenstown would lead us far away from the coast and into the heart of the South Island, through the Southern Alps – another journey certain to cause shock and awe.

Our expectations for the day had been set high, in that we were hoping to travel nearly the full length of the South Island in a day. The distance between Kaikoura and Invercargill was close to 750 kilometres, over ten hours of driving without rest, and after six hours Smiley started to tire. It was the chance I'd been waiting for since we'd met, the opportunity to drive a camper van across New Zealand.

'Yeah, mate, you can take over if you like, don't mind at all, getting a little tired. Ever driven a camper before?' asked Smiley.

'Never,' I replied. 'But I've driven white vans and people carriers so I'm sure I can manage.'

'Sweet. And you've driven an automatic before?'

Automatic? I looked down to my right. No gears. Ah.

'No,' I replied, hoping not to catch a look of fear on Smiley's face, 'but it can't be too difficult, can it?'

'Not at all, mate, you'll be a born natural!' Smiley smiled as he pulled over for us to swap positions. The man was fearless.

I pulled myself onto the driver's side, pushed the seat back and buckled up. Just two pedals under my feet. Brake and accelerator. Stop. And go. How could I possibly get it wrong?

With surprising ease, it turned out. As we took a sharp bend, Smiley spotted traffic heading towards us on a one-way bridge ahead and warned me to slow down. Sixteen years of instinct kicked in and I slammed my left foot down hard on the clutch as the other lifted off the accelerator. Of course it wasn't the clutch, because there was no clutch. It was the brake. First there was panic. The camper van hadn't done what I'd expected it to do. Next there was a noise from Smiley. He wasn't completely fearless after all. Third was the sound of every unsecure item behind us – bags, laptops, blankets, eggs, frying pans – as they continued moving forward from the rear of the van and landed in the front. Finally, we came to a dead stop.

I learned from my mistake and never repeated it during the rest of my time behind the wheel. That didn't stop me causing several hundred dollars' worth of damage to the camper van by careering too close to a verge.

'Sccrrreeeeeeeeeeeeecccchhhh,' said the moulded under-carriage as I tore a lengthy rip in it.

'Mate, I can't afford to repair that,' said the less-than-smiley Smiley after we pulled over to inspect the damage. 'Not sure what we're going to do about it.' His meaning was clear and of course he was absolutely right.

'Don't worry about it,' I replied. 'I mentioned to Ricki at Explore New Zealand that I might be taking a turn to drive. I'm sure he'll have arranged insurance.'

Fingers crossed.

'If he hasn't,' I added, 'then I'll pay for it. It was my fault, please don't worry about it.'

It was a completely empty promise that I'd made to Smiley. I was yet to figure out how I was going to pay for my flight back to the UK; unless I asked Jane and the boys to begin eating out of bins, there wasn't money in the bank for either a camper van undercarriage or a one-way ticket home.

With Smiley reinstated behind the wheel I was left to gawp at the scenery. As dusk settled over New Zealand, we stopped at the Church of the Good Shepherd on the shores of Lake Tekapo, a grey finger of water that reached to faraway frozen peaks. The church is a tourist attraction in its own right, but there were no other visitors to share the experience with. The sight of dolphins in the Marlborough Sounds had brought tears to my eyes; the distant Mount Cook at the head of Lake Tekapo caused them to roll down my face. It was an exhilarating sensation to be moved by beauty.

twitchhiker Flying around the inky black slalom that is the road to Queenstown. Only a couple of brown trouser moments. Good job it's dark.

21:44 PM Mar 26th

Despite our diversion, Ricki had been on the ball and tweeted an offer of a room in Queenstown for the evening. From Kaikoura to Queenstown was nearly 600 kilometres; navigating the skinny mountainous road in darkness had delayed us even further, meaning we didn't arrive at the Base hostel until nearly midnight. Invercargill was still over two hours drive away, meaning that to reach my radio interview the following morning, we'd have to be up at four o'clock.

I did consider climbing into bed, but decided to explore Queenstown instead – I had just four hours and I was unlikely to return. I had attempted to lie down but was distracted by the swaying motion of the ceiling above; it was a faint but discernable nausea that I couldn't shake. And it became apparent that sleep was out of the question anyway; my room was above Altitude Bar, a venue from which the speakers spelled BOOM BOOM BOOM BOOM to everyone in their blast radius. It wasn't just Altitude, it was all of Shotover Street and others nearby, too. Queenstown is the destination for teenage and twenty-something-year-old adventure junkies who want to throw themselves into canyons by way of bungee jumps, parachute over glaciers and seek out other adrenalin-spurting activities I hadn't the slightest wish to indulge in. If that sounds like your Mecca, you're very welcome to Queenstown. Unfortunately, it'll also mean you having to deal with thousands of said adventure junkies when they're smacked out of their skulls on drink every evening. Perhaps I was too old to appreciate the scene, perhaps I was too tired to embrace a lively night out, but I could go to the Bigg Market in Newcastle any night of the week for a similar experience. While Smiley returned home to deal with matters there, I took a couple of drinks in Altitude and another further up the street in the World Bar, trying not to feel so damned old. Eventually I convinced myself that Queenstown didn't need exploring – not at two in the morning, anyway – and concluded that sleep was a perfectly acceptable alternative to teenagers groping one another in bars. And I probably would have gotten it, too, if it hadn't been for the meddlesome kids outside Fergburger.

The hole-in-the-wall burger joint on Shotover Street is well known to all who pass through Queenstown, and my grumbling belly was eager to sample their famous New Zealand beef patties. I opted for a Fergburger with lettuce, tomato, onion and Swiss cheese, paid my eleven dollars, took my number and waited nearby in the street, surrounded by paralytic girls in impossibly short dresses tripping over their stilettos, collapsing in tits and giggles as weasel-faced boys with their arses hanging out of their jeans made a concerted effort to feel them up.

'-king service is a joke, innit. And she doesn't even fucking smile.'

It was difficult not to eavesdrop since the boozy Essex boy was shooting his mouth off to the crowd. The sweet redhead, who had served me without an issue, twisted her face in anger and embarrassment.

'Perhaps you could try being polite and you may get served quicker,' I gently butted in.

The lad spun round with whatever semblance of balance his alcohol intake allowed, and stopped himself shouting his mouth off when he noticed his eyeline didn't reach my shoulders. Instead he swung around once more to his equally inebriated friends, slung his arms over their shoulders and proceeded to take the piss out of me for suggesting a little courtesy. That said, the burgers at Fergburger made the abuse from the spindly framed gobshites almost bearable. Almost. Every place needs to let its hair down, and for New Zealand that place is Queenstown; fortunately, it's an easy place to lose in the vast emptiness of New Zealand if it's not your thing. It's fair to say it wasn't mine.

There were barely two hours remaining in which to sleep and I was too wound up to make use of it, so instead I took up a seat at one of the hostel's Internet terminals to upload photos and chunter on about the Neanderthals I'd encountered. There was still nothing in the way of help beyond Stewart Island, and it was likely there wasn't going to be. Despite being a city, Invercargill offered a population of barely 50,000, and no more than 400 lived on Stewart Island; increasingly I was shouting into a vacuum and my odds of success were collapsing as New Zealand's population became ever sparser.

Chapter 30

Day Twenty-seven – Friday 27 March

Invercargill is rather unfairly referred to by the rest of the country as 'the arsehole of New Zealand'; perhaps that's a purely geographical reference, because first impressions as we drove into the city were of a perfectly pleasant community. No obvious shards of skyscraper or sprawling conurbations, but broad streets flanked by two-storey shops and businesses, no rush hours or rat race. I did see one or two mullets, however, which is one or two too many, whichever continent you happen to be stood on.

Smiley arrived bright and very early, and happy for his brief return home to comfort his distraught girlfriend. I was far less alert, but managed twenty minutes sleep in the back of the camper van as Smiley sped us to More FM for my radio interview. I'd had little rest since arriving in New Zealand, and the adrenalin that had fuelled my conquest of the South Island was beginning to ebb. I was struggling to temper my anxiety, so when breakfast hosts Gretchen and James asked about what I wanted to happen next, my facade slipped.

'Next? I want to see Campbell Island. I want a pilot. I'll settle for seeing it from a hundred miles away through cloud. I don't think I'll find a captain who'll take me to sea, so a pilot with a spare morning, a rich pilot with fuel he needs to burn will do nicely. Anything. I just want to see the bloody island. I'm nearly there, but nearly isn't good enough. I'm going to let so many people down.'

'Wait, isn't your mission to travel as far from home as possible?' asked Gretchen the presenter. 'Because if it is, don't you complete your mission wherever you end up?'

'That's right,' piped up her co-host James, 'wherever you finish in thirty days, you'll have travelled as far from home as possible.'

'...'

I didn't have an answer. They were right. Campbell Island was only a notional target; the aim was always to travel as far as I could from my home with the support of Twitter; wherever I managed to reach would satisfy that aim. Wherever you go, there you are, but it still felt like a cheat.

I polished off another plate of Smiley's award-winning eggs Benedict (at least they would be, if awards were handed out in such places) and we headed on towards the seaport at Bluff, a tiny community of 2,000 residents and the southernmost town on the mainland. Throughout the week I'd told many of my intention to at least reach Stewart Island, and not one person in New Zealand had a good thing to say about the ferry crossing. Smiley told tales of wall-to-wall vomit on one particular trip, to the point that he swore he'd never step foot on board again. Since I've already gone to painstaking lengths to portray Smiley as a particularly fearless bastard, you'll appreciate that this revelation troubled me no end.

Our ferry tickets had been offered on Twitter by Stewart Island Experience (@StewartIslandEx) and I initially mistook their terminal building for a medium-sized post office, with its cashiers sitting behind tempered glass and racks of leaflets, and elderly people milling about in waterproofs for no discernable reason. They were waiting for the Stewart Island ferry, which turned out not to be a ferry at all, but my twin-bowed arch-nemesis of the high seas, a catamaran.

The crossing was relatively smooth, at least according to the locals who happily chuckled to one another over the deteriorating state of the tourists during the hour-long voyage. It was comparable to necking tequila cut with oysters while sitting in the saddle of a bucking bronco. After forty-five minutes of sea-sawing across Foveaux Strait, I felt like I'd been kicked in the guts, and when we finally rounded the craggy black cove and made for port in the harbour at Oban, I was doubled over and threatening to drool. Smiley bundled me off the boat, along the wooden pier and towards the hostel that Ricky had arranged for us; it was less than four hundred metres from the ferry terminal but my legs failed to coordinate their movement and over I went into the black gravel path, clutching my guts, my head and stomach swirling in opposite directions. I was officially sea-sick and would shortly bid good-day to the morning's eggs Benedict.

After a few hours' sleep in my small and pretty room at Bunkers hostel, I felt strong enough to stand and wander back downstairs to the living room. Warmed by a large grated fire, one or two backpackers sat about the light airy space on cushions and beanbags, reading books and airing their bare toes. I sat at the scarred oak dining table and took my first proper look at the view across the rain-swept land; it was like Site B in *The Lost World*, but with fewer Hypsilophodons. A few roads lined with one-and two-storey buildings led back towards the shore, but otherwise the natural landscape still dominated, untamed and unspoilt.

Stewart Island, or Stewart Island/Rakiura to give it its official title, was the remotest place on which I had ever stood, or curled round bathroom porcelain; a fleck of savage rock and fauna barely larger than Greater London, it had a population roughly 19,000 times smaller, most living in the island's only town, the north-eastern port of Oban. Domestic electricity is five times more expensive than on the mainland, due to it being produced by an onshore diesel generator. And there is no mobile phone coverage for anyone other than New Zealanders – only two domestic networks have erected phone towers on land, and neither provides international access for third-party operators.

The arthritic desktop computer in the living room was my only connection to the world and to Twitter, and it was painfully slow – no doubt some elderly telecommunications cable piped in Internet services by the thimbleful from the mainland, but it didn't matter. My journey had been powered by goodwill and generosity through Twitter, and Twitter was a people-powered medium. Two billion people in the world had Internet access; two million of them used Twitter – I worked out the percentages, and realised there was no earthly reason why anyone amongst the 400 residents on Stewart Island should have even heard of Twitter, let alone know I was amongst them.

And so my chance to set foot on Campbell Island slipped away. To reach that mysterious wilderness 600 kilometres away within the thirty days would have meant setting sail that day, so as the sky darkened, I knew it was all but over. I wanted to call home and tell Jane the news, because she'd tell me I hadn't failed, that I'd done something wonderful and unique and that she was so desperately proud of me she could burst. But I couldn't. Aside from a Dutch backpacker thumbing through CDs and a snoring Smiley upstairs, I was alone. There was still the slenderest of chances of a flight across the ocean; it wasn't a lost cause quite yet, but the possibility provided little consolation. I chewed my teeth and turned it all over in my head; I'd let everyone down.

twitchhiker In Bunkers hostel on Stewart Island. Dutch girl picks Rock Anthems CD to play in lounge. Track 1 – The Final Countdown. The end is the beginning.

6:09 PM Mar 27th

twitchhiker Enough. Can't find a CD that doesn't skip and refuse to listen to Final Countdown on loop, so playing my copy of @patricktoneill's CD from LA.

6:47 PM Mar 27th

A single pub served the 400 inhabitants of Stewart Island, and half of them were to be found in there on a Friday night. The South Sea Hotel offered two bars and a restaurant area, little in the way of contemporary decoration, and the sensation you were sitting in your gran's front room. It was less a public house, more a house party for invited islanders and a handful of bemused visitors in garishly coloured waterproofs. Some of the most friendly, drunkard locals you could ever care to topple into propped up the bar; local fishermen slapped each other hard over the back while recalling their tales for tourists, still wearing their oversized wellington boots and roll-neck jumpers. In the lounge next door was a karaoke-style talent competition, accompanied by an amateur pianist capable of playing every third note. Every so often there were roars and cheers, though from our seat neither Smiley nor I could determine whether they supported or detested the vocal efforts. Eventually curiosity led the two of us through to the lounge, where we witnessed a gentleman who bore an uncanny resemblance to Paul Shane belting out 'Burning Love' to the tune of 'In the Ghetto', although not in a manner that suggested it was intentional.

My stomach was aching with retching and hunger as I meekly picked at our fish and chip supper. Smiley and I were in agreement – there was no point remaining on Stewart Island beyond the following day. Any opportunity to proceed further south would come from Invercargill – if the offer of a flight came through, that's most likely where I'd need to be to take advantage of it.

Once I reached Invercargill, I'd wait and hope that Twitter pulled one final rabbit out of its hat. If it didn't, I'd be satisfied I'd come so far, meeting the wonderful, gracious people I had, seeing more of the world than some people see in their lifetimes and having raised a healthy amount of money for *charity: water*.

Through my blog and Twitter I suggested that reaching Stewart Island was indeed an extraordinary accomplishment and everybody who played a part should be proud. Privately, there was the tiniest flicker of disappointment in my mind, that I might have come so close and fallen at the last hurdle. But I could live with it. I could.

Chapter 31

Day Twenty-eight – Saturday 28 March

I was horribly, horribly ill. Wretchedly so. Even while lying perfectly still, I felt myself gently rocking back and forth. The bloated white face in the bathroom mirror looked like it belonged to a raw corpse.

The air above Stewart Island was full of British drizzle as we walked down the short path to the ferry terminal for the afternoon crossing, and the sea in the cove was ruled by white-tipped waves and angry gusts of gale. Despite the wintry conditions, Smiley's sunglasses had never left his head – if not in front of his eyes, they were pushed up across his thick blonde locks. That was until we reached the wooden house at the pier's end that was the ferry terminal, when the wind whipped the glasses from his curls and into the harbour.

'Bollocks, they cost me two hundred dollars,' snapped Smiley in my direction. 'Water can't be that deep. Maybe I can go in and get them.'

It didn't sound a particularly sensible course of action, and the terminal staff agreed.

'Well is there somebody around who doesn't mind slipping on a wetsuit and grabbing them for me? The water can't be very deep, I saw where they landed.'

'Sorry, mate,' replied the member of staff behind the desk, 'hear what you're saying, but can't really have you in the water with boats coming in and out.'

Smiley wasn't taking no for an answer, insisting the staff accompany him outside so he could point at the spot in the water where his glasses had landed. And still the staff insisted there was nobody who could help him. Frustrated, Smiley's demeanour slipped ever so slightly as he turned to me.

'You can pay for them, can't you?' Smiley asked me. My first reaction was that he was joking.

'You must be raking it in on this trip. I wouldn't have lost them if I hadn't brought you here.'

He wasn't joking. Smiley had been wearing a pair of $200 sunglasses in the rain and had lost them, and it was my fault. I laughed off the suggestion the best I could, hoping he'd let the matter drop, and joined the queue for the ferry as it docked outside. Then a stray thought sparked up in a corner of my brain; I couldn't board, not yet, not if Stewart Island would be as far as I'd travel from home.

'I'll be back in a minute,' I said to Smiley, and headed out the door, down the length of the pier, across the main road and into the wild bush.

'What was that all about?' asked Smiley, when I eventually joined him on the deck of the ferry.

I reached into my pocket and pulled out a smooth grey stone, no larger than my palm.

'It's a piece of the moon,' I said.

Smiley looked confused.

'For a promise I made,' I added.

Crossing Foveaux Strait, I'd been repeatedly told, was always worse on the way back. The warnings had meant little until I'd taken the hour-long catamaran journey to reach Stewart Island the previous day, which provided me with a yardstick to judge the return crossing by. Once the vessel skipped over the relatively calm waters of the cove and into the open sea, it was quickly apparent that everyone on board was going to die. The boat was pitching so steeply that the horizon would frequently disappear from sight, and instead the view from the port windows was a solid wall of grey sea.

The feeling of helplessness and relentlessness was similar to air turbulence, except for the rhythm, the endless rhythm of the water slamming the hull. I lasted ten minutes before spewing into a paper bag, as grizzled fishermen stood about drinking tins of lager and talking about how they'd seen the seas far worse. Well fucking hooray for you, mister fishermen, now excuse me while I stagger to the toilet and cough up my organs. Unlike air turbulence, which can sometimes be avoided by adjusting the altitude of the plane, there was no way for the boat's captain to take action, nor any respite until reaching Bluff – the crossing took an hour, and no amount of hoping and wishing from me and the other four passengers chucking up into paper bags would make it any less so.

As the catamaran slowed on approach to the mainland and the chaotic waters found order, I had nothing left to give.

I was sick of being sick, hungry but without an appetite, exhausted but wide awake. And I was done with boats – no seafaring vessel could reach Campbell Island in time, so I could at last give them a wide berth. A little nautical humour for you there.

Explore New Zealand had booked an evening for Smiley and me at the Tuatara Lodge on Dee Street in Invercargill, without a doubt the most impressive hostel I'd checked into during the New Zealand leg of my journey, and on a par with St Christopher's in Paris. The reception area incorporated a cafe with al fresco seating, there were large, clean en-suite rooms available and the staff were perfectly relaxed about our comings and goings. My goings were chiefly to bed as I attempted to put right the motion sickness that plagued me.

Being back on the mainland after my brief sojourn on the island meant two things – a plentiful supply of Internet access and mobile reception. And the former had good news for me:

flyairnz @twitchhiker – we will fly you home!
5:37 PM Mar 28th

Jo from Air New Zealand, one of the guests at The Wine Vault's party in Auckland, had arranged a complimentary one-way ticket from Auckland to London for me. Thank you thank you thank you. I'd secretly hoped somebody might see me fill a spare seat on a flight to the UK, but I

319

hadn't been banking on it. There wasn't a plan B since I didn't have the funds to see myself home; perhaps plan B was to twitchhike back the way I came.

'I can't wait to have you home, husband!' said Jane when I told her the news over Skype, the boys cuddled around her to smile and giggle and wave.

'I know!' I said. 'I'll be there before you know it, wife.'

We'd referred to one another as 'husband' and 'wife' since we were married. They were our pet names, strikingly descriptive as they were.

'Well, we've got news for you too, haven't we boys?' said Jane.

From below the eyeline of the webcam, a little ball of fuzz loomed into view with eyes as wide as the moon, letting out a squeal, a broken meow.

'I called her Daisy,' beamed Jack.

It felt a little too soon after Elly had died, but Elly had been ill for several weeks and there was clearly a void at home; the family was lacking and lonely.

I crossed the street to the camper van, smoke billowing from the roof – Smiley was preparing burritos for supper. He was still sore about the sunglasses, and the tear in the side of the van.

'While you're paying for the damage, you could sling in a new pair of glasses for your mate Smiley!' All said with a smile, but the matter was beginning to cause tension. I'd received an email from Ricki while offshore – as expected, I'd been fully insured to drive the camper, so my wallet was saved the expense.

'Ah, that's great news, mate,' said Smiley. 'Just the glasses to pay for then!'

I switched topics as we sat down with our burritos, and tried not to let myself become irritated. I'd travelled around the world and there had been barely a bad word between my hosts and me; that was perhaps more remarkable than my journey.

I left Smiley to lament at the loss of his beloved headwear and headed back across the street to Speights, a bright and burly bar next to the hostel on Dee Street. There had been a couple of tweets from Invercargill residents so we'd agreed to meet up that evening. The crowd at the bar was bizarre; aside from the mullets and Maori, there were men in kilts. Kilts. In New Zealand. They certainly didn't sound Scottish, nor had they been to a wedding, but according to my fellow tweeps who arrived shortly afterwards, if they weren't from the Highlands then they most likely claimed Scottish lineage. A significant number of the country's first European settlers in the nineteenth century were from Scotland; Dunedin on the South Island's west coast takes its name from the Scottish Gaelic name for Edinburgh. Bagpipes and Hogmanay aren't foreign traditions to the residents of Invercargill, and nor is the Scottish accent; my associates at the bar spoke with accents far removed from the Highlands, but it's not unusual to meet local individuals and families with strong Scottish burrs.

It was a sedate night in Speights, a whimper rather than a bang, but the conversation was dandy and entertaining; Kerryn Smith from the local tourist board (@kezasmith) arrived with a friend in tow, as did Julian (@Julznova), a tech student studying in the city. Over the course of the evening, they confirmed that use of Twitter in the Southland region was embryonic at best; we were far from the bright lights of Auckland, Wellington and Christchurch. Julian was perhaps the most active Twitter user in the city, and he only knew of a dozen or so other users.

Then there was the slightest chink of hope. As the conversation progressed, it turned out that Julian's friend, Andrew, was a pilot. A pilot.

Stop everything.

'Yeah, there are planes that fly out to Stewart Island,' Andrew shouted above the din of the Scottish Kiwis behind us.

I was talking to a pilot based in Invercargill, who flew private planes in and out of the city. What were the chances? This was it, this was the happy ending, the neat bow to tie everything up that you knew was coming all along, ever since I suggested the possibility of failure. You never doubted it would happen, not for a moment, did you? Thank you for showing such faith in this incredible journey.

'But they won't fly any further out to sea,' Andrew concluded. 'You wouldn't want to go up in one even if they did. The air currents above Foveaux Strait knock the small planes about worse than the ferries. Most passengers spend their twenty minutes up in the air screaming.'

It was over.

Boats didn't dare stray there without good cause. Pilots wouldn't fly there on a whim. There was no physical way to reach my destination, that speckle of sand I'd first spied on Google Maps two months before.

My challenge had ended earlier that day, across Foveaux Strait on Stewart Island. I was 18,848 kilometres from north-east England. I'd travelled as far from Newcastle as possible in twenty-eight days and there was no possibility of progressing further. And I wasn't distraught or heartbroken in the end, there were no tears or exasperated sighs, only relief that Twitter had come through for me so magnificently, and that it was time to go home to my family.

Chapter 32

Smiley and I decided not to stay in Invercargill for a second night, and instead headed north to Queenstown. The rules allowed us to stay on until the following day, but the vacuum of interest from the city did nothing to convince me it was wrong to begin the journey home. If the laws of geology saw Campbell Island shift closer to the mainland, if a mystery benefactor with a private plane came through, then we were close enough to turn around and take advantage of it, though the probability of such an event occurring seemed negligible.

The drive from Invercargill back to Queenstown was quiet and bountiful in its beauty. I attempted to photograph the magnificence of Lake Wakatipu as we drove along its eastern shore; in the end, I put my camera away and lost myself in its glory – I couldn't capture the scale and serenity of the blue waters and tumbling, crumbling valleys above. If governments paid for their citizens to take a two-week sightseeing tour of New Zealand instead of investing in nuclear arsenals that could never win a war, the world would no doubt be a far more tranquil place.

'Did I want to stay on in Queenstown for the evening?' enquired Smiley. Not really, said I. It certainly looked a far more peaceful place by daylight, nuzzled into the shores of Lake Wakatipu while the creatures of the night spent their sunlight jumping off cranes or out of planes. I was ready for home, I was aching to be with my family. Jo at Air New Zealand had offered a flight to Auckland from Queenstown that evening, and I had no qualms about accepting it.

'Well, I might have lost my glasses because of you, but I've got you a going-away present,' said Smiley.

Smiley pulled up at Queenstown airport and disappeared into the back of the van, rummaging through his bag of clothes.

'There you go,' said Smiley, dropping a dirty black rag in my hands. 'A driver's polo-shirt. Really nice they are. Needs a wash though.'

I didn't have anything to offer back. The gift exchange had broken down, and the last present I'd received – Narelle's glass globe – had been to me.

'And I have something for you!' I was filling as I went into the back and opened up my bags. There was a month's worth of ticket stubs, door keys, tickets and dirty underwear (I hadn't done any washing since Los Angeles) – there had to be something worthy of a present in there. And there was – the solar gadget charger I'd carried around the world but never once used.

'You won't know how much you've needed this until you use it,' I said, selling it to him in the vain hope the glasses would never be mentioned again.

Smiley really earned his name as I handed it over and explained his mobile phone would be charged wherever he went. Victory rescued from the jaws of defeat. We shook hands and hugged; it was unexpected considering the quietly simmering tension between us, but well received nevertheless.

'Careful how you go, mate,' Smiley beamed as I crossed the road towards the terminal building. 'And if you ever come back and need a driver, I'm your man.'

Over the next two days I made my way home to the UK. The SKYCITY Grand Hotel in Auckland offered me one final night of five-star luxury; I wasn't going to refuse after my week of hostels, camper vans, ferry crossings that Ernest Borgnine would baulk at and cockroaches the size of Shetland ponies.

When I announced news of my journey's end on Twitter, hundreds of pounds in additional donations to *charity: water* were made, messages of congratulations were tweeted from around the globe, from strangers and friends, old and new. At the SKYCITY Grand Hotel, a card from Mel dispelled any lingering notion that my journey was a failure:

You have demonstrated what I have always hoped and dreamed was true– that ultimately we all have a deep love and connection with one another. Twitter strips away social barriers in a way like nothing else I have ever seen.

*I am so honoured that you have seen my country in
the way that you have and met Kiwis who will forever
be your friends.*

*Take care on the journey back home. Kia kaha. Ka
kite anoau i a kōe. Be strong, keep going. I'll see you
again soon.*

Mel x

Air New Zealand saw me safely from Auckland to London via
Los Angeles and, through Twitter, my long-time friends Paul
and Gail offered to save me a five-hour commute by flying me
the last leg of my journey to the north-east. While I travelled
back around the world, the national newspapers published
excitable stories of my journey, the *Mail* and *The Sun* reducing
me to just another crank who'd achieved some outrageous
stunt for the sake of filling their pages. Local newspapers and
television channels were eager to know where I was and when
I'd arrive home so they could send journalists and crews.

I didn't tell them. I avoided Twitter, returned none of the
phone calls; nobody knew where I was in the country once
I arrived home. Nobody was going to slow me down in
reaching my family, and nobody did. When I stepped out
from the Metro station to my waiting family, I sobbed and
I grinned and I cried a month's worth of love. I didn't know
who to hug first when Jane and the boys flew towards me, so
I tried to hug them all and succeeded with absolute success.
My God, my family. I'd travelled the earth to discover what
was waiting for me at home all along.

Home looked odd. The same, but different – in that way it always does when you return after time away. The park opposite was a shade greener, in the full throes of spring, a house a few doors along had been put up for sale, next door had bought a new car. Through the front door, the bags were dumped in the hall, the smell of home familiar and welcome. Both Jack and Sam led me into the living room to the left; the full width and drop of the window was obscured by a poster, twenty sheets of A4 paper taped together; large letters noisily shouted WELCOME HOME DADDY above a less-than-flattering caricature of me atop the globe. New Zealand was where the Falkland Islands should be and the UK appeared to be a similar size to Africa, but it was perfect and delightful nevertheless.

When I landed in Auckland, if you'd asked then whether I'd have settled for reaching Stewart Island and going no further, I'd have told you absolutely not. If you'd told me I stood a slim-to-non-existent chance of peering across to Campbell Island from a distant vessel, I'd have angrily disagreed. But as the week passed, it became disappointingly clear that Stewart Island would see me reach the end of the line.

At every stage of the journey there had been a natural momentum, an irresistible force born out of the ceaseless support on Twitter. Once I reached New Zealand's South Island, that forward motion began to wane. Activity on Twitter started to slow, the re-tweets fell away. Why did it feel as if I'd stalled at that critical stage? Running thirteen hours ahead of the UK meant I lost my home support, as the sleeping majority missed my daytime activity. There was an element of fatigue too – I'd been banging on about Twitchhiker for two months solid, and perhaps people felt they'd shouted themselves hoarse on my behalf.

I had remained out of contact for long stretches of time on my journey across the South Island, either because of a lack of Internet access or mobile phone coverage. On a land mass the size of England and Wales, with just one fiftieth of the population, a cast-iron communications infrastructure simply isn't necessary. So I wasn't able to push my message as hard as I wanted to in the final days of the project. Twitter itself had been unable to aid me to the end; it had been a bond, a commonality shared with the communities I'd visited around the world, up until those last few days. I shouldn't have been so surprised; even a virtual community needed an element of physicality to exist.

So I didn't see Campbell Island, but it honestly didn't matter by the time I arrived home. The aim was to travel as far as I possibly could from home within thirty days, and by reaching Stewart Island I'd travelled to a place the majority of New Zealanders have never set foot on, never mind the rest of the world. The amount of money donated to *charity: water* passed the £5,000 mark, and they received media coverage the world over. Scott and his team would put the money and exposure to excellent use, helping communities in developing countries.

On a personal level, I saw the world, proved it wasn't full of rapists and bastards, and thousands had taken the journey with me. Twitter proved without a shadow of a doubt that it is much more than a social network, but a user-defined infrastructure that can be harnessed to change lives and expectations, to share and enhance unique experiences and viewpoints.

The Twitchhiker project proved beyond doubt that kindness is universal, that the whole can be infinitely greater than the sum of its parts, and that social media may begin online but it will converge with the real world whenever and wherever we let it.

And in the year that has passed since I stood in that supermarket and furrowed my brow at idiot customers, nobody has attempted anything similar. Twitchhiker was a peerless achievement – not only for me, but for the dozens of people who played Good Samaritan along the way, the hundreds who donated to charity, and the thousands who supported the adventure on Twitter. Without a doubt, to be a twitchhiker was something unique, and special. And real.

Acknowledgements

This book represents the efforts of thousands of people around the world. That said, all their names would never fit on the front cover and the individual royalty payments would be pathetic, so I'm going to take credit for the whole thing. Still, there are a number who deserve particular mention, aside from those you've just read about.

First, a bunch of musicians, most of them alive, who provided the soundtrack that accompanied four months of demented typing. Soundtracks pop up throughout the book, so here's one that played behind the scenes:

'Will You Follow Me?' – Rob Dougan
'Wichita Lineman' – Glen Campbell
'Feel Every Beat' – Electronic
'I Will Possess Your Heart' – Death Cab for Cutie
'Invaders Must Die' – The Prodigy
'This Too Shall Pass' – OK Go
'God Only Knows' – The Beach Boys
'I'm Not Calling You a Liar' – Florence & The Machine
'Won't Get Fooled Again' – The Who
'Go With the Flow' – Queens Of The Stone Age

Rob Dougan receives top billing because we follow one another on Twitter and occasionally chat about all sorts of random minutiae. He's @robdougan on Twitter, by the way, and his music is inspirational.

Then there are several tweeps who were involved in the Twitchhiker project, yet for the sake of brevity or bone idleness are not mentioned: Chris Noble (@worldnomads) at WorldNomads.com, who insured me on my quest; James Parton (@jamesparton) and @O2Litmus for their mobile support; Alistair MacDonald (@alistair) for his altogether crucial and mysterious role; Andy Blood (@TheBloodster) and the team at TBWA\Whybin in Auckland for their support and Paddy Healy (@paddyslacker) for the joke about the tea.

Who else? There are two magnificent storytellers responsible for piquing my interest in writing – Douglas Adams and Robert Rankin – and there are knowing nods to both in the book. Also, I have to thank those who have encouraged me in my outlandish attempts to forge a career in writing – Paul Carter, Ken Snowdon, Neil Davey, Jason Deans, Paul Nikkel, Kevin Job, Paul Carr and Andy Dawson have all played a part.

All this scribble needed beating into shape by somebody, and for that I have to thank my editor Lucy York as well as Jennifer Barclay at Summersdale. The fact this book exists at all is down to my agent Barbara Levy and her team.

Down to the nitty-gritty. There are three friends to whom I owe everything, or nothing whatsoever, depending on my mood when you ask – Jon Kirby, Kelly Scott and

Adrian Taylor. Thank you for looking after me over the years, and apologies for screwing up on more occasions than I dare count.

Finally, I wouldn't be the person I am today without the love and care of my parents and my brother, and I wouldn't have the strength to rise on a rainy day without my family – Jane, Jack and Sam. In the words of REM – for you alone, you are the everything.

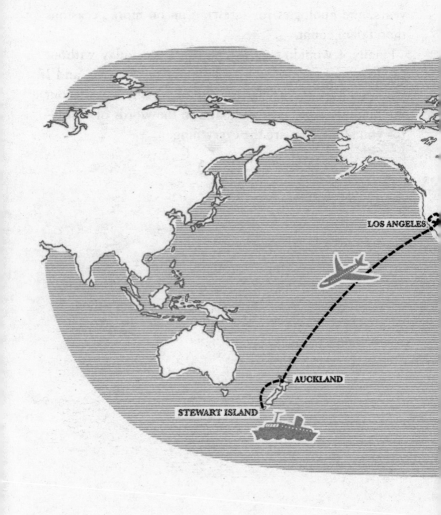

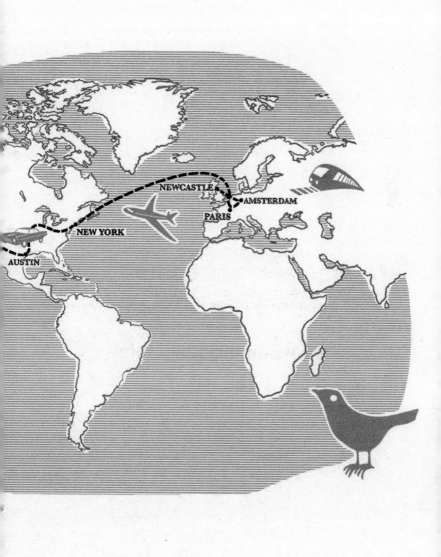

Have you enjoyed this book?
If so, why not write a review on your favourite website?

Thanks very much for buying this Summersdale book.

www.summersdale.com